SIDREA Series in Accounting and Business Administration

This is the official book series of SIDREA - the Italian Society of Accounting and Business Administration. This book series is provided with a wide Scientific Committee composed of Academics by SIDREA. It publishes contributions (monographs, edited volumes and proceedings) as a result of the double blind review process by the SIDREA's thematic research groups, operating at the national and international levels. Particularly, the series aims to disseminate specialized findings on several topics – classical and cutting-edge alike – that are currently being discussed by the accounting and business administration communities. The series authors are respected researchers and professors in the fields of business valuation; governance and internal control; financial accounting; public accounting; management control; gender; turnaround predictive models; non-financial disclosure; intellectual capital, smart technologies, and digitalization; and university governance and performance measurement. This book series is indexed in Scopus.

Lorenzo Leto

Integrating Change Management and Management Accounting Change

New Perspectives on Performance Measurement Systems Implementation

Springer

Lorenzo Leto
Centro di Servizi Polo Universitario Sistemi Logistici (POLOG)
University of Pisa
Livorno, Italy

ISSN 2662-9879 ISSN 2662-9887 (electronic)
SIDREA Series in Accounting and Business Administration
ISBN 978-3-031-84386-0 ISBN 978-3-031-84387-7 (eBook)
https://doi.org/10.1007/978-3-031-84387-7

This Springer imprint is published by the registered company Springer Nature Switzerland AG
The registered company address is: Gewerbestrasse 11, 6330 Cham, Switzerland

Acknowledgments

I would like to thank Prof. Nicola Giuseppe Castellano for his helpful comments and invaluable guidance.

I would also like to express my sincere thanks to the entire management of CAEN for allowing me to conduct the interviews necessary for the preparation of this manuscript. In particular, I would like to thank Michela Givoletti, Claudio Raffo, Alessandro Iovene, Michele Zardetto, and Giorgio Salvadori for their kind availability and for allowing me to learn about their business reality, which allowed me to build a very interesting case study.

All errors and omissions are the sole responsibility of the author.

Competing Interests The author has no competing interests to declare that are relevant to the content of this manuscript.

Contents

List of Figures

List of Tables

Chapter 1
Introduction to the Book

This manuscript examines the process of management accounting change and investigates the role of change management approaches in supporting and explaining the dynamics of the implementation of performance measurement systems (PMS) within organizations. It emphasizes that PMS implementation is not merely a technical task but a complex organizational change process. Specifically, the book analyzes how various human and organizational factors can either enable or hinder successful change.

By applying change management theories, the book explores why some organizations succeed while others fail in adopting PMS, with particular attention to how change management strategies can be adapted to these systems. Through the analysis of a case study, it examines whether the factors identified in organizational change literature can be applied to PMS implementation and management accounting change, offering insights into the dynamics of success and failure.

1.1 Introduction

In today's complex and evolving business landscape, the ability to adapt and implement an effective performance measurement system (PMS) is a critical determinant of organizational success (Melnyk et al., 2014). PMS are advanced management accounting tools that allow companies to have a holistic view of their performance (Franco-Santos et al., 2012). These systems typically include both financial and nonfinancial indicators to track all the elements that affect a company's success. In fact, their purpose is to assess the validity of the company's strategy and the effectiveness of its implementation, which are essential elements for its survival and prosperity. Based on the critical factors underlying the success of the strategy (e.g., customer satisfaction & loyalty, employee retention, know-how), PMS should be

L. Leto, *Integrating Change Management and Management Accounting Change*, SIDREA Series in Accounting and Business Administration,
https://doi.org/10.1007/978-3-031-84387-7_1

adapted and updated accordingly by allowing their regular monitoring. Despite the proved usefulness of these systems, many organizations actually find it difficult to manage the process of implementing and adopting them, often resulting in frustrating and unsuccessful experiences (Van Camp & Braet, 2016). There are also documented cases where companies initially implement PMS but fail to regularly and profitably use them over time, leading to further instances of failure. Since updating and implementing these systems is fundamentally an organizational change that raises issues closely related to human factors, such as resistance to change (Hayes, 2022), the question arises as to whether the use of change management approaches might be useful today to increase the likelihood of successful implementation. Additionally, these approaches may provide a better understanding of the dynamics that contribute to both success and failure.

Change management is a discipline that originated in the 1950s and is still very active in research, business consulting, and practice (Burke, 2023). The goal of this line of research is to study and understand the dynamics of change for scientific purposes. However, it is also very practice-oriented, aiming to provide companies and consultants with a set of tools, methods, and approaches to facilitate and produce organizational change. Indeed, many important contributions in this area have been proposed by professor-consultants (e.g., Kotter, 1996). Particularly visible and popular are, for example, the prescriptive approaches offered by the Harvard Business School (e.g., Kotter et al., 2011, 2021).

The intersection between the change management literature and the literature on PMS implementation and management accounting change has been relatively rare in the academic field and has mostly occurred years ago (e.g., Ansari & Bell, 2009; Argyris & Kaplan, 1994). Although some have strongly suggested potential links (e.g., Bourne et al., 2003; Nudurupati et al., 2011), there has actually been little empirical application of these approaches to PMS.

In light of this, the purpose of this book is to explore the usefulness of change management theories in understanding the PMS implementation dynamics, but also to increase the odds of their successful adoption. In other words, this work aims to contribute to theoretical academic research by proposing the consideration of change management theories in order to gain a more complete understanding of the phenomenon of management accounting change. In particular, one of the objectives is to understand if the enabling and hindering factors identified by organizational change management literature seem to play a role in the acceptance, dissemination, and use of PMS across a company. Moreover, by examining the theories of change management, this study also proposes, through the analysis of a case study, the extension of Bourne et al.'s (2000) framework, thus providing an additional theoretical contribution. This framework, which is specifically focused on the implementation of PMS, divides the implementation process into three phases: design, implementation, and use. Through the inclusion of elements related to the human factor and considered by change management theories, such as the development of the need for change, this work proposes the addition of a predesign phase that allows a more comprehensive view of the phenomenon. This phase turns out to be essential, as suggested by change management theories, for the transition to the actual design phase. From a more practical standpoint, this study also seeks to explore the usefulness of change management tools and prescriptive approaches in supporting practitioners who intend to implement a PMS in their companies to increase the chances of successful adoption. Keeping in mind the challenges and opportunities during the predesign, design, implementation, and use phases of a PMS, as well as the enabling and hindering factors of these processes, can help practitioners manage this type of change. Finally, the case study analysis chapter offers some suggestions and approaches tailored specifically to the implementation of PMS, which may be useful to practitioners. Therefore, this work aims to be of interest to both researchers and managers.

Unlike the previously cited studies, this book applies more contemporary change management theories, specifically the framework proposed by Stouten et al. (2018). By applying it to a case study, this research investigates its relevance and, more in general, the relevance of change management theories and approaches in explaining the dynamics of PMS implementation. Stouten et al.'s (2018) framework is, in the opinion of the author, particularly compelling. Compared to many mainstream models, it is more recent and incorporates the advances that have been made in change management research over the years. Furthermore, it is based solely on scientific evidence and research findings rather than the opinions of gurus or expert consultants (Hughes, 2016; Rosenbaum et al., 2018). For this reason, it can be considered more rigorous and reliable.

Already since the 1980s, a number of factors—including increased competition, advances in information systems, an increased focus on sustainability, and rapid technological innovation—have forced organizations to regularly reassess and adapt their strategic approaches (Deng et al., 2020; Kotter, 1995). These changes have necessitated the integration of increasingly sophisticated management accounting systems (Beusch et al., 2022; Franco-Santos et al., 2012) to assess not only costs and efficiency levels but also the effectiveness of strategic decisions. One of the best-known and most widely used PMS is the balanced scorecard, introduced by Kaplan and Norton (1996). This highly popular management accounting system is designed to evaluate the effectiveness of a company's strategy and its execution by focusing on four key perspectives. These perspectives aim to provide a comprehensive view of the company's performance, encompassing internal processes, market and customer dynamics, level of innovation and learning, and financial results. These elements of analysis can be expanded by including additional perspectives (e.g., sustainability impacts) or by removing those that are of no particular interest to the specific company. As is typical of PMS, the balanced scorecard integrates both financial and nonfinancial performance indicators into dashboards, offering, through its four perspectives, a holistic approach to performance measurement and management. By addressing these diverse areas, the balanced scorecard generally helps to ensure that a company's objectives are not only well-defined but also effectively monitored and achieved (Franco-Santos et al., 2012).

Despite the widespread use of these systems, the process of designing, implementing, and using PMS remains challenging (Bourne et al., 2018; Sgrò et al., 2020). Even the balanced scorecard has been subject to a high implementation failure rate (Hoque, 2014). This could act as a deterrent for many businesses, such as smaller firms, which may be reluctant to allocate their scarce resources to such initiatives if they don't see the benefits or feel the implementation process is too difficult (Heinicke, 2018; Sgrò et al., 2020).

As this book shows later, the process of PMS implementation can be fraught with a number of issues and can be difficult to pursue without the necessary financial and human resources (Castellano & Leto, 2021; Lueg & Vu, 2015). Some issues relate, for example, to the difficulty of adapting these tools to individual companies and identifying the most appropriate metrics for monitoring and measuring company performance (Miraglia, 2012; Prayudi et al., 2024). Alternatively, they may be related to limitations of information systems that do not allow for collecting appropriate and reliable data to feed the PMS (Frezatti et al., 2014; Van Camp & Braet, 2016). In addition, there are a number of elements, such as power shifts, lack of necessary skills and resistance to measurement that can lead to resistance to change from individuals or groups of individuals within the organization (Jakobsen & Lueg, 2014; Yetano, 2013).

Resistance to change is a phenomenon that has been widely addressed and explored in studies related to change management (Mikel-Hong et al., 2023). It is no coincidence that this highly practitioner-oriented field of research has its roots in psychology and organizational studies (Hayes, 2022). Yet, although the human element is considered to be very influential in determining the success or failure of these initiatives, most studies of PMS implementation, or more generally of management accounting change,[1] are actually based on theories far removed from change management and psychology.

Scholars of management accounting change have adopted a massive number of different perspectives and frameworks to explain the complex and multidimensional phenomena of change (Alsharari et al., 2015; Busco et al., 2007). Management accounting change turns out to be, then, an interdisciplinary research field, as it offers studies based on diverse theoretical foundations, ranging from philosophy and sociology to organizational behavior and theory (Macchia, 2019). Yet, the most followed research lines in management accounting change are probably the ones founded on sociological theories and institutionalism (Alsharari, 2019; Alsharari et al., 2015), also thanks to the widespread frameworks by Burns and Scapens (2000) and Brignall and Modell (2000). Research grounded on institutionalism enabled the development of many research works which helped to understand the dynamics of change and stability in management accounting systems (Alsharari et al., 2015; van der Steen, 2011), especially within medium-large (Dossi & Patelli, 2008; Lasyoud & Alsharari, 2017) and public organizations (Akbar et al., 2015; Yetano, 2013). These studies typically view change as incremental and involuntary, and therefore provide little guidance to practitioners seeking to implement a planned management accounting change such as PMS implementation. In general, these

[1] Management accounting change is a widely studied research topic that focuses on the phenomenon of updating and implementing management accounting systems such as PMS (Burns & Scapens, 2000; Vaivio, 1999).

theories seek to examine how the external (e.g., regulatory changes, competitor behavior) and internal (e.g., behavior of specific organizational units or groups within the firm) institutional contexts of companies influence the dynamics of management accounting change (e.g., Brignall & Modell, 2000; Burns & Scapens, 2000). They also seek to explore how existing management control routines within the firm are altered by changes in the institutional context and how new routines are ultimately "institutionalized" or, in other words, become permanent over time. However, it is widely recognized that the implementation of PMS can be planned and actively pursued by individuals within the organization and has the potential to be both revolutionary and disruptive (Bourne et al., 2003), consistent with the claims of the change management literature (Hayes, 2022).

This research diverges from the institutional perspective, rooting itself instead in the disciplines of organization development and change, and the psychological and behavioral sciences, thereby adopting an organizational change management lens. Since change management theories and prescriptive models deal extensively with the issues related to organizational change, adopting a change management perspective to explore PMS implementation appears justified. Moreover, Bourne et al. (2003) have indicated that applying change management theories to PMS implementation studies may help better understand the success and failure dynamics and facilitate PMS adoption. Nudurupati et al. (2011) have argued that change management approaches appear very useful during the implementation, use, and update of PMS and moderately useful during the design phase. Broadbent and Laughlin (2005) have also suggested the intersection between studies on organizational change and accounting change. Still, very few studies of management accounting change have actually attempted to understand whether the approaches of change management (Castellano & Leto, 2021) can favor the success of PMS implementation. Two exceptions in the management accounting literature, which do not refer to the implementation of a PMS but to the implementation of a cost management system, are Ansari and Bell (2009) and Argyris and Kaplan (1994). Ansari and Bell (2009) found partial support for the work of Kotter (1996) and Senge (1990) but also pointed out the existence of gaps in their theories when applied to a technical activity such as accounting change. They suggest that accounting changes are still best approached as organizational changes, but the technical nature of accounting requires an adaptation of existing change management models. Argyris and Kaplan (1994) proposed a structured approach to facilitate activity-based costing implementation based on the organizational development and change studies and approaches offered by Argyris (1990a, 1990b).

Changes in management accounting systems are often linked to or part of other major organizational changes that require careful management. Examples can include changes in the corporate strategy and culture, in the technologies adopted and in the assigned tasks (Ansari & Bell, 2009; Kasurinen, 2002), which are all topics considered by change management literature (Hayes, 2022). Focusing on specific management accounting systems, such as PMS, is legitimate and supported by academic debate (Franco-Santos et al., 2012). In fact, PMS, with their holistic nature, can create specific challenges related to implementation (Vaivio, 1999).

These tools differ from traditional management accounting tools because they are directly or indirectly linked to business strategy and include nonfinancial or qualitative measures (Franco-Santos et al., 2012). Moreover, although their focus is on the assessment of the strategy, they usually offer greater monitoring over the performance of individual managers, which can create resistance to measurement. This organizational change often also includes changes in mindset and measurement approaches, as individuals are held accountable for aspects for which they were not previously responsible (Franco-Santos et al., 2012). For example, changing the criteria by which sales managers are evaluated, such as focusing on a nonfinancial element like customer satisfaction level rather than just revenue, can lead to specific negative individual responses that may require intervention.

The planned implementation of a PMS is regarded here as a disruptive change (Burns & Vaivio, 2001), where a series of difficulties related to individuals' resistance to change, power, politics, and organizational culture may have to be assessed and managed (Carlucci et al., 2015; Mikel-Hong et al., 2023). Therefore, the type of change examined here is not evolutionary, slow, incremental or nonvoluntary as it is usually considered in the management accounting change literature based on institutional theory (Burns & Scapens, 2000). Instead, it is major, radical, revolutionary, and planned (Burke, 2023; Gersick, 1991). The adoption of the planned change perspective not only departs from most of the literature on management accounting change, but also provides potentially useful insights for managers and practitioners that intend to actively pursue the implementation of a PMS in their company.

In conclusion, this study aims to explore the possibility of reintroducing the consideration of change management theories into the scholarly debate on management accounting change, while also investigating their usefulness in assisting practitioners in the implementation of PMS. Both fields share significant points of contact, as they both fundamentally address the phenomenon of organizational change. The prevailing approach in management accounting change may overlook psychological and individual factors that are fundamental to change management studies (Mikel-Hong et al., 2023). In fact, according to these studies, such factors play an essential role for the success or failure of change processes. Completely ignoring change management theories could limit the analysis and prevent the adoption of a broader perspective on the phenomenon of organizational and management accounting change. Moreover, the research area of change management could revitalize the field of management accounting change, as it is currently very active and vital, as evidenced by the continuous publication of books (e.g., Cameron & Green, 2019; Hayes, 2022) and scholarly articles (e.g., Mikel-Hong et al., 2023; Stouten et al., 2018).

This book is structured as follows. Chapter 2 provides an overview of the literature on management accounting change. It delineates key frameworks and scholarly contributions, and allows to underline how different is the theoretical approach guiding this book.

Chapter 3 offers an extensive literature review on PMS and their implementation. This chapter first provides a brief historical overview of why and how PMS developed. After that, a rundown of the main models proposed in the literature is shown, together with their main strength and weaknesses. Next, the characteristics associated with the adopted definition of PMS are outlined, representing the boundaries within which this research is conducted. In the final part of the chapter, a literature review on PMS implementation is presented, taking into account studies on the subject from the fields of management accounting and operations management and strategy. This review summarizes the main topics discussed in the literature, highlights key concerns and issues, and identifies factors that may influence the dynamics of the implementation process across its various phases.

Chapter 4 is entirely devoted to illustrating the main theories of change management and the theoretical framework of Stouten et al. (2018). Here, the history of the development of change management models is presented, together with a description of the characteristics of the most successful proposals. The recent framework of Stouten et al. (2018) is then analyzed in detail, presenting the similarities and differences with the other previously proposed change models. An analysis of the enabling and hindering factors found in the model is also provided, comparing them with the factors identified in the literature related to PMS. This is followed by a summary of the enabling and hindering factors that are considered critical in the change management literature and Stouten et al.'s (2018) framework, but underexplored in the PMS literature. This chapter may be of particular interest to practitioners as it already provides a summary of key elements for managing organizational change. It also further justifies the need for this study as it identifies some gaps in the literature on PMS implementation in terms of examined enabling and inhibiting factors.

Chapter 5 is dedicated entirely to the case study. It begins with a detailed presentation of the methodology for data collection and analysis, including the rationale for case selection, data collection strategies, and the analytical methods used for interpreting the data. Following this, a summary description of the case company is provided, detailing the implementation process and the control system established.

Before presenting the analysis of the implementation process and its phases (Bourne et al., 2000), a list of enabling and hindering factors, identified with the support of Stouten et al.'s (2018) framework, is presented. These factors are discussed based on their effects—either positive or negative—in the specific case study and in light of change management theories. This section offers a lens for better understanding the case study and provides a checklist of factors and practical suggestions applicable to real-world settings. Subsequently, the chapter presents the findings and analyzes the implementation process. Stouten et al.'s (2018) framework is applied to identify enabling and inhibiting factors and to document their occurrence throughout the change process. The final section of the chapter discusses the findings, highlighting the theoretical and empirical contributions of the work.

Chapter 6, the concluding chapter, summarizes the key findings and contributions of the study.

References

Akbar, R., Pilcher, R. A., & Perrin, B. (2015). Implementing performance measurement systems: Indonesian local government under pressure. *Qualitative Research in Accounting and Management, 12*(1), 3–33.

Alsharari, N. M. (2019). Management accounting and organizational change: Alternative perspectives. *International Journal of Organizational Analysis, 27*(4), 1124–1147.

Alsharari, N. M., Dixon, R., & Youssef, M. A. E.-A. (2015). Management accounting change: Critical review and a new contextual framework. *Journal of Accounting & Organizational Change, 11*(4), 476–502.

Ansari, S., & Bell, J. (2009). Five easy pieces: A case study of cost management as organizational change. *Journal of Accounting and Organizational Change, 5*(2), 139–167.

Argyris, C. (1990a). *Overcoming organizational defenses: Facilitating organizational learning*. Allyn & Bacon.

Argyris, C. (1990b). The dilemma of implementing controls: The case of managerial accounting. *Accounting, Organizations and Society, 15*(6), 503–511.

Argyris, C., & Kaplan, R. S. (1994). Implementing new knowledge: The case of activity-based costing. *Accounting Horizons, 8*(3), 83–105.

Beusch, P., Frisk, J. E., Rosén, M., & Dilla, W. (2022). Management control for sustainability: Towards integrated systems. *Management Accounting Research, 54*, 100777.

Bourne, M., Mills, J., Wilcox, M., Neely, A., & Platts, K. (2000). Designing, implementing and updating performance measurement systems. *International Journal of Operations & Production Management, 20*(7), 754–771.

Bourne, M., Neely, A., Mills, J., & Platts, K. (2003). Why some performance measurement initiatives fail: Lessons from the change management literature. *International Journal of Business Performance Management, 5*(2–3), 245–269.

Bourne, M., Melnyk, S., & Bititci, U. S. (2018). Performance measurement and management: Theory and practice. *International Journal of Operations & Production Management, 38*(11), 2010–2021.

Brignall, S., & Modell, S. (2000). An institutional perspective on performance measurement and management in the new public service. *Management Accounting Research, 11*(3), 281–306.

Broadbent, J., & Laughlin, R. (2005). Organisational and accounting change: Theoretical and empirical reflections and thoughts on a future research agenda. *Journal of Accounting & Organizational Change, 1*, 7–26.

Burke, W. W. (2023). *Organization change: Theory and practice* (6th ed.). Columbia University, Sage.

Burns, J., & Scapens, R. W. (2000). Conceptualizing management accounting change: An institutional framework. *Management Accounting Research, 11*(1), 3–25.

Burns, J., & Vaivio, J. (2001). Management accounting change. *Management Accounting Research, 12*(4), 389–402.

Busco, C., Quattrone, P., & Riccaboni, A. (2007). Management accounting issues in interpreting its nature and change. *Management Accounting Research, 18*(2), 125–149.

Cameron, E., & Green, M. (2019). *Making sense of change management: A complete guide to the models, tools, and techniques of organizational change* (6th ed.). Kogan.

Carlucci, D., Schiuma, G., & Sole, F. (2015). The adoption and implementation of performance measurement process in Italian Public Organisations: The influence of political, cultural and rational factors. *Production Planning & Control, 26*(5), 363–376.

Castellano, N., & Leto, L. (2021). Implementazione di Sistemi di Misurazione delle Performance nelle PMI: elementi di analisi nella prospettiva del cambiamento organizzativo. *Management Control, 1*, 129–150.

Deng, W., Feng, L., Zhao, X., & Lou, Y. (2020). Effects of supply chain competition on firms' product sustainability strategy. *Journal of Cleaner Production, 275*, 124061.

Dossi, A., & Patelli, L. (2008). The decision-influencing use of performance measurement systems in relationships between headquarters and subsidiaries. *Management Accounting Research, 19*(2), 126–148.

Franco-Santos, M., Lucianetti, L., & Bourne, M. (2012). Contemporary performance measurement systems: A review of their consequences and a framework for research. *Management Accounting Research, 23*(2), 79–119.

Frezatti, F., Carter, D. B., & FG Barroso, M. (2014). Accounting without accounting: Informational proxies and the construction of organisational discourses. *Accounting, Auditing & Accountability Journal, 27*(3), 426–464.

Gersick, C. J. G. (1991). Revolutionary change theories: A multilevel exploration of the punctuated equilibrium paradigm. *Academy of Management Review, 16*(1), 10–36.

Hayes, J. (2022). *The theory and practice of change management*. Bloomsbury Publishing.

Heinicke, A. (2018). Performance measurement systems in small and medium-sized enterprises and family firms: A systematic literature review. *Journal of Management Control, 28*(4), 457–502.

Hoque, Z. (2014). 20 years of studies on the balanced scorecard: Trends, accomplishments, gaps, and opportunities for future research. *British Accounting Review, 46*(1), 33–59.

Hughes, M. (2016). Leading changes: Why transformation explanations fail. *Leadership, 12*(4), 449–469.

Jakobsen, M., & Lueg, R. (2014). Balanced scorecard and controllability at the level of middle managers–the case of unintended breaches. *Journal of Accounting & Organizational Change, 10*(4), 516–539.

Kaplan, R. S., & Norton, D. P. (1996). *The balanced scorecard: Translating strategy into action*. Harvard Business School Press.

Kasurinen, T. (2002). Exploring management accounting change: The case of a balanced scorecard implementation. *Management Accounting Research, 13*, 323–343.

Kotter, J. P. (1995). *The new rules: How to succeed in today's post-corporate world*. Harvard Business Review Press.

Kotter, J. P. (1996). *Leading change*. Harvard Business Review Press.

Kotter, J. P., Brown, T., Martin, R. L., & Rigby, D. K. (2021). *HBR's 10 must reads on change management, Vol. 2 (with bonus article "accelerate!" by John P. Kotter)*. Harvard Business Press.

Kotter, J. P., Kim Chan, W., & Mauborgne, R. A. (2011). *HBR's 10 must reads on change management (including featured article "leading change," by John P. Kotter)*. Harvard Business Review Press.

Lasyoud, A., & Alsharari, N. M. (2017). Towards an understanding of the dimensions and factors of management accounting change. *Asia-Pacific Management Accounting Journal, 12*(1), 105–142.

Lueg, R., & Vu, L. (2015). Success factors in balanced scorecard implementations: A literature review. *Management Revue, 26*(4), 306–327.

Macchia, S. (2019). A review on management accounting change. What's next? *Economia Aziendale Online, 10*(1), 107–134.

Melnyk, S. A., Bititci, U., Platts, K., Tobias, J., & Andersen, B. (2014). Is performance measurement and management fit for the future?. *Management Accounting Research, 25*(2), 173–186.

Mikel-Hong, K., Li, N., Yu, J., & Chen, X. (2023). Resistance to change: Unraveling the roles of change strategists, agents, and recipients. *Journal of Management*, 01492063231198189.

Miraglia, R. A. (2012). Nuove tendenze nei sistemi di controllo e di misurazione delle performance. *Management Control, 2*, 1–14.

Nudurupati, S. S., Bititci, U. S., Kumar, V., & Chan, F. T. S. (2011). State of the art literature review on performance measurement. *Computers and Industrial Engineering, 60*(2), 279–290.

Prayudi, M. A., Nurkholis, N., Saraswati, E., & Rusydi, M. K. (2024). Top management characteristics, performance measurement systems design and strategic change of reformed public hospitals in Indonesia. *Australasian Accounting, Business and Finance Journal, 18*(1), 44–60.

Rosenbaum, D., More, E., & Steane, P. (2018). Planned organisational change management: Forward to the past? An exploratory literature review. *Journal of Organizational Change Management, 31*(2), 286–303.

Senge, P. M. (1990). *The fifth discipline: The art and practice of the learning organization.* Doubleday.

Sgrò, F., Palazzi, F., Ciambotti, M., & Gelsomini, M. (2020). The design, implementation and use of intellectual capital measurements: A case study. *Management Control, Suppl. 1*, 19–38.

Stouten, J., Rousseau, D. M., & De Cremer, D. (2018). Successful organizational change: Integrating the management practice and scholarly literatures. *Academy of Management Annals, 12*(2), 752–788.

Vaivio, J. (1999). Exploring a "non-financial" management accounting change. *Management Accounting Research, 10*(4), 409–437.

Van Camp, J., & Braet, J. (2016). Taxonomizing performance measurement systems' failures. *International Journal of Productivity and Performance Management, 65*(5), 672–693.

van der Steen, M. (2011). The emergence and change of management accounting routines. *Accounting, Auditing & Accountability Journal, 24*(4), 502–547.

Yetano, A. (2013). What drives the institutionalization of performance measurement and management in local government. *Public Performance and Management Review, 37*(1), 59–86.

Chapter 2
The Process of Management Accounting Change

This chapter provides a concise review of the literature on management accounting change, outlining the key frameworks and studies that have shaped the field. Traditionally, research in this area has been rooted in sociological theories, such as institutional theory, and has aimed to explain the dynamics and implications of change. However, this manuscript departs from most approaches by incorporating concepts from change management, specifically from the fields of psychology, organizational theory, and organizational development and change.

This chapter helps the reader to understand how this manuscript's approach differs from established frameworks, while still addressing key themes of management accounting change. It also emphasizes that while performance measurement systems are part of the discourse, management accounting change theories and frameworks are intended to be more generally applicable to management accounting systems, from traditional to advanced and holistic.

2.1 Chapter Summary

This chapter provides a brief review of the literature and main frameworks belonging to the research field of management accounting change. Foundational research in this area has generally aimed to understand how changes in management accounting systems occur. Specifically, much research has focused on identifying the catalysts and dynamics driving these changes, the elements that support or impede progress, and the wide-ranging implications—both positive and negative—associated with their implementation. As mentioned in the introduction, most of the literature in this field is based on the use of sociological theories, such as institutional theory. Despite the aim remains fundamentally the same of management accounting change studies, this study sets itself apart from established approaches within the

L. Leto, *Integrating Change Management and Management Accounting Change*, SIDREA Series in Accounting and Business Administration,
https://doi.org/10.1007/978-3-031-84387-7_2

field. Rather than following the prevailing literature, this work is informed by concepts and theories from change management, including those from psychology, organizational theory and behavior, and organizational development and change. Therefore, this chapter is useful for the reader both to understand how the approach taken in this book differs from the usual one, and to get an overview of the insights that this field of research provides for understanding performance measurement systems (PMS) implementation dynamics.

Before reviewing the main theories and frameworks of management accounting change, it is important to make an initial point. While these theories are useful for understanding the specific phenomenon of PMS implementation and adoption, they often have a broader focus on management accounting change in general. The introduction of PMS that measure qualitative elements and use nonfinancial indicators is also fundamental to the discourse of management accounting change (Chenhall & Moers, 2015), as these characteristics create specific implementation issues and dynamics. Nevertheless, the theories, frameworks, and studies in this field usually target the implementation or change of any management accounting system, ranging from the most traditional to the most advanced and evolved.

Interestingly, studies on management accounting change began to emerge in the early 1990s (e.g., Innes & Mitchell, 1990; Scapens & Roberts, 1993) and gained considerable momentum from the late 1990s to the early 2000s (e.g., Brignall & Modell, 2000; Burns & Scapens, 2000; Cobb et al., 1995; Dillard et al., 2004; Kasurinen, 2002; Vaivio, 1999). This period coincides with the development and adoption by companies of more advanced performance measurement and management accounting systems. Scholars of organizational change see this period as a significant break with the past, leading to increased competition among firms and the need for more frequent and rapid organizational change due to rapid technological advances, globalization, and a greater focus on sustainability (Kotter, 1995; Weick & Quinn, 1999). Thus, it can be assumed that these phenomena have all contributed to a greater interest in studies related to organizational change.

2.2 A Brief Overview of Management Accounting Change

In the research on management accounting change, many contributions have been made, often adopting different perspectives and research methodologies. The studies in this field frequently entail the development of frameworks to analyze and explain the change process (e.g., Alsharari et al., 2015; Arroyo, 2012; Bogt & Scapens, 2019; Brignall & Modell, 2000), as well as the interpretation of the dynamics and determinants that can impact its implementation through the analysis of case or field studies (e.g., Pigatto et al., 2023; Alsharari & Daniels, 2024; Giannetti et al., 2021; Kasurinen, 2002). These analyses were initially developed using an exploratory and inductive approach (e.g., Innes & Mitchell, 1990; Scapens & Roberts, 1993). Instead, recent research in this area usually applies established frameworks to examine the phenomenon of change, while still proposing occasionally new ones

(Alsharari et al., 2015). Some of these established frameworks originate from other areas of research (e.g., Chenhall & Moers, 2015; Giannetti et al., 2021), while others are specific to management accounting change (e.g., Teklay & Bobe, 2023).

One of the earliest contributions in the field of management accounting change is probably the framework of Innes and Mitchell (1990), which presented the factors that can support the implementation of a change in management accounting systems. These factors are divided into *catalysts*, *facilitators*, and *motivators*. *Motivators* are elements that broadly influence change, such as intense market competition, technological advances, and changes in the operating environment. *Facilitators*, while not sufficient to produce change on their own, are essential to enable management accounting change. These include the knowledge and skills available within the organization and the availability of financial and technological resources. *Catalysts* are factors that directly trigger a particular type of change (e.g., the introduction of a specific PMS or management accounting tool). Examples include regulatory changes and the entry of new competitors or substitute products. Innes and Mitchell (1990) highlight that both *motivators* and *catalysts* can drive change, but their effectiveness depends on the presence of *facilitators*. This framework was later expanded to include new elements by Cobb et al. (1995), namely the role of *leaders* and *momentum*, while also recognizing the existence of elements that inhibit change. *Leader*s are subjects that play a critical role as *catalysts* in the early stages of change processes and remain essential supporters throughout implementation. Because of their influence and power in the organization and their ability to motivate their employees, they can play a significant role in bringing about change. *Momentum* refers to the sense of progress that drives people to pursue implementation. In other words, it is realized when the implementation project keeps going and keeps people working on it. A final expansion of this framework was then proposed by Kasurinen[1] (2002), who detailed the factors that tend to inhibit or prevent the realization of change, namely *confusers*, *frustrators*, and *delayers*. *Confusers* are factors that disrupt the change process and create doubt about the goals and impact of the change. Examples include key sponsors withdrawing from the project, misunderstandings about usefulness of the PMS, or disagreements about the change goals.

Frustrators are elements that impede specific change efforts. These can include an organizational culture that is resistant to implementing new tools or specific changes, or managers who resist because they fear changing power dynamics. *Delayers* are temporary technical obstacles that affect both the planning and implementation phases. These include the lack of a reliable information system or an unclear strategy.

In essence, the successive developments of the framework have sought to incorporate new elements not previously considered and to provide a more comprehensive view of the dynamics and factors that may influence a management accounting

[1] Kasurinen's (2002) framework is discussed in more detail in Sect. 3.4.2, which focuses specifically on PMS implementation. This framework was, in fact, developed and applied to analyze a PMS implementation case.

change process. Kasurinen (2002) proposal has been used in research to identify factors that help or hinder the implementation of specific tools (Farneti, 2009; Munir et al., 2013). It can also help managers by highlighting potential problems and opportunities that can be managed, avoided, or seized during an organizational change process.

Despite this notable example, most of management accounting change studies has actually been based on the use of institutionalist theories (Goretzki et al., 2013). This has led to the creation of various frameworks designed to explain and analyze the change process, along with the events and factors that contribute to its success or failure. The two main streams of institutional theories applied in the field of management accounting change concern old institutional economics (OIE) and new institutional sociology (NIS) (Alsharari et al., 2015). Often, the two have been treated separately and in contrast to each other, as the former lends itself better to explaining intraorganizational dynamics (Bogt & Scapens, 2019; Burns & Scapens, 2000) while the latter more the dynamics of the external operating environment (Lasyoud et al., 2018; Rashid et al., 2024). However, a few studies related to management accounting change have also attempted to highlight the existence of points of contact and the complementarity of the two types of theories (e.g., Fahlevi et al., 2022; Alshahari et al., 2015). In any case, both types of theories have been used with essentially the same goal: to understand how internal (organizational units, interorganizational groups with significant influence) or external institutions (regulations, competitors, markets) generate organizational change and the institutionalization or permanence of new practices and routines.

While institutionalist theories are predominant, there are also some studies and frameworks based on other sociological theories. Notably, Giddens' (1984) structuration theory has been frequently cited and employed in research related to management accounting change (e.g., Makrygiannakis & Jack, 2016). This theory is sometimes utilized in tandem with institutionalist theories (e.g., Alsharari & Abougamos, 2017; Hassan, 2005) or independently (e.g., Coad et al., 2016; Englund & Gerdin, 2008).

To begin with, one of the most relevant examples of management accounting change framework is the one provided by Burns and Scapens (2000), which is based on the institutionalist perspective proposed by Scapens (1994) and OIE (Veblen, 1898, 1919). According to the authors, this framework adopts a dynamic approach to overcome the limitations of other theories, such as Giddens' (1984) structuration theory, which does not allow the change process to be adequately investigated due to its static nature.

Basically, this framework recognizes the existence of two "realms": the realm of institutions and the realm of action. Institutions, according to the authors, "comprise the taken-for-granted assumptions which inform and shape the actions of individual actors.[2]" Such institutions are encoded in rules and routines. Rules represent the formalized way of doing things in an organization (e.g., the rules to be followed

[2] P.8, Burns and Scapens (2000).

when preparing a budget), while routines are the patterns of thought and action that are habitually adopted by groups of individuals (e.g., the way a budget is usually prepared). In turn, established rules and routines tend to influence the realm of action, i.e., how individuals apply and reproduce these rules and routines over time. Although changes in the realm of institutions occur more rapidly, both the realm of institutions and the realm of action are subject to changes of a cumulative nature. Individuals may consciously or unconsciously adopt attitudes and actions that are not exactly in line with what is established by either institutions or rules and routines. The adoption of different behaviors could influence the rules and routines present in a company, which in turn remain influenced by the institutions in place and the changes occurring within them.

An interesting aspect of the Burns and Scapens (2000) framework is its rejection of an atomistic approach focused on analyzing individual realities and individuals, striving instead to understand how changes occur within groups and organizations. Moreover, unlike most studies based on institutional approaches, it focuses on what happens inside an individual organization rather than outside, contemplating, in other words, the interactions that occur within it.

As mentioned above, this framework has been applied extensively in research to explain certain management accounting change processes and has undergone numerous extensions to address and overcome some of its limitations (Bogt & Scapens, 2019; Teklay & Bobe, 2023). For example, it was used by Siti-Nabiha and Scapens (2005) through a longitudinal case study analysis to understand and explain the process of management accounting change in a company. A significant modification of it was, instead, proposed by Quinn (2011) by taking inspiration from the work of Feldman and Pentland (2003) about organizational routines and the distinction they provided between the ostensive and performative dimensions of routines. In particular, compared to the original proposal, this study explores more deeply the nature of rules and routines in management accounting, aiming at better applicability in less formal organizations where interorganizational institutions are less obvious and formalized, such as small and medium-sized enterprises (SMEs).

The framework of Burns and Scapens (2000) has also undergone a recent revision and expansion by Bogt and Scapens (2019) to encompass the dynamics related to the external environment. In expanding the framework, the authors integrated broader field-level and extra-organizational institutions, acknowledging also the influence of situated actors and incorporating the concept of "situated rationality." This modification aims to enable the exploration of the rationalities of different organizational groups and differentiates between situated rationality and the more generalized forms of rationality rooted in institutional logics. This revised framework was developed to consider agency and situated actions, accepting that choosing suitable routines involves deliberation. It also examines the potential dominance of influential actors within and outside the organization who can mandate rules or enforce "generalized practices" prevalent in the broader environment. Finally, this expansion also addresses critical issues that were ignored, such as the role of trust, power, and agency in the change process.

The limited consideration of the influence of the external environment on the change process in the original framework (Burns & Scapens, 2000) has also led to the emergence of different frameworks based on NIS. In fact, NIS theories can include concepts such as legitimation and decoupling, which can provide a more comprehensive view of the phenomenon and consideration of the influence of the external environment (Alsharari et al., 2015). According to these theories, legitimation helps explain how new management accounting practices gain acceptance within an organization and its broader environment, thereby driving management accounting change. Practices become legitimate when they conform to widely accepted norms and values within the institutional environment, such as societal norms, industry standards, or professional guidelines. Decoupling, on the other hand, refers to situations where organizations adopt new practices or policies to demonstrate conformity with external pressures and expectations, but these practices are not actually implemented or are only superficially integrated into day-to-day operations.

The issue of Burns and Scapens' (2000) framework incapability to consider the operating environment and social context was openly addressed by Dillard et al. (2004), who proposed a new framework based on NIS. In particular, this framework is based on both the concept of Weber's (1968) axes of tension and Giddens' (1984) structuration theory. This framework aims to provide a better consideration of the social context and the effects of elements such as the distribution of power, the perception of rationality in the choice of accounting systems and the way reality is framed or symbolically described.

Another framework of significant importance, but attributable more to the strand of NIS than OIE, is that of Brignall and Modell (2000). The authors, in fact, while not explicitly claiming to be inspired by NIS, develop it on the basis of studies belonging to that strand (e.g., DiMaggio & Powell, 1983). This framework is specifically aimed at analyzing the adoption and use of multidimensional PMS in the public sector. In particular, it focuses on the sociopolitical dynamics and the operational context of public sector organizations, examining their impact on the adoption of such tools. In their study, they identify three key groups of stakeholders that affect the design and implementation of PMS in the public sector, which are: funding bodies, groups of professional service providers within the focal organization, and purchasers of its services. Given the complex interplay of power dynamics and the presence of diverse stakeholders with varied interests, the authors suggest that grasping the related institutional pressures is essential for a clearer understanding of the changes in management accounting systems in the public sector.

A further framework worth mentioning that remains within the institutionalist strand of management accounting change is that of Alsharari et al. (2015). In their work, these authors illustrate the points of contact and differences between OIE and NIS theories. They underscore that OIE has been criticized for its predominant focus on organizational-level views, overlooking the extensive societal, political, and economic elements that frame the organizational context. On the other hand, they argue that NIS, with its emphasis on extra-organizational dimensions, lacks an in-depth analysis of the internal dynamics of organizational change, leaving unexplored the varied organizational responses to similar institutional pressures.

To overcome the inherent limitations in both OIE and NIS theories, Alsharari et al. (2015) proposed a hybrid framework that aims to give a holistic view of the forces that shape change both inside and outside the companies. This framework integrates the frameworks of Dillard et al. (2004) and Burns and Scapens (2000) and also incorporates Hardy (1996) model of power mobilization. This last incorporation also addresses the influence of power dynamics on the adoption and implementation of management accounting systems. In the author's opinion, their work can facilitate the study of the interactions between extra- and intraorganizational elements impacting the development of management accounting systems and considers aspects such as power, agency, and institutional resistance in management accounting change processes.

Arroyo (2012) also attempted to bridge the gap between OIE and NIS theories. Drawing inspiration from the works on institutional entrepreneurship by DiMaggio (1988), Dacin et al. (2002), and Greenwood and Suddaby (2006), Arroyo proposed a framework that addresses the limitations of both types of institutional theories. This framework concurrently considers the dynamics within the external environment and operational context, as well as the intraorganizational dynamics among different groups of individuals. This work is still based on the framework of Burns and Scapens (2000) to analyze intraorganizational dynamics, while it is also informed by the framework of Tolbert and Zucker (1999) and Greenwood et al. (2002) for conducting analysis of the extra-organizational dynamics.

Although the frameworks seen so far can be used to analyze both the internal dynamics and the dynamics in the operating environment that lead to change, it's interesting that only a few studies apply management accounting change frameworks to small companies. In other words, they have been mostly applied in large companies or public companies (e.g., Alsharari & Daniels, 2024; Lasyoud & Alsharari, 2017; Youssef, 2013).

For instance, Alsharari and Abougamos (2017) applied institutional and structuration theory to examine the process of management accounting change within the Jordanian Ministry of Finance and the Jordanian public sector. Their study suggests that accounting changes in these entities are deeply intertwined with broader socioeconomic and political contexts (e.g., public and fiscal reforms), highlighting the shift from traditional bureaucratic systems to New Public Management approaches in response to external challenges and pressures. Another example is provided by Rashid et al. (2024) focused on 20 listed companies in Bangladesh to examine the nature of management accounting change in the context of an emerging economy. In order to explain the phenomenon of management accounting change, the authors applied the NIS theory to show that coercive, mimetic, and normative institutional pressures significantly drive these changes. They argue that these pressures, together with economic factors, influence the adoption and implementation of new management accounting techniques. In other words, they suggest that the interplay between these institutional pressures and economic forces shapes the extent and nature of management accounting change in these firms.

Another aspect that emerges, in addition to the prevalence of studies focused on large or public companies, is the consistent use of sociological theories to analyze and explain the phenomenon of change. Theories grounded in psychology or those developed within the field of research organizational behavior & theory are less frequently considered or employed, with notable but dated exceptions such as Argyris and Kaplan (1994).

The heavy reliance on sociological theories might narrow the lens of analysis for the management accounting change process, potentially providing a less holistic view of the factors that shape and influence it. For example, the issue of resistance to change, a challenge acknowledged since the early stages of management accounting change research (Hassan, 2005; Liguori & Steccolini, 2011), has been extensively addressed by scholars in human resources (e.g., Choi, 2011; Rafferty & Restubog, 2017), change management (e.g., Kotter, 2012; Stouten et al., 2018), psychology (e.g., Lewin, 1947; Schein, 1996), and organizational behavior & theory (e.g., Buchanan et al., 2005; Weick & Quinn, 1999). These theories have been applied to understand the dynamics surrounding acceptance or resistance to change in groups within organizations, as well as individual behaviors. Yet, their application in PMS implementation and management accounting change studies appears less common. This is particularly surprising given that psychology and human resource management theories seem appropriate for analyzing individual dynamics and reactions to change.

Following this brief introduction to management accounting change, attention is now turned to the specific phenomenon of PMS implementation.

References

Alsharari, N. M., & Abougamos, H. (2017). The processes of accounting changes as emerging from public and fiscal reforms: An interpretive study. *Asian Review of Accounting, 25*(1), 2–33.

Alsharari, N. M., & Daniels, B. (2024). Management accounting practices and organizational change aspects in the public sector: Contextual/processual approach. *Journal of Accounting & Organizational Change, 20*(1), 177–204.

Alsharari, N. M., Dixon, R., & Youssef, M. A. E.-A. (2015). Management accounting change: Critical review and a new contextual framework. *Journal of Accounting & Organizational Change, 11*(4), 476–502.

Argyris, C., & Kaplan, R. S. (1994). Implementing new knowledge: The case of activity-based costing. *Accounting Horizons, 8*(3), 83–105.

Arroyo, P. (2012). Management accounting change and sustainability: An institutional approach. *Journal of Accounting & Organizational Change, 8*(3), 286–309.

Bogt, H. J., & Scapens, R. W. (2019). Institutions, situated rationality and agency in management accounting: A research note extending the Burns and Scapens framework. *Accounting, Auditing & Accountability Journal, 32*(6), 1801–1825.

Brignall, S., & Modell, S. (2000). An institutional perspective on performance measurement and management in the new public service. *Management Accounting Research, 11*(3), 281–306.

Buchanan, D., Fitzgerald, L., Ketley, D., Gollop, R., Jones, J. L., Lamont, S. S., & Whitby, E. (2005). No going back: A review of the literature on sustaining organizational change. *International Journal of Management Reviews, 7*(3), 189–205.

Burns, J., & Scapens, R. W. (2000). Conceptualizing management accounting change: An institutional framework. *Management Accounting Research, 11*, 3–25.

Chenhall, R. H., & Moers, F. (2015). The role of innovation in the evolution of management accounting and its integration into management control. *Accounting, Organizations and Society, 47*, 1–13.

Choi, M. (2011). Employees' attitudes toward organizational change: A literature review. *Human Resource Management, 50*(4), 479–500.

Coad, A., Jack, L., & Kholeif, A. (2016). Strong structuration theory in accounting research. *Accounting, Auditing & Accountability Journal, 29*(7), 1138–1144.

Cobb, I., Helliar, C., & Innes, J. (1995). Management accounting change in a bank. *Management Accounting Research, 6*, 155–175.

Dacin, M. T., Goodstein, J., & Scott, W. R. (2002). Institutional theory and institutional change: Introduction to the special research forum. *Academy of Management Journal, 45*(1), 45–56.

Dillard, J. F., Rigsby, J. T., & Goodman, C. (2004). The making and remaking of organization context: Duality and the institutionalization process. *Accounting, Auditing & Accountability Journal, 17*(4), 506–542.

DiMaggio, P. J. (1988). Interest and agency in institutional theory. *Institutional Patterns and Organizations*, 3–21.

DiMaggio, P. J., & Powell, W. W. (1983). The iron cage revisited: Institutional isomorphism and collective rationality in organizational fields. *American Sociological Review*, 147–160.

Englund, H., & Gerdin, J. (2008). Structuration theory and mediating concepts: Pitfalls and implications for management accounting research. *Critical Perspectives on Accounting, 19*(8), 1122–1134.

Fahlevi, H., Irsyadillah, I., Indriani, M., & Oktari, R. S. (2022). DRG-based payment system and management accounting changes in an Indonesian public hospital: Exploring potential roles of big data analytics. *Journal of Accounting & Organizational Change, 18*(2), 325–345.

Farneti, F. (2009). Balanced scorecard implementation in an Italian local government organization. *Public Money & Management, 29*(5), 313–320.

Feldman, M., & Pentland, B. (2003). Reconceptualising organizational routines as a source of flexibility and change. *Administrative Science Quarterly, 48*(1), 94–118.

Giannetti, R., Cinquini, L., Miolo Vitali, P., & Mitchell, F. (2021). Management accounting change as a learning process: A longitudinal analysis. *Qualitative Research in Accounting & Management, 18*(4–5), 484–515.

Giddens, A. (1984). *The constitution of society. Outline of the theory of structuration*. University of California Press.

Goretzki, L., Strauss, E., & Weber, J. (2013). An institutional perspective on the changes in management accountants' professional role. *Management Accounting Research, 24*(1), 41–63.

Greenwood, R., & Suddaby, R. (2006). Institutional entrepreneurship in mature fields: The big five accounting firms. *Academy of Management Journal, 49*(1), 27–48.

Greenwood, R., Suddaby, R., & Hinings, C. R. (2002). Theorizing change: The role of professional associations in the transformation of institutional fields. *Academy of Management Journal, 45*(1), 58–80.

Hardy, C. (1996). Understanding power: Bringing about strategic change. *British Journal of Management, 7*(s1). https://doi.org/10.1111/bjom.1996.7.issue-s1. https://doi.org/10.1111/j.1467-8551.1996.tb00144.x

Hassan, M. K. (2005). Management accounting and organisational change: An institutional perspective. *Journal of Accounting & Organizational Change, 1*(2), 125–140.

Innes, J., & Mitchell, F. (1990). The process of change in management accounting: Some field study evidence. *Management Accounting Research, 1*(1), 3–19.

Kasurinen, T. (2002). Exploring management accounting change: The case of a balanced scorecard implementation. *Management Accounting Research, 13*, 323–343.

Kotter, J. P. (1995). *The new rules: How to succeed in today's post-corporate world*. Harvard Business Review Press.

Kotter, J. P. (2012). Accelerate! *Harvard Business Review, 90*(11), 45–58.
Lasyoud, A., & Alsharari, N. M. (2017). Towards an understanding of the dimensions and factors of management accounting change. *Asia-Pacific Management Accounting Journal, 12*(1), 105–142.
Lasyoud, A. A., Haslam, J., & Roslender, R. (2018). Management accounting change in developing countries: Evidence from Libya. *Asian Review of Accounting, 26*(3), 278–313.
Lewin, K. (1947). Frontiers in group dynamics. *Human Relations, 1*, 5–41.
Liguori, M., & Steccolini, I. (2011). Accounting change: Explaining the outcomes, interpreting the process. *Accounting, Auditing & Accountability Journal, 25*(1), 27–70.
Makrygiannakis, G., & Jack, L. (2016). Understanding management accounting change using strong structuration frameworks. *Accounting, Auditing & Accountability Journal, 29*(7), 1234–1258.
Munir, R., Baird, K., & Perera, S. (2013). Performance measurement system change in an emerging economy bank. *Accounting, Auditing & Accountability Journal, 26*(2), 196–233.
Pigatto, G., Cinquini, L., Tenucci, A., & Dumay, J. (2023). Serendipity and management accounting change. *Meditari Accountancy Research, 31*(7), 88–115.
Quinn, M. (2011). Routines in management accounting research: Further exploration. *Journal of Accounting & Organizational Change, 7*(4), 337–357.
Rafferty, A. E., & Restubog, S. L. D. (2017). Why do employees' perceptions of their organization's change history matter? The role of change appraisals. *Human Resource Management, 56*, 533–550.
Rashid, M. M., Hossain, D. M., & Alam, M. S. (2024). An institutional explanation of management accounting change in an emerging economy: Evidence from Bangladesh. *Journal of Accounting & Organizational Change, 20*(3), 513–535.
Scapens, R. W. (1994). Never mind the gap: Towards an institutional perspective on management accounting practice. *Management Accounting Research, 5*, 301–321.
Scapens, R., & Roberts, J. (1993). Accounting and control: A case study of resistance to accounting change. *Management Accounting Research, 4*(1), 1–32.
Schein, E. H. (1996). Kurt Lewin's change theory in the field and in the classroom: Notes toward a model of managed learning. *Systems Practice, 9*(1), 27–47.
Siti-Nabiha, A. K., & Scapens, R. (2005). Stability and change: An institutionalist study of management accounting change. *Accounting, Auditing & Accountability Journal, 18*(1), 44–73.
Stouten, J., Rousseau, D. M., & De Cremer, D. (2018). Successful organizational change: Integrating the management practice and scholarly literatures. *Academy of Management Annals, 12*(2), 752–788.
Teklay, B., & Bobe, B. J. (2023). Quality management adoption and management accounting change in a sub-Saharan African firm. *Accounting, Auditing & Accountability Journal, 37*(3), 713–742.
Tolbert, P. S., & Zucker, L. G. (1999). The institutionalization of institutional theory. *Studying Organization. Theory & Method, 1*, 169–184.
Vaivio, J. (1999). Examining the quantified customer. *Accounting Organizations and Society, 24*(8), 689–715.
Veblen, T. (1898). Why is economics not an evolutionary science? *Quarterly Journal of Economics, 12*, 373–397. Reprinted in Veblen, T., (1919). The Place of Science in Modern Civilisation and Other Essays, New York, Huebsch, 56–81.
Veblen, T. (1919). *The place of science in modern civilization and other essays*. Huebsch.
Weber, M. (1968). *Economy and society: An outline of interpretive sociology, two volumes*. Bedminster.
Weick, K., & Quinn, R. (1999). Organizational change and development. *Annual Review of Psychology, 50*, 361–386.
Youssef, M. A. (2013). Management accounting change in an Egyptian organization: An institutional analysis. *Journal of Accounting & Organizational Change, 9*(1), 50–73.

Chapter 3
Performance Measurement Systems Implementation Literature Review

This chapter provides a comprehensive literature review on the implementation of performance measurement systems (PMS). It begins by tracing the history of management accounting and control systems, explaining the evolution towards modern, integrated PMS. The discussion continues by highlighting key features of popular PMS models as well as their strengths and weaknesses.

The chapter then examines the various definitions of PMS given in different fields, including management accounting, strategic management, and operations management.

A significant part of the chapter is then devoted to a detailed review of literature on PMS implementation. Using Bourne et al.'s (2000) framework, which divides the process of PMS adoption into design, implementation, and use phases, the chapter systematically reviews studies that focus on each stage. It highlights the dynamics, challenges, and enabling factors related to PMS implementation phases, drawing on research from several disciplines to provide a broad understanding of the benefits and potential drawbacks organizations face when adopting these systems.

3.1 Chapter Summary

This chapter provides a literature review on the implementation of performance measurement systems (PMS). Therefore, its purpose is to provide an overview of the prevailing research related to the process of implementing and updating such systems in organizations, as well as to present the main related issues and concerns. The chapter begins with a section on the history of PMS. This section briefly outlines the history of early management accounting and control systems. It then examines the reasons that led to the development of the modern, integrated, and holistic systems in use today. It also provides a brief analysis of the most popular PMS

L. Leto, *Integrating Change Management and Management Accounting Change*, SIDREA Series in Accounting and Business Administration,
https://doi.org/10.1007/978-3-031-84387-7_3

models, highlighting their key features, strengths and weaknesses. The first section concludes with a description of the specific attributes that define a PMS for the purposes of this study, distinguishing it from other management accounting systems sometimes considered under the umbrella of PMS in other works.

The second section delivers an overview of the different definitions prevalent across the various strands of research that have ventured into the topic of PMS, such as management accounting, strategic management, and operations management. Subsequently, it presents two holistic theoretical frameworks by Otley (1999) and Ferreira and Otley (2009) from the management control field of research, offering insight into the main concerns surrounding the research about PMS design, adoption, and use. The third section focuses specifically on the literature review pertaining PMS implementation. This section opens with a presentation of Bourne et al.'s (2000) framework, which is particularly useful for analyzing this type of phenomenon because it adopts a processual, rather than a static, perspective. Their framework, which breaks down the process of introducing PMS into the respective stages of design, implementation, and use, is then employed to systematize the literature review. In other words, the literature review about PMS implementation process is partitioned into further subsections, each corresponding to the stages identified by Bourne et al. (2000). In this way, the studies are divided and presented in three categories: those that focus on the design of the system, those that focus on the implementation of the system, and those that focus on the use of the system. Finally, the contributions collected span a variety of research areas to provide a broad view of the dynamics, difficulties, enabling factors, benefits, and drawbacks associated with the implementation of PMS.

3.2 PMS Brief History and Main Models

3.2.1 PMS Historical Development

Through historical reconstructions based on archival records, it has been established that the forerunners of multidimensional PMS are none other than cost accounting systems (Bititci et al., 2012). The practice of preparing reports and accounting documents is extremely ancient and dates back to well before the years of the Industrial Revolution and the advent of capitalism. According to Johnson (1981), the accounting practice started with the use of double-entry bookkeeping, which can be traced back to the late thirteenth century (Bititci et al., 2012). However, these accounting documents primarily served to keep track of the relationships and transactions between the merchant or entrepreneur and their customer. Therefore, they only concerned the relationships outside the organizations.

The development and use of management accounting tools, which looked internally at the organization, is a relatively recent practice and can be found starting from the nineteenth century (Johnson & Kaplan, 1987). Specifically, the first companies to need internal accounting information for making decisions and monitoring were the cotton textile mills that appeared in that period in England and the United States (Johnson, 1981).

The Industrial Revolution marked a heightened need for control. In fact, Johnson (1981) observes that this era was characterized, among other things, by a transition from piecework payment to the wage and salary system. This shift led to the need to better assess and control the costs incurred and the level of employee efficiency. Consequently, these phenomena also made it necessary for companies to develop a set of new tools to measure these dimensions.

By the 1930s, in the span of just over 100 years, all the more traditional management accounting tools would have already been developed (Johnson & Kaplan, 1987). In 1912, Donaldson Brown, a financial executive and corporate director at Dupont, invented a formula for breaking down the return on equity (ROE) index known as the Dupont Analysis or ROE tree. This approach included calculating a series of economic-financial indices, namely, in addition to ROE itself, return on assets (ROA), and return on investments (ROI) (Chandler, 1962). These indicators have become extremely widespread and are still used today to evaluate the performance of companies.

The budget is also a tool that is still extremely used today, but that has relatively distant origins. In fact, the first concept of a business budget was developed at General Motors in the 1920s (Chandler, 1962). Previously, the concept of budgeting was already known, but it was only applied at the governmental level. Thus, prior to the General Motors case, it was not common practice to develop a budget, while in later years, it would become, relatively quickly, one of the most widely used tools for American companies. Between 1930 and 1980, there were no more significant innovations in relation to management accounting tools (Bourne et al., 2003a). However, from the 1970s, traditional tools were increasingly viewed as outdated and inadequate for supporting business decision-making processes.

With the advent of the concepts of differentiation and cost leadership strategy, developed at the end of the 1970s (Porter Michael, 1985), these tools began to show their limitations even more (Neely & Bourne, 2000). As mentioned, some U.S. companies introduced traditional tools such as Dupont Analysis or budgeting in the early decades of the twentieth century, a period when the strategy most applied by companies was cost leadership (Neely & Bourne, 2000). Therefore, these tools proved more effective in encouraging strategies focused on reducing costs through increased efficiency and productivity, rather than on offering "premium" services or products. In other words, they did not provide adequate guidance for companies pursuing differentiation strategies that rely on charging premium prices for the unique qualities, benefits or superior performance of their products and services. Until the 1950s, when the phenomenon of globalization had not yet fully established itself, the focus of enterprises in strategic terms continued to be devoted entirely to reducing costs and increasing efficiency and productivity. The need to develop alternative tools was, therefore, not actually perceived. Since the 1960s, with the postwar economic recovery of many countries and the effective advent of globalization, the differentiation strategy has become more prevalent among companies (Bititci et al., 2012). In particular, previously less considered elements such as product quality, innovation, production and delivery time, and customer satisfaction gained significance, making it necessary to monitor several new critical success factors previously nonexistent (Neely & Bourne, 2000).

To be precise, the criticisms made at the time against these tools were numerous and varied and not connected only to the concept of differentiation strategy. The most important ones were to encourage short-termism and managerial myopia,[1] to focus excessively on identifying deviations to be corrected rather than seeking continuous improvement, to constrain responsiveness and favor barriers to change, to assume a backward-looking, to be disconnected from organization strategy, to focus too much on the inside of the company, to favor manipulation of short-term performance measures (Bourne et al., 2000; Neely & Bourne, 2000).

By encouraging managerial myopia and an excessive focus on economic-financial variables, tools such as Dupont analysis have even been accused of harming the competitiveness of the U.S. manufacturing industry (Hayes & Abernathy, 1980) at a time when globalization was increasing competition among firms. It can be argued that the perception of the inadequacy of the traditional tools culminated with the landmark work of Johnson and Kaplan (1987), who reported the declining relevance of management accounting, attributing it to the obsolescence of the prevailing systems and methods. Within this influential work, the authors proposed the activity-based costing system, designed to refine the calculation and management of business costs, offering an advanced alternative to traditional techniques.

Despite the great innovativeness of the new cost accounting approaches, this was only the beginning of a revolution in management control. As early as the beginning of the 1990s, new management accounting systems that were more holistic and integrated and capable of monitoring more qualitative and nonfinancial aspects would emerge (Bourne et al., 2003a).

To be accurate, by the late 1970s, the need to introduce tools to monitor more qualitative and nonfinancial factors was already widely perceived, but the initiatives at the company level were still somewhat limited (Neely & Bourne, 2000). Typically, early attempts involved management control tools that allowed the measurement of nonfinancial indicators but lacked a holistic perspective completely. Moreover, these indicators were not systematized through frameworks that facilitated the readability and comprehension of information at higher hierarchical levels.

Academics and consultants developed more modern PMS in response to this lack of system integration, the need to provide a holistic view of corporate performance, and the need to better monitor corporate strategy (Neely & Bourne, 2000). Thus, it can be said that the new models and emerging techniques were specifically designed to overcome the limitations of more traditional approaches.

[1] *Managerial myopia* is an expression that refers to a short-term focus by managers on immediate financial goals.

3.2.2 PMS Main Models

Although the most modern PMS have been developed since the 1990s, there were also earlier cases of tools and frameworks possessing some of their distinctive characteristics. Many consider the tableau de bord, a tool developed in France at the end of the 1800s, to be a forerunner, if not the first example of PMS (Pezet, 2009). An examination of the prevalent models reveals some common characteristics, suggesting that each model has cumulatively contributed to the development of new models throughout the evolution of PMS. In other words, each contribution on the topic has supported or influenced the development of subsequent proposals. Looking specifically at the tableau de bord, it already included the construction of dashboards of financial and nonfinancial indicators aimed at monitoring business performance and critical success factors, echoing already the multidimensional approach of later models. Moreover, the principles that should guide the construction of dashboards of indicators of the tableau de bord framework (Pezet, 2009) have many similarities with the balanced scorecard of Kaplan and Norton (1996). Examples of these principles include the limited use of indicators to provide a clear and easy-to-understand summary of performance, and the possibility to use detailed dashboards that provide more information about specific items included in the summary dashboards. However, although this tableau de bord aimed to assess the degree of success of the organization, it lacked an explicit connection with the company's strategy. Moreover, nonfinancial indicators concerned elements that were easily measurable physically (e.g., number of discarded raw materials, defective products, and delivery time) rather than aspects of a more qualitative nature (e.g., creativity, customer satisfaction, and degree of innovation).

Moving to much more recent times, one of the earliest examples of modern PMS is probably the one developed in the field of operations management by Sink (1985) and refined by Sink and Tuttle (1989). The model is based on the assumption that the performance of a company depends on the complex interrelationships existing among seven performance criteria, namely (I) effectiveness, (II) efficiency, (III) quality, (IV) productivity, (V) quality of work-life, (VI) innovation, and (VII) profitability. While hailed as a seminal work, the model is not without its limitations, most notably its failure to adopting a holistic view, given its primary focus on the value chain. For the latter reason, it can be said that, unlike holistic models, its focus was only on the inside of the company. Some factors considered essential such as the level of customer satisfaction, the strategy, the growth and learning, or the organizational culture, are not subject to monitoring in this proposal.

The performance pyramid by Lynch & Cross (1991; Cross & Lynch, 1988), sometimes called the SMART Model, is another of the first examples of more advanced and recent PMS. This tool represents in a structured form a series of elements to which the company must pay attention in order to obtain satisfactory strategic and financial results (Castellano, 2012). Unlike its predecessors, it integrates both internal aspects, such as costs and processes, and external facets like market presence and client relations. Another innovative element of the SMART model, which will be taken up in even more evolved systems, consists in creating an explicit connection between the strategy pursued and the level of external effectiveness achieved by the company. In this case, the nonfinancial indicators already included elements of a more qualitative nature, given that among the dimensions of analysis, there is also that of clients and their degree of satisfaction. However, while aiming to give a more complete and holistic view than the systems used previously, the proposal of Lynch & Cross (1991) leaves out some elements considered fundamental for the success of companies by other scholars, such as learning, innovation, and organizational culture (Kaplan & Norton, 1996; Sveiby, 1997).

Shortly after the performance pyramid came the balanced scorecard as proposed by Kaplan and Norton (1996) across a series of publications. This PMS is still one of the most "mainstream," given its widespread use in companies (Marchi & Maraghini, 2018). Consequently, it is also one of the most considered tools by practitioners and in the field of research, as evidenced by the numerous publications on the subject (Sigalas, 2015; Hoque, 2014).

This framework distinguishes four perspectives of analysis: financial, internal business process, customer, and innovation and learning. Nevertheless, unlike the performance pyramid, the balanced scorecard has a notably much more flexible structure. Its proponents argue that it can be potentially applied to many different contexts and adapted to the companies' needs because the elements of analysis can be significantly modified, adding additional perspectives or removing some of them. Indeed, Lueg and Silva (2013) identified 27 studies featuring various balanced scorecard adaptations. A typical example of these "augmented" balanced scorecards is the so-called sustainability balanced scorecard (Hansen & Schaltegger, 2016), which basically adds to the four classic perspectives, a fifth perspective related to environmental and social issues. This version of the balanced scorecard became widespread in many companies due to the increasing importance of the topic of environmental and social sustainability at a strategic level (Cinquini et al., 2016).

The balanced scorecard remains, first and foremost, a strategic control tool; therefore, the indicators that make it up must help understand the quality of the strategy adopted and the effectiveness and efficiency with which it is implemented (Strohhecker, 2016). According to its developers, the number of indicators that compose the system should be limited to at least 15 but no more than 20 in order to give the organization's top management a holistic but concise view of corporate performance. However, it is possible to develop a series of secondary dashboards that provide greater detail on the performance of certain elements and allow a better understanding and monitoring of certain phenomena and processes for the managers of the lower levels (Kaplan & Norton, 1996). Another feature of originality compared to other proposals is the consideration of the distinction between leading and lagging indicators. Lagging indicators represent elements, often of greatest interest to the company, that are directly influenced by the results achieved in the leading indicators. According to Kaplan and Norton (1996), achieving positive results at the level of leading indicators promotes and enables the achievement of positive results also at the level of lagging indicators. A simplistic example of this might be the interplay between customer satisfaction and sales volume. In this case, customer satisfaction can be a leading indicator, potentially influencing the volume of sales, while the volume of sales can be a lagging indicator, reflecting the effects of various factors, including the level of customer satisfaction.

Aside from versatile tools such as the balanced scorecard, which are designed for broad applicability, there exist tools tailored for businesses operating in particular sectors or with unique operational contexts (Choong, 2013; Parida et al., 2015; Saunila, 2016). Among these, two noteworthy systems stand out for their widespread adoption by practitioners and their prominence in research: the intangible assets monitor (Sveiby, 1997) and the performance prism (Neely et al., 2002).

Sveiby (1997) created the intangible assets monitor to explain the discrepancy between a company's market and book value through the evaluation of business performance and intangible elements. Unlike the balanced scorecard or SMART model, this tool exclusively targets the qualitative, nonfinancial aspects that contribute to an organization's success, such as its image, brand, capacity for innovation, and know-how. Sveiby (1997) identifies three key dimensions for analysis: internal structure, external structure, and individual competencies.

The external structure addresses the company's relationships with external parties, including stakeholders, customers, and suppliers, as well as factors like corporate and brand reputation that influence the company's strategic success. The internal structure takes into account internal elements such as the type of organizational structure, the way work is divided up among individuals, the type of patents and copyrights that the company holds, the climate in the organization, and the type of culture. Finally, the individual competencies dimension takes into account the experience, characteristics, know-how, and skills possessed by the people working in the company. According to this approach, for each element or asset identified as essential to business success, at least one indicator should be found to assess its level of growth, one to analyze its level of renewal/innovation, one to monitor its level of efficiency, and one to assess its stability/durability. While a tool such as the balanced scorecard relies heavily on the synthesis and keeping the number of indicators to no more than 25, in this framework, the number of indicators is significantly greater, although the financial dimension is not considered.

Finally, another notable PMS is Neely's (2002) performance prism, designed for companies whose success depends on satisfying their stakeholders. This model aims to provide a holistic view of an organization's performance by considering the needs of all key stakeholders and their contributions to the company's success. Therefore, it focuses significantly on measuring the factors that impact stakeholder satisfaction. In this case, the term "stakeholder" is defined broadly to include a wide array of parties interested in the company's performance, such as shareholders, clients, local communities, and internal members of the organization like employees and management.

To conclude, it can be said that there are various proposals regarding PMS, each having its strengths and weaknesses. There are tools such as SMART or the intangible assets monitor, which focus on specific aspects of performance. On the other hand, there are systems such as the balanced scorecard or the performance prism, which offer a broader view, covering a wide range of performance dimensions.

Nevertheless, from the experiences of both academics and practitioners, the superiority of one system over another has not been established (Choong, 2013). The balanced scorecard is indeed the most prevalent and researched tool (Hoque, 2014), yet this alone does not confirm its appropriateness for all circumstances. As discussed, certain tools are crafted with particular applications in mind, potentially offering greater utility in those specific situations. For example, for firms prioritizing stakeholder satisfaction, the performance prism might prove more effective. Or, again, when firms base their success on intangible factors, the intangible assets monitor may be the best choice.

The challenges and costs associated with implementing a PMS are another element that should not be overlooked when choosing a system. Although the most advanced tools might be potentially the most useful, some companies do not have the resources or skills to implement them. For example, the balanced scorecard generally requires fairly well-developed information systems in order to be able to gather and systematize information to make up the system's indicators, but small companies rarely have them (Amir, 2014; Malagueño et al., 2018; Papulová et al., 2021).

The impossibility of finding a successful universal approach regarding the choice of model and how to design, implement, and use PMS is an issue widely espoused in the management accounting literature (Gatti & Chiucchi, 2017; Otley, 2016). Companies therefore need to make informed decisions about which performance measurement system to adopt, based on their own knowledge, resources and specific needs for control and monitoring. Moreover, even once the model to be used has been chosen, an effort to adapt the system itself remains necessary by selecting the indicators, elements, and phenomena that are to be controlled and managed (Cheng & Humphreys, 2016). Yet, it is not a given that the process of implementing such systems starts with the choice of a precise and predefined model. There are cases of companies using performance measurement tools that do not explicitly refer to one of the "mainstream" models found in the literature (Giovannoni & Maraghini, 2013; Sousa & Aspinwall, 2010). Second, the literature also reports cases where PMS have been developed incrementally, starting from the analysis and monitoring of single specific processes. In these cases, systems have only, over time, acquired the feature of multidimensionality typical of such systems (Presti, 2021).

3.2.3 Setting Boundaries to This Research: What Type of PMS?

To conclude this introductory section on PMS, it is important to establish the boundaries of this research and clarify what kind of tools are here considered PMS. In fact, various proposals for management accounting systems have been presented over the years, but not all align with the definition of PMS intended in this study.

In this research, it is adopted the framework for contemporary PMS outlined by Franco-Santos et al. (2012), which provides the defining traits these systems should have. According to these scholars, there are four distinct types of PMS, characterized by their components and primary functions. All four of these typologies incorporate a mix of financial and nonfinancial performance indicators, but in some cases, there is an explicit link with the strategy, while in others, the link is implicit but still present. Concerning the key use, they find that these tools may be used (I) only to inform managerial decision-making and assess organizational performance. They may be used (II) to inform managerial decision-making and assess organizational and managerial performance. Finally, they may be used (III) to inform managerial decision-making, assess organizational and managerial performance, and influence monetary rewards. By combining the kind of use and the presence of an explicit or implicit link to strategy, the authors define the four types of PMS. To begin with, there is type A, which involves employing financial and nonfinancial indicators that are explicitly or implicitly linked to strategy to inform decision-making and evaluate organizational performance. Type B is similar to type A but includes clear cause-and-effect relationships between the various measures that make up the system and an explicit link to strategy. Type C is similar to type B but also includes the assessment of managerial performance. Finally, type D shares the same characteristics of type C but also includes a link between monetary rewards and performance targets.

In light of the characteristics suggested by Franco-Santos et al. (2012), PMS here refers to tools that include financial and nonfinancial measures, which are implicitly or explicitly linked to the company's strategy. In this study, the main defining characteristic of PMS is not, however, related to their specific purpose of use. In other words, PMS are considered here as tools that have the above characteristics and can be used to inform managerial decisions, evaluate business performance, assess managerial performance, and/or provide incentives. In any case, to be considered successful, their implementation requires in any case some kind of regular use of the system within the organization, not just its availability (Nudurupati et al., 2011). As the change management literature suggests, changes are only considered successful if they result in behavioral change among employees (Hayes, 2022). Therefore, in the case of PMS, this change in behavior must involve their consistent use.

Considering the classification provided by Franco-Santos et al. (2012), the most classical management accounting systems, such as Dupont's analysis, or the traditional budget and cost accounting tools, like activity-based costing and time-driven activity-based costing, are excluded from consideration in this work.[2] In fact, in Dupont's analysis, the traditional budget ad cost accounting tools typically do not have an explicit connection to the companies' strategies and do not make use of nonfinancial indicators.

---

[2] This exclusion is specific to this work precisely because it adopts the defining characters proposed by Franco-Santos et al. (2012). The tools mentioned here are treated elsewhere as PMS in their own right (Lizza, 2007; Marasca, 2011).

On the other hand, tools such as the performance pyramid (Lynch & Cross, 1991), the balanced scorecard (Kaplan & Norton, 1996), the performance prism (Neely et al., 2002), and the intangible assets monitor (Sveiby, 1997) are here considered as PMS. Indeed, these tools are geared toward the strategic evaluation and control of the company and involve the use of financial and nonfinancial variables.

3.3 Definition and Theoretical Background

The definitions of PMS are numerous and highlight different aspects (Franco-Santos et al., 2007). In fact, this subject has involved scholars from multiple disciplines who have often taken diverse analytical lenses and perspectives. Because of the holistic nature of these tools, this topic has been addressed not only by scholars of management accounting and control (Lizza, 2007; Marasca, 2011) but also by researchers belonging to the fields of marketing, human resources, information systems, strategy, and operations management (Neely, 2008; Franco-Santos & Doherty, 2017).

For example, the balanced scorecard itself, although created by management accounting scholars (Kaplan & Norton, 1996), is a widely analyzed, studied, and applied tool in the disciplines of operations management (Perkins et al., 2014), human resources (Sharma et al., 2016), and strategic management (Hasan & Chyi, 2017).

While the variety of approaches and perspectives is probably a positive element that contributes to a more comprehensive view of the methodologies applied to measure business performance, this has also fostered confusion and ambiguity in defining what PMS are (Franco-Santos et al., 2007).

The most widely accepted definition in operations management is probably the one given by Neely et al. (1995, p. 81), who define PMS as a "set of metrics used to quantify both the efficiency and effectiveness of actions." Another often-cited definition is the one from Bititci et al. (1997, p. 533), who suggest that PMS is "the heart of the performance management process and it is of critical importance to the effective and efficient functioning of the performance management system" and that it may be used as a "reporting process that gives feedback to employees on the outcome of actions."

In examining the research field of strategic management, one of the most cited definitions comes from Atkinson et al. (1997), who affirm that "performance measurement focuses on one output of strategic planning: senior management's choice of the nature and scope of the contracts that it negotiates, both explicitly and implicitly, with its stakeholders. The performance measurement system is the tool the company uses to monitor those contractual relationships."

There are also definitions developed in the management accounting and control field that basically see these tools as an evolution of the more traditional management accounting systems. In this area of study, one of the most considered is Otley's (1999, p. 364) definition, which describes PMS as a "system that provides the information that is intended to be useful to managers in performing their jobs and to assist organizations in developing and maintaining viable patterns of behavior." Another is provided by Broadbent and Laughlin (2009, p. 293), who define PMS as "a control framework which attempts to ensure that certain ends are achieved, and particular means are used to attain these ends."

According to Otley (1999), the elements that compose a performance measurement system are (1) objectives, (2) strategy, (3) targets, (4) rewards, and (5) information flows (feedback and feedforward). Within this conceptual framework, it becomes evident that Otley's emphasis extends to both the measurement and management of performance. This work was subsequently further elaborated and expanded upon by Ferreira and Otley (2009), who provided a broader view of the key aspects of the performance measurement and management systems and the issues connected to their design, implementation, and use. The elements that compose this framework are namely (1) mission and vision, (2) key success factors, (3) organization structure, (4) strategies and plans, (5) key performance measures, (6) target setting, (7) performance evaluation, (8) reward system, (9) information flows, systems, and networks, (10) PMS use, (11) PMS change, and (12) strength and coherence.

According to Ferreira and Otley (2009), the first step in developing a PMS entails identifying and delineating the company's:

(1) Mission and vision, the mission explicates the company's fundamental purpose and activities, while the vision outlines the desired future state that the company wants to achieve. These elements are indispensable for recognizing the phenomena that hold relevance for the organization and necessitate monitoring and managing.

(2) Key success factors, sometimes referred to as critical success factors, constitute the areas, activities, attributes, competencies, and capabilities that are crucial to an organization's success. These elements have received numerous definitions over the years (Anthony, 1965; Rockart, 1982) and have also assumed a central role in the practice of performance measurement (Parmenter, 2015). The achievement of satisfactory results at the level of critical success factors or areas is generally considered fundamental to the success and survival of organizations (Rockart, 1982). It is for this reason that for the company to thrive, it can be useful to identify these factors and consequently choose measures and indicators to monitor the results achieved in these areas (Rangone, 1997).

(3) Organizational structures consist in how work, tasks, and roles are assigned and divided among the individuals who are part of a company. This element is also recognized within other frameworks as an aspect of management control systems (Merchant & Van der Stede, 2017) because it delineates in some way the range of the activities, actions, and performances expected from, or permitted to, each individual present in the company. Thus, it can be said that organizational structures are part of management control as they establish what individuals should or should not do in the company.

(4) Strategies represent the direction of the firm and the long-term goals the organization intends to fulfill. They are deemed an indispensable component in the

construction of any contemporary performance measurement system. Indeed, strategy undergoes continual monitoring and assessment in the most recent models (Castellano, 2011; Franco-Santos et al., 2012), as discussed in the preceding section. Franco-Santos et al. (2012), who have provided an extensive literature review on PMS, also state that strategy monitoring is one of the defining features of contemporary performance measurement tools. Kaplan and Norton (2004) have even developed the concept of "strategy maps" to describe the strategy's key elements more easily and thus facilitate the implementation of the balanced scorecard and the identification of indicators that are actually useful for strategic management and control.

(5) Key performance measures, whether financial or nonfinancial, serve as indicators at various organizational levels to evaluate a company's performance and its ability to realize its strategy and objectives. As previously noted, the implementation of a PMS within an organization often involves substantial effort to determine the appropriate metrics to be measured. On the one hand, there is the matter of understanding which indicators are most useful to the firm (Carlucci, 2010). On the other hand, there is also the issue of identifying indicators that are actually measurable for the company based on its capabilities and information systems (Marchi, 2011; Neely, 2008). In some instances, potentially useful indicators are excluded because the organization lacks the capacity to gather the necessary data. For example, not all companies have the resources to compose a customer satisfaction index based on the administration of questionnaires or interviews, even though such an indicator could hold considerable interest.

(6) Target setting is the process of identifying objectives to be assigned in order to evaluate and reward performance. According to Ferreira and Otley (2009), this element is of fundamental importance because it makes it possible to verify whether the company is achieving the objectives it has set itself and to compare the results actually achieved with the desired ones. Where targets have not been met, it creates an opportunity to understand why the desired results have not been achieved and what future action needs to be taken. More sophisticated systems may even offer predictive insights, signaling when objectives are at risk of not being met, thus enabling proactive responses to potential setbacks. In addition, target setting plays a key role in terms of management control because it makes individuals realize what elements they need to focus their efforts on. Therefore, it guides and aligns the actions of subjects who can be held accountable for achieving certain goals. With regard to this last aspect, there have been many studies aimed at investigating which are the most effective approaches to target setting. For example, some studies have examined the effect of setting challenging versus easily attainable goals, or the methods of setting targets that create greater commitment to achieving them (Bol et al., 2010; Webb, 2004).

(7) Performance evaluation encompasses a spectrum of activities ranging from formal performance appraisal to the informal guidance provided by managers regarding priority areas. Some companies adopt a formalized performance appraisal system in order to evaluate individuals according to well-defined criteria. In other cases, the approach may be less formal and based rather than on specific parameters

on managers' subjective perceptions (Franco-Santos et al. 2012). The latter approach becomes "unavoidable" where the performance measurement system is underdeveloped or lacks the sophistication to produce accurate individual or organizational performance data.

(8) Rewards are the outcome of performance evaluations and may include expressions of approval and recognition by senior managers, financial rewards, and promotions. Many studies have focused on the topic of incentive and reward systems (Rizzotti, 2019; Speckbacher & Wentges, 2012) to understand how and when they are used, what is their effectiveness in improving performance and pushing individuals to engage in desired behaviors, and what are their effects on motivation. For example, Cardinaels and Yin (2015) found that the way managers use incentives can influence the use of truthful or manipulated reports and signal trust or distrust, but also leak important information about the social norm to which employees are trying to conform.

(9) Information flows, systems, and networks are essential for the functioning of a PMS and the collection of information needed to compose the performance indicators. Information systems thus constitute, to some extent, the backbone of management accounting & control systems and PMS (Marchi, 1993, 2011). Indeed, the type of indicators that can be adopted within a PMS depends on the type and amount of data the company may have at its disposal and on its ability to process them. In our times, where phenomena such as big data are emerging, the challenge for companies has become not only to gather information but also to refine it in order to obtain indicators that are actually useful for understanding the company's performance and guiding decision-making processes (Huerta & Jensen, 2017; Kamble & Gunasekaran, 2020; Nudurupati et al., 2016). Recent IT developments related to the Internet and social media have given companies the opportunity to access a whole range of new information, which, if not turned into synthetic indicators, may prove challenging to interpret. The information harnessed through these channels can provide either feedback, aiding in the identification and adoption of corrective measures without fundamentally altering organizational activities, or feedforward insights, potentially prompting a rethinking of strategies and organizational processes already put in place (Ferreira & Otley, 2009).

(10) The use of PMS consists of managers' use of information and control systems. Indeed, the literature delineates a diversity of modalities and objectives behind managers' employment of these systems. For example, there are instances where these systems are used with a strictly diagnostic and decision-support approach (Tessier & Otley, 2012). Still, there are also many situations in which these systems are actually used to influence people's behavior toward the assumption of desired attitudes and achievement of performance standards (Castellano, 2012).

(11) PMS change expresses the need to adapt and update PMS over time to address and align with strategic shifts within the company, as well as to the evolving competitive, economic, social, and political environment (Melnyk et al., 2014). More generally, as mentioned in the introduction to this work, the issue of change has been addressed extensively both in the field of management accounting systems research, giving rise to the internal strand of management accounting change

studies (Alsharari et al., 2015), and specifically in the field of PMS, with contributions given not only by accounting experts but also by strategy and operations management scholars.

(12) Strength and coherence pertain to the level of alignment and coordination among the different components of the whole system to deliver efficient and effective outcomes. In fact, Ferreira and Otley (2009) point out that the system is more than its single components because of the virtuous relationships among the elements that are part of it. Still, it may happen that although the system is designed well at the level of particular components, the lack of integration and coordination among them can adversely impact the organization's management and control capabilities.

Otley's (1999) and Ferreira and Otley's (2009) frameworks significantly contributed to defining the conceptual nature of any PMS (Broadbent & Laughlin, 2009). In the field of research, these frameworks can be used to determine the elements to consider when conducting studies on performance measurement and management systems. In practice, managers can use them to analyze and improve the alignment of organizational structures, strategies, and control mechanisms to improve overall performance and strategic coherence.

Another relevant conceptual framework for analyzing PMS use has been proposed by Broadbent and Laughlin (2009), who developed it to extend the work of Otley (1999). In their paper, the two authors define two macro-types of PMS, within which any management control system can be categorized, i.e., transactional PMS and relational PMS. This dichotomy draws inspiration from the extensive discourse on rationalization by the seminal works of Weber (1968) and Habermas (1984). In particular, Broadbent and Laughlin (2009) argue that relational PMS are driven by the exercise of communicative rationality among stakeholders, which is the process by which they discuss and attain consensus on the goals the company needs to achieve. In the presence of relational PMS, the management tends to be more comfortable with qualitative performance indicators, although quantitative indicators are also used. The performance indicators and relative targets are assumed to be discursively agreed upon among the stakeholders, who feel the ownership of the PMS.

On the other hand, they claim that transactional PMS are driven by the application of instrumental rationality to choose measures and targets, which can be defined as highly functional and directed to specific outcomes process. This time, ownership of the PMS is "associated and linked either to a particular sub-group of stakeholders or to an abstract requirement seemingly owned by no-one" (Broadbent & Laughlin, 2009, p. 293). In this category of PMS, there is a focus on avoiding a lack of precision in the system, which impacts the choice and use of means to achieve the targets, making managers more comfortable with the use of precise and quantitative performance indicators.

While the frameworks proposed by Otley (1999), Ferreira and Otley (2009) and Broadbent and Laughlin (2009) shed some light on the conceptual nature of performance measurement, they are quite broad in scope. The frameworks can be applied to both traditional and innovative management accounting and control tools. In fact,

Otley (1999) employed the initial iteration of his framework to both companies that use advanced PMS, such as the balanced scorecard, and to companies that use only traditional tools, such as the budget. More in general, the authors of these frameworks see performance management activity as a natural evolution of management control, and these frameworks should therefore be viewed in this light. In other words, their focus is not only on performance measurement systems but also on the ways in which performance is controlled, influenced, and managed.

Therefore, these models do not specifically delineate the features that a PMS must possess to determine which management control systems are to be classified as PMS (Franco-Santos et al., 2012). In addition, Ferreira and Otley's (2009) framework itself, while presenting a dimension specifically dedicated to the change and updating of systems used in companies, it does not specifically outline what are the phases, steps, or sequence of events related to the implementation process of a PMS.

For these reasons, while acknowledging the substantial utility of the aforementioned frameworks, as evidenced by the volume of literature based on them, this study has chosen to adopt Bourne et al.'s (2000) theoretical framework to systematize the literature review. This framework focuses on the process of PMS implementation and the sequence of phases that characterize it (Bourne et al., 2018). In particular, the adoption of this framework allows for a more structured ordering of the literature regarding the dynamics and the facilitating or hindering elements observed in each of the different stages of implementation described by Bourne et al. (2000).

3.4 PMS Implementation Process

According to Bourne et al. (2000) and Nudurupati et al. (2011), the process of implementing and using a PMS can be segmented into three phases, which are respectively (I) design, (II) implementation, and (III) use. These stages occur both when a system is introduced for the first time and when an existing tool is updated to maintain its effectiveness in meeting business needs (Bourne et al., 2018). According to these authors, PMS should be updated regularly to remain useful for the company over time as the company's strategy or critical success factors change (Baird, 2017). In fact, we recall that PMS are designed to measure the effectiveness of a company's strategy, the appropriateness of the activities it implements to pursue it, and how well those activities are executed. As a result, it is normal for many companies today to update their PMS frequently due to frequent regulatory, technological, and competitive changes. Yet, it has been acknowledged that there is often some lag in updating PMS even when changes in the external environment evidently point to doing so, leading to significant discrepancies in alignment with the organization's environment and strategy (Bititci et al., 2012; Melnyk et al., 2014; Nudurupati et al., 2016). Okwir et al. (2018) suggest that this delay may sometimes be related to the level of organizational complexity and the intricate relations between the elements that compose the PMS in use, which are getting increasingly sophisticated to respond to the escalating complexity of the external environment. These authors basically identify six sources of complexity, which are role, task, procedural, methodological, analytical, and technical. They suggest that understanding and managing these complexities is crucial for the effective design, implementation, and use of PMS. According to them, to manage role complexity, roles within the organization should be well designed and clearly defined, through effective communication and training. Tasks should also be clearly delineated, and the use of multiskilled teams can facilitate the process of updating the PMS. Methodological and analytical complexity can be addressed by selecting the best measures to monitor strategy and understanding the relationships between different measures. Finally, technical complexity can be managed by using reliable information systems and technologies.

The phases outlined by Bourne et al. (2000) basically describe a linear sequence through which the process of PMS implementation should progress. Nonetheless, they admit that these phases are conceptual and can overlap in practice since the different individual measures and elements composing a PMS may be rolled out with different timelines. At least within certain limits, the overlap between these phases is, in fact, taken for granted in many studies (Wouters & Wilderom, 2008).

According to Bourne et al. (2000), the (I) design phase consists of determining the key objectives to be measured and the development of appropriate performance measures. The (II) implementation phase is concerned with establishing the necessary systems and procedures to collect and analyze data for regular performance assessment. The (III) use phase entails measuring the efficacy of strategy implementation, challenging the assumptions of the company's strategy, and testing the strategy's validity. This framework comes across as more simplified than Ferreira and Otley's (2009) framework and arguably provides a less broad view of the issues surrounding performance measurement and management. However, it places a greater emphasis with respect to the sequential activities required for developing, applying, and revising these systems.

Keeping in mind the framework by Bourne et al. (2000) seems particularly fruitful here, as it promotes an understanding of the PMS implementation process as a series of distinct yet interconnected stages. This perspective seems particularly appropriate as the challenges associated with each phase tend to be different (Nudurupati et al., 2011). A closer examination of the literature on PMS, focusing on these three phases, is now presented.

3.4.1 Performance Measurement System Design

The first phase, which, as mentioned, involves the design and development of the PMS, can already pose some significant challenges. The proper conduct of this phase is usually considered essential as how the system is design has direct impact on its effectiveness (Kaplan, 2012). In general, it has been often suggested that the more the development and implementation of these tools come successfully to completion, the more companies tend to gradually see both financial and nonfinancial benefits (Gong & Ferreira, 2014; Malagueño et al., 2018), provided that the system is well designed (Grigoroudis et al., 2012; Lucianetti, 2012). The way the system is designed is also relevant because it may have significant effects on how incentives are allocated; therefore, an incomplete or flawed PMS could generate feelings of inequality and injustice in the rewards system. In other words, an incomplete[3] or flawed PMS might lead to a sense of inequality and injustice in the members of the company. If the design does not cover all relevant aspects, individuals may perceive their performance as not being fairly or objectively evaluated compared to their colleagues. Moreover, they may feel that the metrics used do not accurately reflect the commitment and effort they have put into carrying out the tasks they are responsible for (Palaiologos et al., 2011). Managers might see the incompleteness of a PMS as a deterrent to its use, particularly if they perceive it fails to provide an accurate assessment of strategic performance and lacks supporting strategy management (Huelsbeck et al., 2011; Islam et al., 2018). In summary, the design of the system not only affects its strategic control and management effectiveness, but also determines its managerial application in the firm (Agostino & Arnaboldi, 2011, 2012). For example, Artz et al. (2012) suggest that the alignment of the indicators chosen at the level of individual functions with the goals of the company and the perceived reliability in measurement positively influences the use of the PMS to support strategic decision-making processes and hold individuals accountable. A study by Guenther and Heinicke (2019) shows evidence that a PMS with a sophisticated design may produce greater benefits when there is an interactive use of the system but may produce fewer benefits or even be detrimental if the tools are used only for diagnostic purposes. Lucianetti (2012) pointed out that the level of development and integration of the balanced scorecard influences both its effectiveness and the managers' perceived utility and use of the PMS, reaching its full potential when it guides strategy and incentive allocation.

In order for a PMS to be defined as well-designed, the various contributions in the literature have emphasized that the tool should comprise performance measures and targets that are strategically aligned, controllable, timely, technically valid, and interlinked through cause-and-effect relationships (Franco-Santos et al., 2012; Pavan & D'Onza, 2013). In other words, they should help measure the effectiveness of strategy implementation and the validity of the strategy itself, but they should also be timely to support decision-making and measurable using the company's existing information systems. In addition, it should be clear how achieving particular levels of performance in specific areas contributes to the overall success of the business and the achievement of business objectives (e.g., how customer retention and satisfaction lead to better financial results).

---

[3]Wouters & Widerom (2008) claim that "the inherent incompleteness of PMS in terms of the inability to reflect the various dimensions of operational performance and tradeoffs among these and therefore user involvement needs to be mobilized, both in terms of existing experience with quantification of performance, and also throughout the design and implementation process of new measures" (p. 489).

As highlighted in the literature review by Franco-Santos et al. (2012), there are numerous studies that support the existence of different types of positive and desired benefits associated with a good design, including those of a nonfinancial nature. In particular, these scholars determined three categories of consequences related to the use of such systems, namely (I) people's behavior, (II) organizational capability, and (III) performance. More specifically, the benefits identified are (I) improved teamwork performance, (II) reduced bonus allocation bias, (III) better strategic outcomes in terms of delivery, flexibility, and low cost, (IV) improved managerial performance, (V) better understanding of what is expected of individuals at work, (VI) improved strategic focus, (VII) increased motivation, (VIII) better support for managerial learning, and (IX) better corporate control of subsidiaries.

Conversely, Franco-Santos and Otley (2018) also point out the existence of unintended and sometimes adverse consequences associated with the use of PMS, many of which relate to the way the system is designed. Although there have been fewer studies on unintentional outcomes than on intentional outcomes, the review they conducted on the subject revealed a number of unintentional outcomes, namely: (I) gaming, sometimes associated with the violation of ethical norms; (II) manipulation of information, ranging from creative accounting to outright fraud; (III) selective attention in terms of what and when to measure; (IV) illusion of control; (V) transformation of relationships associated with increased competitiveness and reduced cooperation; (VI) administrative and managerial overload; (VII) stress and reduced well-being and morale; (VIII) reduced responsiveness and increased organizational rigidity and resistance to change; (IX) reduced risk-taking and innovation; and (X) perceptions of unfairness and inequity in the way employees and managers are evaluated and treated. In particular, they claim that many of these issues may arise depending on the design and reliability of performance management systems, as "the more the 'assumed' reality about the state of goal-alignment and goal-uncertainty diverges from the 'real' state of affairs, the more the resultant system is likely to create perverse unintended consequences, leading to poor organizational outcomes" (Franco-Santos & Otley, 2018, p. 696).

Several scholars have identified notable challenges in the initial stages of PMS development, particularly concerning the selection of metrics and the composition of indicators within the system. Many consultants have cleverly proposed apparently revolutionary or at least fashionable solutions to companies' managers and contributed significantly to disseminating PMS (Qu & Cooper, 2011). Still, although innovative, their proposals have sometimes proved unsuitable for the specific situations in which they were being introduced (Sgrò et al., 2020).

To begin with, PMS need considerable effort to adapt to the company in which they are being introduced to deliver the desired outcomes (Hansen & Schaltegger, 2016; Hoque, 2014). According to several scholars, the system should be composed only of indicators that are actually relevant to understanding how the company is doing and to plan actions and decisions accordingly (Franceschini et al., 2019). In fact, the use of irrelevant indicators that do not provide insight into the actual strategic performance of the company is considered problematic, as well as an excess of selected indicators that, although seemingly relevant, could lead to confusion in management.

Adapting the tool to the needs of the company is often a rather complex process, mainly because the choice of indicators remains fundamentally subjective (Lillis et al., 2022), consequently risking creating the perception of unfairness and of favoritism in the granting of rewards when the system is used to incentivize individuals (Voußem et al., 2016). As Wouters and Sportel (2005) suggested, existing informal control and information systems significantly influence and shape the design and implementation of a new PMS. Therefore, the introduction of these tools could also become quite complex as the information is often scattered and not unified in an integrated process, thus requiring considerable effort in information retrieval and systematization.

Moreover, many studies report difficulties related to the design of the PMS in specific settings.

For example, Giovannoni and Maraghini (2013) argue that companies that base their success on creativity may have difficulties in identifying the best performance measures and translating them into a coherent set of targets. This element is also supported by Mettänen (2005), who analyzed the process of designing and implementing a PMS in an organization that does research, whose success is based on the creativity of its members and elements of a more qualitative nature. Even when the system is introduced in firms whose performance can be effectively measured using more quantitative indicators, it has been found that the design process is iterative and trial and error as new measures need to be tested to understand whether they are actually useful to guide the management (Wouters & Wilderom, 2008). It is, therefore, clear that, depending on the type of company, there may be difficulties in identifying what should be measured, while on other occasions, it may be difficult even to establish shared and accepted indicators by all those involved in designing the PMS.

The size of the company is another significant determinant in the PMS design and implementation process (Guenther & Heinicke, 2019), as evidenced by the numerous studies focusing on small companies (Heinicke, 2018; Pešalj et al., 2018; Sousa & Aspinwall, 2010). Specifically, company size appears to be related to the sophistication level of the PMS; as size increases, there tends to be a trend toward more complex, holistic, and integrated PMS (Amir, 2014). Moreover, the introduction of advanced systems such as the balanced scorecard requires substantial financial and human resources and a reliable information system (Taylor & Taylor, 2013), which small companies often do not have (Neubauer et al., 2012). Since PMS typically incorporates measures and methodologies for tracking strategy effectiveness and implementation progress (Maraghini & Riccaboni, 2019), the capability to effectively define a business strategy to be measured is fundamental. Yet, many small- to medium-sized companies do not routinely formulate and establish their own strategies, adding another significant barrier to determining appropriate indicators (Castellano, 2012). An excessive focus on short-term objectives, common in small companies, can result in the selection of indicators that are not meaningful or useful for managing business performance (Izvercian et al., 2016).

Another significant obstacle may be the absence of a reliable information system: the PMS should be connected to it and be based on valid data (Cavalluzzo & Ittner, 2004; Mithas et al., 2011). If the results given by the PMS are not well-founded, the decision-making process will be negatively affected. This issue is most easily encountered in small companies because they tend not to have a particularly advanced and reliable information system (Cerchione & Esposito, 2017).

Further issues, not necessarily related to size, depend on who designs the system. For example, if the PMS is developed exclusively with a top-down logic by the top management, middle managers might be assigned goals they cannot influence, or they may be given irrelevant indicators for their specific unit or function (Decoene & Bruggeman, 2006; Yigitbasioglu & Velcu, 2012). However, involving managers and employees in the design and collective testing of the system's measures, when possible, can mitigate this problem and promote the selection of useful indicators and increased satisfaction among members of the organization (Jang et al., 2023). This involvement in the design and collective testing of performance measurement systems can be effectively achieved through workshops and brainstorming sessions, focus groups, surveys and questionnaires, pilot testing, and feedback loops (Castellano, 2012).

The presence or absence of training or prior experience in the use of performance measurement tools, combined with insufficient knowledge of their structure, possible indicators and their characteristics, can be another element that significantly affects the quality of design (Panno, 2020; Van Camp & Braet, 2016). However, sometimes the issues that arise in the design of the system are strictly related to computer literacy (Bourne et al., 2000). Subjects with adequate expertise in management accounting & control might effectively contribute to articulating the system in terms of indicators and the elements or areas that should be monitored and controlled. However, it is not a given that these experts also have the IT skills to compose and articulate IT data into dashboards of indicators. Even tools such as the balanced scorecard are usually set up in the company through the use of computer tools and software, which is why Bourne et al. (2000) point out that one of the reasons for failure in the system design phase may also be related to the lack of the necessary computer skills. In any case, it can be assumed that this issue may diminish with the increasing level of computer literacy and the gradual integration of big data and coding studies into accounting courses (Vasarhelyi et al., 2015).

Finally, the lack of "fit" between the environment, the business strategy, the organizational culture, and what is being measured through the PMS is a critical problem (Melnyk et al., 2014), which can result from a bad design or a failure to update the system when needed (Franco-Santos et al., 2012; Hoque, 2014). However, designing a performance measurement system that perfectly fits a particular organization is also a complex, if not impossible, undertaking.

Precisely because of issues that arise in the design of PMS, there are numerous contributions in the literature aimed at providing a methodology and suggestions to prevent or minimize difficulties and guide managers in the development of the system (Chalmeta et al., 2012; Parmenter, 2015; Sousa & Aspinwall, 2010; Yigitbasioglu & Velcu, 2012). Some of these approaches are meant to be applied to companies operating in specific industries or possessing a certain size, while others have more general applicability. For example, Abernethy et al. (2005) proposed an approach for constructing causal performance maps for PMS development in companies that have expert knowledge workers performing complex processes, the results of which are qualitative in nature and, therefore, difficult to quantify. Their methodology could help overcome the problems associated with identifying quantifiable indicators in this type of context, facilitating the design process. Yigitbasioglu and Velcu (2012) conducted a literature review on the design of PMS dashboards and their impact on performance management, showing that they need to be designed with flexibility, allowing users to switch between different presentation formats. They emphasized the importance of effective visualization and synthesis of relevant data, while recognizing the need for interactive drill-down capabilities when required. According to them, these elements are critical in reducing information overload and improving decision-making effectiveness by allowing users to access detailed data on demand. Cocca and Alberti (2010) and Pekkola et al. (2016) developed frameworks specifically aimed at evaluating and supporting the design of small and medium-sized enterprises' (SMEs) PMS to help companies identify problems and shortcomings in the tools in use and introduce corrections and changes if necessary. These approaches were designed to aid SMEs in both developing their systems and assessing their effectiveness, recognizing that more traditional approaches and models often proved more suitable for larger organizations. Purbey et al. (2007) tailored a framework for the healthcare sector, categorizing performance measures that are beneficial in this context to help managers in the PMS design process and in deciding what should be measured. This method should facilitate the identification of indicators in the specific context of healthcare, where "mainstream" models specifically intended for this sector are lacking. Taticchi et al. (2012) conducted a literature review on PMS and provided a framework composed of a series of guidelines to support managers in the development of the system. Moullin (2017) proposed an extension of the balanced scorecard, called the public sector scorecard, which is specifically designed for use in the public sector. Specifically, this PMS should allow public sector organizations to effectively track their unique critical success factors, which are significantly different from those in the private sector. Finally, even Kaplan and Norton (1996) offered an approach for designing and implementing the balanced scorecard aimed at overcoming and preventing issues that may arise, such as difficulties in identifying the most useful indicators or choosing indicators that are accepted by all individuals.

3.4.2 Performance Measurement System Implementation

The second essential phase in the process of implementing a PMS, as outlined by Bourne et al. (2000) and Nudurupati et al. (2011), is the actual implementation of the systems with their respective measures and dashboards. In this phase, as the systems are gradually implemented, managers and employees begin to use the system to measure performance and make decisions based on the new data available. Some individuals may even begin to be held accountable for meeting certain goals and performance standards, and these goals may be linked to a reward system. Despite the undeniable importance of the design phase, proper management of this phase is also critical to the success of the overall initiative, as evidenced by a significant number of studies focused on this step (Gao & Gurd, 2015; Nudurupati et al., 2011).

When focusing specifically on this phase, the kinds of issues that can be identified are generally more related to individuals and organizational factors (De Waal, 2003; Nudurupati et al., 2011). Indeed, even in the presence of a theoretically well-designed system from a strictly technical standpoint, both studies on change management and those related to PMS suggest that poor management of the implementation phase can block or slow down the adoption of the system by the individuals who compose the organization (Nudurupati et al., 2011; Bourne et al., 2003b). For this reason, several studies have tried to understand both the drivers that facilitate or encourage implementation and the factors that hinder it (e.g., Beusch et al., 2022; Bourne et al., 2002; Lueg & Vu, 2015; Madsen & Stenheim, 2014).

In the field of management accounting change, one of the most relevant contributions about the hindering and enabling factors is probably that of Kasurinen (2002). The author proposed a framework derived from the analysis of a case study on the implementation of a balanced scorecard to classify the factors that play a role in management accounting change processes and understand their effects, expanding on what was done in two earlier works by Cobb et al. (1995) and Innes and Mitchell (1990). Several studies have used this framework to support the identification and analysis of the elements that favor or inhibit implementation (e.g., Farneti, 2009; Munir et al., 2013).

Enabling factors, according to this framework, include *motivators*, *facilitators*, *catalysts*, *leaders*, and *momentum*. The first three are the only ones to compose what was the original framework of Innes and Mitchell (1990), while the last two have been recognized in the development of the framework proposed by Cobb et al. (1995).

To begin with, *motivators* are elements that influence change in a general manner. Some examples may be a high level of market competition and complexity, the stage of the product lifecycle, technology advancements, the rate of product innovation, or changes in the operating environment.

While not sufficient to produce change on their own, *facilitators* are believed to be conducive to management accounting change and often essential for its achievement. Some examples may be the type of knowledge and skills (e.g., accounting, computer) possessed in the company or the type and amount of resources available.

Catalysts are factors directly related to change, and their occurrence corresponds closely to the timing of change (Innes & Mitchell, 1990). Such factors comprise major issues like deterioration in financial performance, loss of market share, major regulatory changes, and the arrival of substitute products or new competitors, but also incentive elements such as the arrival of new managers and subjects with skills previously unknown in the company. According to Innes and Mitchell (1990), both *motivators* and *catalysts* can foster change, but they are really effective only in the presence of *facilitators*.

What fundamentally distinguishes *motivators* from *catalysts* is their scope of influence. *Motivators* can drive more broad and holistic changes. For example, a company in a highly competitive market where rapidly evolving technologies and practices are employed may feel pressured to frequently update its technology, tools, organizational structure, and processes. *Catalysts*, on the other hand, favor the initiation of specific changes. For example, a new manager with expertise in PMS may join a company and make a concerted effort to implement them.

Leaders are individuals who act as *catalysts*, especially in the early stages of change processes, but also prove to be essential supporters and sponsors of these projects throughout the implementation phase (Cobb et al., 1995). This factor was probably recognized as essential also because a relevant part of the organizational change literature in those very years was increasingly preaching the importance of leadership as a central factor in the success of change processes (Stouten et al., 2018). This factor remains central in several subsequent studies that emphasize that leadership, provided it is committed to the project, has the ability to influence and motivate people toward adopting and using the system (Bianchi & Rivenbark, 2013; Taylor & Taylor, 2013).

The *momentum* of change is another often recurring term in the organizational change literature. It expresses the fact that the sense of the progress of change and the gradual realization of a worthwhile project drives people to pursue its implementation. The literature on organizational change emphasizes the importance of not losing *momentum*. For this reason, it is generally suggested to not stop at the first positive results and insisting on implementing the change before people lose focus and energy toward the project (Hayes, 2022; Kotter, 2012).

With regard to hindering factors for management accounting change processes, Kasurinen's (2002) framework expands on what was suggested by Cobb et al. (1995) by classifying them into three different types, namely: *confusers*, *frustrators*, and *delayers*.

Confusers are factors that disrupt the process of change. Some examples might be the withdrawal from the project of one of the main sponsors or leaders of the change, misunderstandings with respect to the implications or usefulness of the tool in the company, and disagreement with respect to what should be the goals of the change.

Frustrators are factors that suppress the change attempt. In this category falls an organizational culture that does not support the tool's implementation or organizational changes in general and resistance from managers who fear that the tool may change power distribution.

Finally, *delayers* are temporary and rather technical hindering factors and have a decisive influence both in the early stages of project design and in the proper implementation phase. Examples include the absence of a reliable information system and the absence of a formulated and clear strategy.

Both in the field of management accounting change and others, various studies have employed case study analysis or surveys to pinpoint specific issues or factors that affect the implementation of PMS (Bourne et al., 2002; Franco-Santos et al., 2012; Munir et al., 2013). These works often do not refer to Kasurinen's (2002) framework, although the factors identified can fit into the author's classification. Indeed, some studies from disparate fields of research have attempted to identify the different factors that positively or negatively influence the introduction of PMS (e.g., Beusch et al., 2022; De Waal, 2003) or have focused only on single elements in order to understand better their effects on implementation dynamics (e.g., Bourne et al., 2002; Cavalluzzo & Ittner, 2004; Rowland & Hall, 2012).

One of the most reported enabling factors for the success of this kind of initiative is probably management commitment (Beusch et al., 2022; Wickramasinghe et al., 2007), while its absence is generally regarded as one of the most common reasons for failure (Bourne et al., 2002; Bourne et al., 2003b). The commitment may be present or absent at the outset of the implementation project and can be sustained or lost during the implementation and use of the system. The lack of perceived benefits during the implementation phase (Elkmash et al., 2022; Munir et al., 2013), coupled with the time and effort required to develop and introduce the system, which can be substantial, are some of the factors that can produce a failure of the project (Bourne et al., 2003b). Consequently, it cannot be ruled out that as time progresses, other seemingly more stringent priorities emerge, shifting the attention of top management to other issues and processes to be managed. The choice of targets and objectives that are not effectively shared by leadership is another element that could negatively influence commitment toward using the tool and achieving assigned targets (Webb, 2004). Moreover, the low attractiveness of the given goals can generate a loss of commitment and even produce real resistance toward the control tool (Rowland & Hall, 2012).

Competency in IT and management accounting, crucial in the design phase, is also vital during implementation (Frederico et al., 2021; Panno, 2020). A PMS may be developed by a select few with requisite expertise in-house or with external consultants, but for it to be widely and consistently used by managers across the company, a broad base of users must have the relevant skills and expertise. In other words, individuals may struggle to use the system and interpret its data without the necessary knowledge. For this reason, it has been pointed out that the administration of training specifically geared toward the use of PMS can also foster adoption and increase the likelihood of successful implementation (Cavalluzzo & Ittner, 2004). Neglecting to offer specific training can adversely affect not only the ability to use the tool but also the understanding of its implications and benefits, leading to confusion and frustration (Munir et al., 2013).

Another fairly recurrent enabling factor involves sponsorship, active support, and participation in the implementation process by those with senior positions in the company (Argyris & Kaplan, 1994). In particular, it was found that the use of PMS by top management for evaluating performance and holding individuals accountable can encourage the interest in adopting and regularly utilizing the system (Cavalluzzo & Ittner, 2004). In addition, holding individuals accountable for meeting performance targets can help them understand which elements are important for business success and where to focus their attention (Castellano, 2012).

Another frequently reported enabling factor in the literature concerns people's involvement in the implementation process. This has already been reported in the normative process proposed by Kaplan and Norton (1996) in order to facilitate the identification of measures and dashboards that are more in line with the needs of the company. Involvement seems to produce positive effects toward generating commitment and reducing resistance to change (Tayler, 2010). Furthermore, it fosters a feeling of transparency in the management of the implementation process, encouraging employees to take a positive attitude toward the tool (Rowland & Hall, 2012).

Many studies have noted that for a project to succeed, a company must possess or encourage an organizational culture that aligns with the tool being implemented (Carlucci et al., 2015). Some studies also report how a culture oriented toward organizational learning, performance improvement, and entrepreneurship significantly enhances the success of PMS implementation initiatives (De Waal, 2003; Taylor & Taylor, 2013, 2014). A quality-oriented culture may also support the introduction of a PMS, as it can lead to more effective monitoring of compliance with desired quality standards in services and products (Taylor & Taylor, 2013). Moreover, introducing new metrics might necessitate a cultural shift and the development of new mindsets among managers who will use the tool. This is particularly significant when introducing elements like nonfinancial measures or different metrics for management accountability for the first time (Chiucchi, 2013a, 2013b).

As reported by Bititci et al. (2006), it is the system itself that influences, as it is developed, introduced, and used the way managers reason and behave with their employees. This suggests that cultural change is not only a precursor to facilitating the implementation of certain tools but also a consequence of the system's influence on company personnel once introduced (Franco-Santos et al., 2012). Initially, an authoritarian management culture may favor implementation, but as the system takes hold, a participatory leadership style and goal-oriented culture should prevail (Bititci et al., 2006). This further suggests that the adoption of a participatory style in system development and introduction is associated with successful system adoption.

Finally, the perception of benefits associated with the system is another crucial aspect both early in the design phase by project participants and during implementation. In particular, the perception of advantages associated with the change should be shared by those employees who will be affected by the new system (De Waal, 2003). This is why an effective communication strategy and dialogue among managers of different levels could reduce some situations of confusion and resistance (Beusch et al., 2022; Sharma & Gadenne, 2011; Umashev & Willett, 2008), as well as the creation of moments of participation for employees and managers of specific organizational units in the design and implementation of the system (Groen, 2018; Madsen & Stenheim, 2014).

Concerning the hindering factors, resistance to change stands as a considerable obstacle in the implementation and utilization of PMS (Macchia, 2021). Many case studies on PMS implementation and management accounting change have reported resistance to change as a factor that can slow down or even lead to project failure (Bourne et al., 2003b; Lueg & Vu, 2015; Scapens & Roberts, 1993; Tuomela, 2005).

One type of resistance to change quite specific to this type of project is the so-called resistance to measurement (Nudurupati et al., 2011), reported in the literature even before the development of modern holistic PMS (Deming, 1986). Such kind of resistance to change arises when performance metrics are closely associated with individual or organizational unit accountability, potentially threatening perceived autonomy or power within the organization (Carlucci et al., 2015).

Other instances of resistance could be related to strict cultural aspects. Indeed, while, as mentioned just before, cultural change or the presence of an organizational culture already oriented toward the adoption and use of these tools is reported as an enabling factor (Mendibil & MacBryde, 2006), on the other hand, a culture that is not very oriented toward change or the use of these tools could create a barrier (Madsen & Stenheim, 2014). If a company has already been in business for several years and, therefore, has a series of deep-rooted practices, it is likely that its members have already developed a certain mindset and have become accustomed to using specific tools (Kotter, 2012). Employing new systems that require new knowledge, in addition to demanding some learning effort, may necessitate a different mentality and behaviors that not everyone may be able to embrace. The same kind of culture that has settled over the years may have fostered the creation of an organizational structure and a set of relationships between different organizational units that may not be conducive to the implementation of integrated tools. In this case, resistance may arise when the organization adopts holistic tools requiring greater integration of processes and terminology used among different units (Scapens & Roberts, 1993). Yet, the organizational culture that underpins the company's routine and performance management & measurement activities could be challenged when the company faces a crisis (Busco et al., 2006). In other words, in scenarios where the prevailing organizational culture is subjected to scrutiny due to the company's adverse circumstances, there may be a more conducive environment for the implementation of tools that can also transform the management mindset and routine operational practices.

In general, as the change management literature also suggests (Bourne et al., 2003b), if there is a perception that introducing a certain tool will bring disadvantages to the individual or the organization, there is likely to be some form of resistance. Resistance may originate not only from the anxiety surrounding a potential alteration in the power dynamics but also from a variety of perceived disadvantages. These may include concerns over the potential for the new system to reduce organizational flexibility (Franco-Santos & Otley, 2018), the excessive effort or cost of implementation compared to the anticipated benefits (De Waal & Counet, 2009; Sgrò et al., 2020), the creation of mistrust in the accuracy of the information system that feeds data into the PMS (De Waal, 2003; Taylor & Taylor, 2014), and the emergence of discord due to the perceived inadequacy or inequity of the selected targets and performance indicators (Sharma et al., 2016).

3.4.3 *Performance Measurement System Use*

In addressing the final phase of Bourne et al. (2000) framework, this study selectively and briefly examines the most significant findings related to the use of PMS, being the implementation and not the use, the focus of this work. Most of the research has sought to understand the effects associated with the employment of performance measurement tools and how individuals use these tools (Franco-Santos et al., 2012; Franco-Santos & Otley, 2018).

Nonetheless, it is critical to acknowledge that the efficacy of PMS use is inextricably linked to its antecedent phases of design and implementation. The design of the system, its attributes, and the extent to which it is integrated and disseminated throughout the organization invariably influence its subsequent utilization and the outcomes it produces (Bourne et al., 2003b; Franco-Santos et al., 2012; Wouters & Wilderom, 2008).

As already said, early studies on the subject already reported the existence of generally visible benefits in terms of better intellectual capital mobilization (Chiucchi, 2013a, 2013b). This is not surprising given the existence of PMS specifically designed to measure and manage intellectual capital (Sveiby, 1997). In particular, nonfinancial indicators in PMS can provide a clearer and more complete view of the company's intellectual capital elements, such as human capital with its skills and knowledge, or know-how and copyrights, and their contribution to the company's success. Moreover, PMS can help managers become familiar with intellectual capital concepts and their practical applications (Chiucchi, 2013a, 2013b).

In any case, the use of PMS is generally associated with higher organizational and financial performance, which remains the main reason for their adoption (Franco-Santos et al., 2012). However, there are certain contingent factors—such as the lack of reliable information systems or organizations whose success depends on scarcely quantifiable critical factors—that may limit these advantages or even generate detrimental effects (Abernethy et al., 2005; Franco-Santos & Otley, 2018). Research has tried to shed more light on this topic. For example, Franco-Santos and Otley (2018) found that in some organizations where the use of PMS is perceived to be heavily focused on controlling and guiding employee behavior and performance through strict rules, detailed instructions and specific performance targets, it can create significant pressure on managers and employees. This pressure is often considered threatening, leading to detrimental behaviors such as manipulating performance data or lying. These behaviors can even become internalized over time, eroding trust and ruining social interactions within the organization. Another example is provided by Bourne et al. (2005), who conducted a comparative analysis of case studies of organizational units within an organization, contrasting the use of PMS between high and average performing units. They found that units that achieved higher performance levels were characterized by unit managers' more significant understanding regarding performance drivers and how to manage them, more sophisticated use of available measures in monitoring activities, and an "interactive" (Simons, 1995) use of the PMS.

As mentioned previously, Franco-Santos et al. (2012) & Franco-Santos and Otley (2018) provide an extensive collection of the positive or negative consequences reported in the literature and associated with the use of PMS.[4]

In examining PMS application, numerous studies, particularly within the field of management accounting, have sought to understand how managers employ these systems through the lens of Simons' (1995) levers of control framework and its subsequent elaborations (Tessier & Otley, 2012). In particular, this framework identifies four levers of control. There are belief and interactive control systems, which are considered "positive" control systems because they can facilitate motivation and learning. Then there are boundary and diagnostic control systems, which are considered "negative" control systems and are associated with setting behavioral constraints and monitoring performance. Belief systems essentially consist of formal definitions communicated by management and leadership to outline the purpose, values, and direction of the organization. Interactive control systems are represented by the formal information systems that managers use to support their decision-making processes. Boundary systems consist of the formal rules established in the organization to control and influence the behavior of its members. Finally, diagnostic control systems are the formal information systems that managers use to monitor results and address deviations from established performance standards. One example of study on PMS that employed this framework is provided by Tuomela (2005). The author applied the framework to investigate the use of a PMS for strategic control in a firm, showing that such a system could be used both diagnostically and interactively, and that its use reinforced the core values of the organization and clarified the explicit limits and rules that outline acceptable behavior and actions of the employees. The study highlights that interactive use of the system might allow for more evident improvement in company performance and greater commitment to assigned targets but may be pretty time-consuming when collecting the data and when interactively discussing the results.

What emerges in general from the studies regarding the use of PMS is that while it is undisputed that their use can bring benefits, the relationship is not straightforward, and it would be overly simplistic to attribute a priori advantages to the use of these systems (Franco-Santos et al., 2012; Okwir et al., 2018). These benefits depend on how the system is designed, how it is used, and how it fits the specific measurement and control needs of the organization.

References

Abernethy, M. A., Horne, M., Lillis, A. M., Malina, M. A., & Selto, F. H. (2005). A multi-method approach to building causal performance maps from expert knowledge. *Management Accounting Research, 16*(2), 135–155.

Agostino, D., & Arnaboldi, M. (2011). How the BSC implementation process shapes its outcome. *International Journal of Productivity and Performance Management, 60*(2), 99–114.

[4] Please refer to the section relating to the design of PMS for more detail on the consequences identified.

Agostino, D., & Arnaboldi, M. (2012). Design issues in balanced scorecards: The 'what' and 'how' of control. *European Management Journal, 30*(4), 327–339.

Alsharari, N. M., Dixon, R., & Youssef, M. A. E.-A. (2015). Management accounting change: Critical review and a new contextual framework. *Journal of Accounting & Organizational Change, 11*(4), 476–502.

Amir, A. M. (2014). Performance measurement system design in service operations: Does size matter? *Management Research Review, 37*(8), 728–749.

Anthony, R. (1965). *Planning and control systems: A framework for analysis*. Division of Research, Harvard University.

Argyris, C., & Kaplan, R. S. (1994). Implementing new knowledge: The case of activity-based costing. *Accounting Horizons, 8*(3).

Artz, M., Homburg, C., & Rajab, T. (2012). Performance-measurement system design and functional strategic decision influence: The role of performance-measure properties. *Accounting, Organizations and Society, 37*(7), 445–460.

Atkinson, A. A., Waterhouse, J. H., & Wells, R. B. (1997). A stakeholder approach to strategic performance measurement. *MIT Sloan Management Review*.

Baird, K. (2017). The effectiveness of strategic performance measurement systems. *International Journal of Productivity and Performance Management, 66*(1), 3–21.

Beusch, P., Frisk, J. E., Rosén, M., & Dilla, W. (2022). Management control for sustainability: Towards integrated systems. *Management Accounting Research, 54*, 100777.

Bianchi, C., & Rivenbark, W. C. (2013). Alla ricerca dei fattori rilevanti nell'adozione dei sistemi di gestione della performance nelle amministrazioni pubbliche territoriali. L'analisi di due casi di studio. *Azienda Pubblica, 1*, 35–59.

Bititci, U. S., Carrie, A. S., & Mcdevitt, L. (1997). Integrated performance measurement systems: A development guide. *International Journal of Operations & Production Management, 17*(5-6), 522–534.

Bititci, U., Garengo, P., Dörfler, V., & Nudurupati, S. (2012). Performance measurement: Challenges for tomorrow. *International Journal of Management Reviews, 14*, 305–327.

Bititci, U. S., Mendibil, K., Nudurupati, S., Turner, T., & Garengo, P. (2006). Dynamics of performance measurement and organizational culture. *International Journal of Operations and Production Management, 26*, 1325–1350.

Bol, J. C., Keune, T. M., Matsumura, E. M., & Shin, J. Y. (2010). Supervisor discretion in target setting: An empirical investigation. *The Accounting Review, 85*(6), 1861–1886.

Bourne, M., Kennerley, M., & Franco-Santos, M. (2005). Managing through measures: A study of impact on performance. *Journal of Manufacturing Technology Management, 16*(4), 373–395. https://doi.org/10.1108/17410380510594480

Bourne, M., Melnyk, S., & Bititci, U. S. (2018). Performance measurement and management: Theory and practice. *International Journal of Operations & Production Management, 38*(11), 2010–2021.

Bourne, M., Mills, J., Wilcox, M., Neely, A., & Platts, K. (2000). Designing, implementing and updating performance measurement systems. *International Journal of Operations and Production Management, 20*(7), 754–771.

Bourne, M., Neely, A., Mills, J., & Platts, K. (2003a) Implementing performance measurement systems: A literature review. *International Journal of Business Performance Management, 5*(1), 1–24. https://doi.org/10.1504/IJBPM.2003.002097

Bourne, M., Neely, A., Mills, J., & Platts, K. (2003b). Why some performance measurement initiatives fail: Lessons from the change management literature. *International Journal of Business Performance Management, 5*(2–3), 245–269. https://doi.org/10.1504/IJBPM.2003.003250

Bourne, M., Neely, A., Platts, K., & Mills, J. (2002). The success and failure of performance measurement initiatives—Perceptions of participating managers. *International Journal of Operations & Production Management, 22*(11), 1288–1310.

Broadbent, J., & Laughlin, R. (2009). Performance management systems: A conceptual model. *Management Accounting Research, 20*, 283–295.

Busco, C., Riccaboni, A., & Scapens, R. W. (2006). Trust for accounting and accounting for trust. *Management Accounting Research, 17*(1), 11–41.

Cardinaels, E., & Yin, H. (2015). Think twice before going for incentives: Social norms and the principal's decision on compensation contracts. *Journal of Accounting Research, 53*, 985–1015.

Carlucci, D. (2010). Evaluating and selecting key performance indicators: An ANP-based model. *Measuring Business Excellence, 14*(2), 66–76.

Carlucci, D., Schiuma, G., & Sole, F. (2015). The adoption and implementation of performance measurement process in Italian public organisations: The influence of political, cultural and rational factors. *Production Planning & Control, 26*(5), 363–376.

Castellano, N. (2011). Modelli e misure di performance aziendale: analisi della letteratura e spunti di ricerca. *Management Control, 1*, 41–63.

Castellano, N. (2012). *La misurazione delle performance per le piccole imprese. Strumenti di misurazione e processi di controllo*. Giappichelli Editore.

Cavalluzzo, K. S., & Ittner, C. D. (2004). Implementing performance measurement innovations: Evidence from government. *Accounting, Organizations and Society, 29*(3–4), 243–267.

Cerchione, R., & Esposito, E. (2017). Using knowledge management systems: A taxonomy of SME strategies. *International Journal of Information Management, 37*(1), 1551–1562.

Chalmeta, R., Palomero, S., & Matilla, M. (2012). Methodology to develop a performance measurement system in small and medium-sized enterprises. *International Journal of Computer Integrated Manufacturing, 5*, 716–740.

Chandler, A. D. (1962). *Strategy and structure*. MIT Press.

Cheng, M. M., & Humphreys, K. A. (2016). Managing strategic uncertainty: The diversity and use of performance measures in the balanced scorecard. *Managerial Auditing Journal, 31*(4/5), 512–534.

Chiucchi, M. S. (2013a). Intellectual capital accounting in action: Enhancing learning through interventionist research. *Journal of Intellectual Capital, 14*(1), 48–68.

Chiucchi, M. S. (2013b). Measuring and reporting intellectual capital: Lessons learnt from some interventionist research projects. *Journal of Intellectual Capital, 14*(3), 395–413.

Choong, K. K. (2013). Understanding the features of performance measurement system: A literature review. *Measuring Business Excellence, 17*(4), 102–121.

Cinquini, L., Miraglia, R. A., & Giannetti, R. (2016). Strumenti di gestione dei costi e misure di performance negli attuali contesti competitivi. *Management Control, 2*, 5–14.

Cobb, I., Helliar, C., & Innes, J. (1995). Management accounting change in a bank. *Management Accounting Research, 6*, 155–175.

Cocca, P., & Alberti, M. (2010). A framework to assess performance measurement systems in SMEs. *International Journal of Productivity and Performance Management, 59*(2), 186–200.

Cross, K. F., & Lynch, R. L. (1988). The "SMART" way to define and sustain success. *National Productivity Review, 8*(1), 23–33. https://doi.org/10.1002/npr.v8:1. https://doi.org/10.1002/npr.4040080105

De Waal, A. (2003). Behavioral factors important for the successful implementation and use of performance management systems. *Management Decision, 41*(8), 688–697.

De Waal, A. A., & Counet, H. (2009). Lessons learned from performance management systems implementations. *International Journal of Productivity and Performance Management, 58*(4), 367–390.

Decoene, V., & Bruggeman, W. (2006). Strategic alignment and middle-level managers' motivation in a balanced scorecard setting. *International Journal of Operations & Production Management, 26*(4), 429–448.

Deming, W. E. (1986). *Out of crisis*. Centre for Advanced Engineering Study, Massachusetts Institute of Technology.

Elkmash, M. R. M., Abdel-Kader, M. G., & Badr El Din, B. (2022). An experimental investigation of the impact of using big data analytics on customers' performance measurement. *Accounting Research Journal, 35*(1), 37–54.

Farneti, F. (2009). Balanced scorecard implementation in an Italian local government organization. *Public Money & Management, 29*(3), 313–320.

Ferreira, A., & Otley, D. (2009). The design and use of performance management systems: An extended framework for analysis. *Management Accounting Research, 20*(4), 263–282.

Franceschini, F., Galetto, M., Maisano, D., & Neely, A. D. (2019). Designing performance measurement systems. *Management for Professionals*.

Franco-Santos, M., & Doherty, N. (2017). Performance management and well-being: A close look at the changing nature of the UK higher education workplace. *International Journal of Human Resource Management, 28*, 2319–2350.

Franco-Santos, M., Kennerley, M., Micheli, P., Martinez, V., Mason, S., Marr, B., Gray, D., & Neely, A. (2007). Towards a definition of a business performance measurement system. *International Journal of Operations & Production Management, 27*, 784–801.

Franco-Santos, M., Lucianetti, L., & Bourne, M. (2012). Contemporary performance measurement systems: A review of their consequences and a framework for research. *Management Accounting Research, 23*(2), 79–119. https://doi.org/10.1016/j.mar.2012.04.001

Franco-Santos, M., & Otley, D. (2018). Reviewing and theorizing the unintended consequences of performance management systems. *International Journal of Management Reviews, 20*(3), 696–730.

Frederico, G. F., Garza-Reyes, J. A., Kumar, A., & Kumar, V. (2021). Performance measurement for supply chains in the Industry 4.0 era: A balanced scorecard approach. *International Journal of Productivity and Performance Management, 70*(4), 789–807. https://doi.org/10.1108/IJPPM-08-2019-0400

Gao, T., & Gurd, B. (2015). Meeting the challenge in performance management: The diffusion and implementation of the balanced scorecard in Chinese hospitals. *Health Policy and Planning, 30*(2), 234–241.

Gatti, M., & Chiucchi, M. S. (2017). Context matters. Il ruolo del contesto negli studi di controllo di gestione. *Management Control, 3*, 5–10.

Giovannoni, E., & Maraghini, M. P. (2013). The challenges of integrated performance measurement systems: Integrating mechanisms for integrated measures. *Accounting, Auditing and Accountability Journal, 26*(6), 978–1008.

Gong, M. Z., & Ferreira, A. (2014). Does consistency in management control systems design choices influence firm performance? An empirical analysis. *Accounting and Business Research, 44*(5), 497–522.

Grigoroudis, E., Orfanoudaki, E., & Zopounidis, C. (2012). Strategic performance measurement in a healthcare organisation: A multiple criteria approach based on balanced scorecard. *Omega, 40*(1), 104–119.

Groen, B. A. C. (2018). A survey study into participation in goal setting, fairness, and goal commitment: Effects of including multiple types of fairness. *Journal of Management Accounting Research, 30*(2), 207–240.

Guenther, T. W., & Heinicke, A. (2019). Relationships among types of use, levels of sophistication, and organizational outcomes of performance measurement systems: The crucial role of design choices. *Management Accounting Research, 42*(1), 1–25.

Habermas, J. (1984). *The theory of communicative action volume 1: Reason and rationalisation of society*. Heinemann.

Hansen, E. G., & Schaltegger, S. (2016). The sustainability balanced scorecard: A systematic review of architectures. *Journal of Business Ethics, 133*, 193–221.

Hasan, R. U., & Chyi, T. M. (2017). Practical application of balanced scorecard - A literature review. *Journal of Strategy and Performance Management, 5*(3), 87.

Hayes, J. (2022). *The theory and practice of change management* (6th ed.). Palgrave Macmillan.

Hayes, R. H., & Abernathy, W. J. (1980). Managing our way to economic decline. *Harvard Business Review, 58*(4), 7–8.

Heinicke, A. (2018). Performance measurement systems in small and medium-sized enterprises and family firms: A systematic literature review. *Journal of Management Control, 28*(4), 457–502.

Hoque, Z. (2014). 20 years of studies on the balanced scorecard: Trends accomplishments gaps and opportunities for future research. *The British Accounting Review, 46*(1), 33–59. https://doi.org/10.1016/j.bar.2013.10.003

Huelsbeck, D. P., Merchant, K. A., & Sandino, T. (2011). On testing business models. *The Accounting Review, 86*(5), 1631–1654.

Huerta, E., & Jensen, S. (2017). An accounting information systems perspective on data analytics and big data. *Journal of Information Systems, 31*(3), 101–114.

Innes, J., & Mitchell, F. (1990). The process of change in management accounting: Some field study evidence. *Management Accounting Research, 1*(1), 3–19.

Islam, S., Adler, R., & Northcott, D. (2018). Managerial attitudes towards the incompleteness of performance measurement systems. *Qualitative Research in Accounting and Management, 15*(1), 84–103.

Izvercian, M., Miclea, Ş., & Potra, S. (2016). Marketing practices in SMEs. Case study: Romania vs. Malta. *Procedia-Social and Behavioral Sciences, 221*, 135–141.

Jang, S., Chung, Y., & Son, H. (2023). Employee participation in performance measurement system: Focusing on job satisfaction and leadership. *International Journal of Productivity and Performance Management, 72*(7), 2119–2134.

Johnson, H. T. (1981). Towards an understanding of 19th century cost accounting. *Accounting Review, 56*, 510–518.

Johnson, H., & Kaplan, R. (1987). *Relevance lost: The rise and fall of management accounting*. Harvard Business School Press.

Kamble, S. S., & Gunasekaran, A. (2020). Big data-driven supply chain performance measurement system: A review and framework for implementation. *International Journal of Production Research, 58*(1), 65–86.

Kaplan, R. S. (2012). The balanced scorecard: Comments on balanced scorecard commentaries. *Journal of Accounting & Organizational Change, 8*(4), 539–545.

Kaplan, R. S., & Norton, D. P. (1996). *The balanced scorecard: Translating strategy into action*. Harvard Business School Press.

Kaplan, R. S., & Norton, D. P. (2004). *Strategy maps: Converting intangible assets into tangible outcomes*. Harvard Business School Press.

Kasurinen, T. (2002). Exploring management accounting change: The case of a balanced scorecard implementation. *Management Accounting Research, 13*, 323–343.

Kotter, J. P. (2012). Accelerate! *Harvard Business Review, 90*(11), 45–58.

Lillis, A. M., Malina, M. A., & Mundy, J. (2022). The role of subjectivity in mitigating incentive contracting risks. *The Accounting Review, 97*(1), 365–388.

Lizza, P. (2007). *Controllo di gestione e performance aziendale*. Giuffrè.

Lucianetti, L. (2012). L'adozione della Balanced Scorecard: i risultati di una ricerca empirica. *Management Control, 3*, 39–66.

Lueg, R., & Silva, A. L. C. (2013). When one size does not fit all: A literature review on the modifications of the balanced scorecard. *Problems and Perspectives in Management, 11*(3), 86–94.

Lueg, R., & Vu, L. (2015). Success factors in balanced scorecard implementations: A literature review. *Management Revue, 26*(4), 306–327.

Lynch, R. L., & Cross, L. F. (1991). Cross. Measure up!: The essential guide to measuring business performance.

Macchia, S. (2021). Are we ready to change?: A case study of management accounting change (MAC) in an Italian co-operative. *Management Control, Special Issue, 1*, 141–164.

Madsen, D. Ø., & Stenheim, T. (2014). Perceived problems associated with the implementation of the balanced scorecard: Evidence from Scandinavia. *Problems and Perspectives in Management, 12*(1), 121–131.

Malagueño, R., Lopez-Valeiras, E., & Gomez-Conde, J. (2018). Balanced scorecard in SMEs: Effects on innovation and financial performance. *Small Business Economics, 51*, 221–244.

Maraghini, M. P., & Riccaboni, A. (2019). Performance e execution oppure performance è execution? *Management Control, 2*, 5–12.

Marasca, S. (2011). *Misurazione della performance e strumenti di controllo strategico*. Esculapio.

Marchi, L. (1993). *I Sistemi Informativi Aziendali*. Giuffrè.

Marchi, L. (2011). L'evoluzione del controllo di gestione nella prospettiva informativa e gestionale esterna. *Management Control, 3*, 5–16.

Marchi, L., & Maraghini, P. M. (2018). *Analisi e pianificazione economico-finanziaria*. Knowità.

Melnyk, S., Bitici, U., Platts, K., Tobias, J., & Anderson, B. (2014). Is performance measurement and management fit for the future? *Management Accounting Research, 25*(2), 173–186.

Mendibil, K., & MacBryde, J. (2006). Factors that affect the design and implementation of team-based performance measurement systems. *International Journal of Productivity and Performance Management, 55*(2), 118–142.

Merchant, K. A., & Van der Stede, W. A. (2017). *Management control systems: Performance measurement, evaluation and incentives* (2nd ed.). Pearson Education.

Mettänen, P. (2005). Design and implementation of a performance measurement system for a research organization. *Production Planning and Control, 16*(2), 178–188.

Mithas, S., Ramasubbu, N., & Sambamurthy, V. (2011). How information management capability influences firm performance. *MIS Quarterly*, 237–256.

Moullin, M. (2017). Improving and evaluating performance with the public sector scorecard. *International Journal of Productivity and Performance Management, 66*(4), 442–458.

Munir, R., Baird, K., & Perera, S. (2013). Performance measurement system change in an emerging economy bank. *Accounting, Auditing and Accountability Journal, 26*(2), 196–233.

Neely, A. (2008). *Business performance measurement unifying theory and integrating practice* (2nd ed.). Cambridge University Press.

Neely, A., & Bourne, M. (2000). Why measurement initiatives fail. *Measuring Business Excellence, 4*, 3–6.

Neely, A., Gregory, M., & Platts, K. (1995). Performance measurement system design. *International Journal of Operations & Production Management, 15*(4), 80–116.

Neely, A. D., Adams, C., & Kennerley, M. (2002). *The performance prism: The scorecard for measuring and managing business success*. Pearson Education Ltd.

Neubauer, H., Mayr, S., Feldbauer-Durstmüller, B., & Duller, C. (2012). Management accounting systems and institutionalization in medium-sized and large family businesses—Empirical evidence from Germany and Austria. *European Journal of Management, 12*(2), 41–60.

Nudurupati, S. S., Bititci, U. S., Kumar, V., & Chan, F. T. S. (2011). State of the art literature review on performance measurement. *Computers and Industrial Engineering, 60*(2), 279–290.

Nudurupati, S. S., Tebboune, S., & Hardman, J. (2016). Contemporary performance measurement and management (PMM) in digital economies. *Production Planning and Control, 27*, 226–235.

Okwir, S., Nudurupati, S. S., Ginieis, M., & Angelis, J. (2018). Performance measurement and management systems: A perspective from complexity theory. *International Journal of Management Reviews, 20*(3), 731–754.

Otley, D. (1999). Performance management: A framework for management control system design. *Management Accounting Research, 10*, 363–382.

Otley, D. (2016). The contingency theory of management accounting and control. *Management Accounting Research, 31*, 45–62.

Palaiologos, A., Papazekos, P., & Panayotopoulou, L. (2011). Organizational justice and employee satisfaction in performance appraisal. *Journal of European Industrial Training, 35*(8), 826–840.

Panno, A. (2020). Performance measurement and management in small companies of the service sector; evidence from a sample of Italian hotels. *Measuring Business Excellence, 24*(2), 133–160.

Papulová, Z., Gažová, A., Šlenker, M., & Papula, J. (2021). Performance measurement system: Implementation process in SMES. *Sustainability, 13*(9), 4794.

Parida, A., Kumar, U., Galar, D., & Stenström, C. (2015). Performance measurement and management for maintenance: A literature review. *Journal of Quality in Maintenance Engineering, 21*(1), 2–33.

Parmenter, D. (2015). *Key performance indicators: Developing, implementing, and using winning KPIs*. John Wiley & Sons.

Pavan, A., & D'Onza, G. (2013). Innovare i Sistemi di Controllo e di Governance per Gestire il Cambiamento. *Management Control, 2*, 5–7.

Pekkola, S., Saunila, M., & Rantanen, H. (2016). Performance measurement system implementation in a turbulent operating environment. *International Journal of Productivity and Performance Management, 65*(7), 947–958.

Perkins, M., Grey, A., & Remmers, H. (2014). What do we really mean by "balanced scorecard"? *International Journal of Productivity and Performance Management, 63*(2), 148–169.

Pešalj, B., Pavlov, A., & Micheli, P. (2018). The use of management control and performance measurement systems in SMEs: A levers of control perspective. *International Journal of Operations & Production Management, 38*(11), 2169–2191.

Pezet, A. (2009). The history of the French Tableau de Bord (1885-1975): Evidence from the archives. *Accounting, Business & Financial History, 19*(2), 103–125.

Porter Michael, E. (1985). *Competitive advantage: Creating and sustaining superior performance*. Free Press.

Presti, C. (2021). Performance management as a part of the management control system. In C. Presti (Ed.), *Integrating performance and risk in a management control system* (pp. 43–64). Springer.

Purbey, S., Mukherjee, K., & Bhar, C. (2007). Performance measurement system for healthcare processes. *International Journal of Productivity and Performance Management, 56*, 241–251.

Qu, S. Q., & Cooper, D. J. (2011). The role of inscriptions in producing a balanced scorecard. *Accounting, Organizations and Society, 36*(6), 344–362.

Rangone, A. (1997). Linking organisational effectiveness, key success factors and performance measures: An analytical framework. *Management Accounting Research, 8*, 207–219.

Rizzotti, D. (2019). Incentivi, Sistemi di Misurazione delle Performance e allocazione dell'impegno manageriale, Management. *Control, 2*, 13–37.

Rockart, J. (1982). The changing role of the information systems executive: A critical success factors perspective. *Sloan Management Review, 24*(1), 3–13.

Rowland, C. A., & Hall, R. D. (2012). Organizational justice and performance: Is appraisal fair? *EuroMed Journal of Business, 7*(3), 280–293.

Saunila, M. (2016). Performance measurement approach for innovation capability in SMEs. *International Journal of Productivity and Performance Management, 65*(2), 162–176.

Scapens, R., & Roberts, J. (1993). Accounting and control: A case study of resistance to accounting change. *Management Accounting Research, 4*(1), 1–32.

Sgrò, F., Palazzi, F., Ciambotti, M., & Gelsomini, M. (2020). The design, implementation and use of intellectual capital measurements: A case study. *Management Control, Suppl. 1*, 19–38.

Sharma, B., & Gadenne, D. (2011). Balanced scorecard in a local government authority: Issues and challenges. *The Australian Journal of Public Administration, 70*(2), 167–184.

Sharma, N. P., Sharma, T., & Agarwal, M. N. (2016). Measuring employee perception of performance management system effectiveness: Conceptualization and scale development. *Employee Relations, 38*(2), 224–247.

Sigalas, C. (2015). Empirical investigation of balanced scorecard's theoretical underpinnings. *Journal of Accounting & Organizational Change, 11*(4), 546–572.

Simons, R. (1995). *Levers of control: How managers use innovative control systems to drive strategic renewal*. Harvard Business School Press.

Sink, D. S. (1985). *Productivity management: Planning, measurement and evaluation, control and improvement*. John Wiley and Sons.

Sink, D. S., & Tuttle, T. C. (1989). *Planning and measurement in your oganization of the future*. Industrial Engineering and Management Press.

Sousa, S., & Aspinwall, E. (2010). Development of a performance measurement framework for SMEs. *Total Quality Management and Business Excellence, 21*(5), 475–501.

Speckbacher, G., & Wentges, P. (2012). The impact of family control on the use of performance measures in strategic target setting and incentive compensation: A research note. *Management Accounting Research, 23*(1), 34–46.

Stouten, J., Rousseau, D. M., & De Cremer, D. (2018). Successful organizational change: Integrating the management practice and scholarly literatures. *Academy of Management Annals, 12*(2), 752–788. https://doi.org/10.5465/annals.2016.0095

Strohhecker, J. (2016). Factors influencing strategy implementation decisions: An evaluation of a balanced scorecard cockpit, intelligence, and knowledge. *Journal of Management Control, 27*(1), 89–119.

Sveiby, K. E. (1997). The intangible assets monitor. *Journal of Human Resource Costing & Accounting, 2*(1), 73–97.

Taticchi, P., Balachandran, K., & Tonelli, F. (2012). Performance measurement and management systems: State of the art, guidelines for design and challenges. *Measuring Business Excellence, 16*(2), 41–54.

Tayler, W. B. (2010). The balanced scorecard as a strategy-evaluation tool: The effects of implementation involvement and a causal-chain focus. *The Accounting Review, 85*(3), 1095–1117.

Taylor, A., & Taylor, M. (2013). Antecedents of effective performance measurement system implementation: An empirical study of UK manufacturing firms. *International Journal of Production Research, 51*(18), 1–14.

Taylor, A., & Taylor, M. (2014). Factors influencing effective implementation of performance measurement systems in small and medium-sized enterprises and large firms: A perspective from contingency theory. *International Journal of Production Research, 52*(3), 847–866.

Tessier, S., & Otley, D. (2012). A conceptual development of Simons' levers of control framework. *Management Accounting Research, 23*(3), 171–185.

Tuomela, T.-S. (2005). The interplay of different levers of control: A case study of introducing a new performance measurement system. *Management Accounting Research, 16*(3), 293–320.

Umashev, C., & Willett, R. (2008). Challenges to implementing strategic performance measurement systems in multi-objective organizations: The case of a large local government authority. *Abacus, 44*(4), 377–398.

Van Camp, J., & Braet, J. (2016). Taxonomizing performance measurement systems' failures. *International Journal of Productivity and Performance Management, 65*(5), 672–693.

Vasarhelyi, M. A., Kogan, A., & Tuttle, B. M. (2015). Big data in accounting: An overview. *Accounting Horizons, 29*(2), 381–396.

Voußem, L., Kramer, S., & Schäffer, U. (2016). Fairness perceptions of annual bonus payments: The effects of subjective performance measures and the achievement of bonus targets. *Management Accounting Research, 30*, 32–46.

Webb, R. A. (2004). Managers' commitment to the goals contained in a strategic performance measurement system. *Contemporary Accounting Research, 21*, 925–958.

Weber, M. (1968). *Economy and society: An outline of interpretive sociology, two volumes.* Bedminster.

Wickramasinghe, D., Gooneratne, T., & Jayakody, J. (2007). Interest lost: The rise and fall of a balanced scorecard project in Sri Lanka. *Advances in Public Interest Accounting, 13*, 237–271.

Wouters, M., & Sportel, M. (2005). The role of existing measures in developing and implementing performance measurement systems. *International Journal of Operation & Production Management, 25*(11), 1062–1082.

Wouters, M., & Wilderom, C. (2008). Developing performance-measurement systems as enabling formalization: A longitudinal field study of a logistics department. *Accounting, Organizations and Society, 33*(4–5), 488–516.

Yigitbasioglu, O. M., & Velcu, O. (2012). A review of dashboards in performance management: Implications for design and research. *International Journal of Accounting Information Systems, 13*(1), 41–59.

Chapter 4
Intersecting Change Management Theories with the PMS Implementation Literature

This chapter provides a review of key theoretical contributions in the field of change management, with the aim of determining their relevance to the implementation of performance measurement systems. It begins with a historical overview of change management models, tracing their evolution over time and examining different frameworks, their characteristics, and common topics.

A significant part of the chapter focuses then on the change management model developed by Stouten et al. (2018), which serves as the conceptual basis for this research. This framework was chosen because, while it has significant similarities with models developed previously, it is based, unlike them, solely on scientific evidence and it is published in a high-ranking journal. This section also highlights factors which, according to the framework, facilitate or hinder change.

In the final section, these factors are compared with those from PMS implementation literature, highlighting key similarities and differences. Common suggestions and approaches between the change management and PMS literature provide a solid foundation for supporting management accounting change initiatives. Those factors that are less prominent in PMS research are examined in the case study presented in the next chapter, with the goal of assessing their relevance for both academic and practical applications.

4.1 Chapter Summary

The following chapter is devoted to an in-depth examination of the main theoretical contributions in the field of change management in order to understand whether these theories may also have relevance in the field of PMS implementation for explaining why certain measurement initiatives succeed or fail. Specifically, the next section is dedicated to a historical examination of this stream of research,

L. Leto, *Integrating Change Management and Management Accounting Change*, SIDREA Series in Accounting and Business Administration,
https://doi.org/10.1007/978-3-031-84387-7_4

presenting the predominant change management models. Here, the evolution of these models over time is delineated, presenting the various types of frameworks, their characteristics, and the most frequently addressed themes. The third section delves into the examination of the change management model proposed by Stouten et al. (2018), which serves as the conceptual foundation for the empirical part of this research. This framework was chosen because, while it has significant similarities with some distinguished models developed previously, it is based, unlike them, solely on scientific evidence, it is relatively recent, and it is published in a high-ranking scientific journal. This section progresses to identify factors that appear to facilitate or inhibit organizational change initiatives from the analysis of this model. The fourth and final section of this chapter aims to compare the factors identified through the analysis of Stouten et al. (2018) framework with what has been found in the literature related to the implementation of PMS. In this way, it is also possible to understand which factors deemed important in the change management literature are also considered as relevant in the research field of PMS. These elements thus represent a solid foundation that practitioners can consider in managing the change implementation process. The factors that seem to receive less attention in PMS research are examined in the case study in the following chapter to determine their relevance, if any, to both research and practice.

4.2 Brief History and Introduction to Change Management Models

4.2.1 Organizational Change Models

Over the past 40 years, many prescriptive change models have been proposed to support managers and practitioners in the successful implementation of organizational change. Typically, the studies of change management do not focus on one specific type of change because they concentrate on the human factor and not on elements of a strictly technical nature. Fundamentally, they assume the replicability of the findings on which they are based to different types of organizational changes (Rosenbaum et al., 2018). The organizational changes considered by this literature usually involve the introduction of new technologies, tools, methodologies, activities, and processes, as well as changes in tasks, roles, organizational culture, and strategy (Hayes, 2022). Some examples of the most addressed topics and strategies for change in the change management literature are the development of the need for change (Armenakis & Bedeian, 1999; Hayes, 2022), the communication of the reasons and implications of change (Whelan-Berry & Somerville, 2010), the analysis and creation of *change readiness* (Armenakis et al., 1993; Bordia et al., 2011; Rafferty et al., 2013), the administration of the required training to manage the new situation (Hiatt, 2006), the management of resistance (Pardo Del Val & Martínez Fuentes, 2003), and the creation of commitment to change (Bartunek et al., 2006; Choi, 2011).

Typically, proposals in this area come from scholars in organization development and behavior (Van De Ven & Poole, 1995), but there are also some proposals from scholars in strategic management (Judson, 1991) and operations management (Bourne et al., 2003b; Hunsucker & Loos, 1989).

Typically, prescriptive models of organizational change fall into the category of teleological models of change identified by Van de Ven and Poole (1995), as they are based on the assumption that organizations change to pursue a purpose and that the process of change can be initiated when dissatisfaction with the status quo is generated. However, the other categories of change models identified by Van de Ven and Poole (1995), which include life-cycle, evolutionary, and dialectical models, also play a critical role in the field of change management. In fact, their depiction of change processes provides valuable insights and guidance for the successful implementation of change initiatives. Life-cycle models, such as those offered by Greiner (1998) and Miller and Friesen (1984), are considered useful tools for predicting, preventing, and managing the difficulties and organizational changes that a company is likely to face throughout its life in relation to its growth and expansion (Hayes, 2022). In general, they focus only on the inside of the organization, without considering the mutation that is happening in a company's operating environment. Instead, evolutionary theories inspired by Darwinism focus primarily on the external environment. In fact they fundamentally assert that only companies that adapt to the needs of the environment will survive and thrive. Finally, dialectical theories view change as a dialog between different stakeholder groups, where change occurs only when it is supported by a group of stakeholders with sufficient decision-making power within the company. According to these theories, change is, in any case, achieved through a compromise that synthesizes the desires of different stakeholder groups.

Continuing on the theme of prescriptive organizational change models, according to many scholars, the first change management model is the "changing as three steps" (Burnes & Bargal, 2017; Cummings et al., 2016; Rosenbaum et al., 2018) model proposed by Lewin (1947, 1951), who is considered as one of the founders of the disciplines of organization development and change management. The framework delineates the organizational change process into three distinct phases: unfreezing, moving, and freezing. It did not offer much guidance for managing change, and its approach was not prescriptive since the main goal was rather to explain how change occurs within individuals who belong to certain groups. Nevertheless, the scholar suggested that it could also be used to understand how change happens within organizations and to favor organizational change and performance improvement (Lewin, 1947). A particular feature of this model is the emphasis placed on the sustainability of change. In fact, it includes a refreezing phase precisely because Lewin postulated that behaviorally, individuals have an inherent inclination to return to previous patterns and habits. He contended that change could be deemed successful when the newly adopted behaviors are routinized and come to be perceived as the status quo and the norm (Buchanan et al., 2005; Hayes, 2022). This model was developed along with his studies about force field analysis, in which the author focused much of his attention on the drivers of resistance to change and the forces that support it. Through his theory of force field analysis, he suggested that in order to successfully introduce radical change, it is better to decrease the forces that resist change rather than increase the forces that push for it. This is because, on a psychological level, he had noticed that in situations of change where the "push" forces were increased, there was a significant increase in the level of anxiety in individuals, as well as a greater tendency to return to old habits once these "push" forces were removed. For example, when a manager authoritatively enforces change, there's an increased risk that employees will revert to old habits once the manager shifts focus from the project or leaves the organization (Hayes, 2022).

To this day, Lewin's theories remain quite widespread, especially in consulting and among change practitioners, being quite simple to explain (Cameron & Green, 2019) and having laid the foundation for a number of subsequent models. The model has received much criticism over the years (Rosenbaum et al., 2018), calling it outdated and inadequate to support managers in managing organizational change (Weick & Quinn, 1999). However, many relatively recent studies reaffirm its importance and defend its applicability even in the modern context (Burke, 2023; Burnes, 2004; Burnes & Bargal, 2017; Weick & Quinn, 1999), where companies need to change frequently and quickly.

The early expansions of Lewin's model were proposed precisely for consulting purposes. These developments were, in fact, offered by consultant "action" researchers who, in the tradition of Lewin (1946), developed their proposals by adopting the action research method. Some examples include the models from Lippitt et al. (1958), Kolb and Frohman (1970), and Bullock and Batten (1985).

These models basically augmented the steps of Lewin's model and made it more detailed, including suggestions on how to actively manage organizational change. Since these works originated with the idea that change had to be carried out with the support of an external facilitator or consultant, called change agent, these models take into account the presence of this subject. In Fig. 4.1, an example of these developments can be observed by looking at how Lippitt et al. (1958) expanded Lewin's model.

The new steps involve, among other things, diagnosing existing problems to be solved and opportunities to be harvested by the client organization, building a relationship between the client organization and the change agent, and closing the relationship with the consultant.

Another notable evolution of Lewin's model is offered by Schein (1996), who claims to have based much of his work on organizational culture change (Schein, 2010) on Lewin's concepts. The main difference with Lewin's original work involves identifying subprocesses within the three phases of change, offering more detailed guidance on its implementation. In the first phase, the *unfreezing* step, Schein (1996) delineates three specific processes:

- Disconfirmation
- Induction of guilt or survival anxiety
- Creation of psychological safety or overcoming of learning anxiety

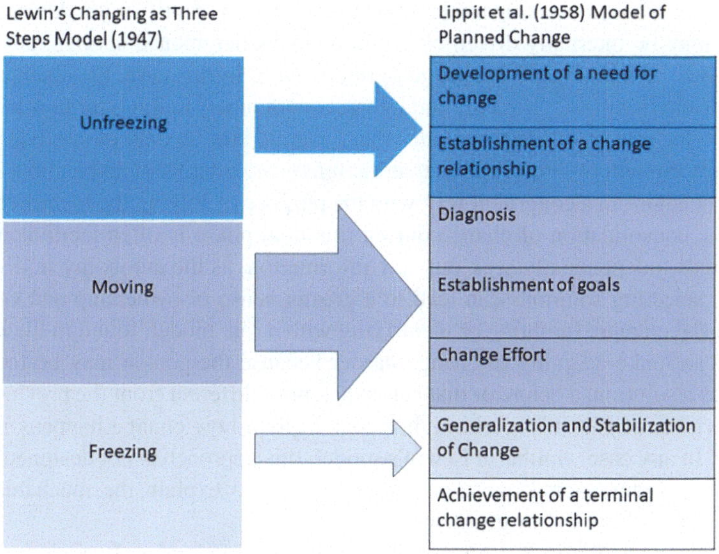

Fig. 4.1 The expansion of Lewin's model (Lewin, 1947) made by Lippitt et al. (1958)

According to Schein (1996), disconfirmation is the first process and begins when an individual feels frustrated or dissatisfied with the status quo. If the subject realizes and accepts the existence of issues with the current situation, it is possible to create a motivation to change and start the induction of the guilt or survival anxiety process. The second step can, therefore, only begin after the person has accepted the disconfirming information: the more the subject has accepted and gained conscience about the disconfirming data, the higher the anxiety about survival will be. However, disconfirmation and survival anxiety may be countered by learning anxiety (Schein, 1996). The person may react defensively and refuse to develop an awareness of the need for change because that would imply him accepting that something is not perfect, with a possible repercussion on individual self-esteem. Moreover, accepting the existence of a problem may imply the necessity to acquire new knowledge and, more in general, an effort. Therefore, he argues that it is fundamental to create a good level of "psychological safety" for the potential learner, where mistakes are accepted and not punished or criticized. The third process is specifically about that. Since motivation is not enough, Schein (1996) asserts that the change agent must employ different tactics with the aim of producing psychological safety in all the people impacted by an organizational transformation.

The *moving* phase is composed of a "cognitive redefinition" and one of two possible processes, namely (I) "Imitation and positive or defensive identification with a role model" and (II) "Scanning." Cognitive redefinition is about redefining a believed concept or modifying evaluation standards with the new information received. The assimilation of new information can happen in two ways. One can occur through engagement with an individual who offers a contrasting perspective and who then becomes a role model to be imitated or to identify with. Alternatively, change may be internally driven by an individual's heightened survival anxiety in the absence of someone to exchange opinions with. In this case, the change target scans the environment, "travels," and interacts with others looking for new information with the aim of solving the issues that generated the anxiety of survival.

Finally, Schein (1996) suggests that the *refreezing* phase should be about changing the behavior in a congruent way with the purpose of solving the identified problem. The consolidation of change during this final phase is often facilitated when individuals independently seek out new information, as the autonomy in discovering and selecting solutions can lead to a greater sense of ownership and commitment to the change. Imitating or identifying with a role model, found in the *moving* phase, can make adapting to change harder because the person may be forced to adopt, as a solution, a behavior that is too distant or different from the previous one. This revision of Lewin's work might better explain how change happens in individuals. In any case, similar to Lewin's model, this approach is not designed exclusively for organizational contexts; rather, it aims to explain the mechanisms of change at the individual or group level.

Like Lewin's approach, later prescriptive models of change often adopted a linear or sequential view of the change process, even when they did not explicitly refer to his model (Rosenbaum et al., 2018; Stouten et al., 2018).

Before moving to the most recent models, it is worth mentioning the "Change Equation" because it emerged as one of the most popular contributions to change management, at least in the practitioners' field. David Gleicher originally formulated it in the 60s while working at the international management consulting firm "Arthur D. Little" (Cady et al., 2014), and it was precisely thought to be used to understand what are the barriers that stop change and consequently help managers identify how to favor acceptance. Even though the original formulation is attributed to Gleicher, it made its first official appearance in a paper written by Beckhard (1975). It was subsequently reprised by Beckhard and Harris (1987) in their change model and expanded and revised by Dannemiller and Jacobs (1992). Curiously, in the updated version of their change model, Beckhard and Harris (1987) don't attribute the formula's origin to Gleicher anymore. The change equation, which is

$$C = A \times B \times D > X$$

aims to demonstrate that organizational change (C) only happens when the dissatisfaction with the status quo (A) multiplied by the desired clear state (B) and practical steps to the desired state (D) is higher than the cost of change. If only one of the three between A, B, and D is near zero, the change project will probably fail because resistance to change won't be overcome. Although the authors do not explain how to calculate the elements of the formula, the change equation is a very simple tool that, according to these authors, can help assess the odds of success of a change process approximately.

Compared to the old ones, the models from the 1980s onward would begin to be more complex and comprehensive, placing greater emphasis on managerial and organizational concepts that were becoming more widely known, such as leadership, strategic change, total quality management, lean organization, and business process reengineering.

The critical role of leadership in the success of change initiatives has become increasingly apparent thanks to models such as the ones from Beckhard and Harris (1987), Beer et al. (1990), Kanter et al. (1992), Kotter (1996, 2012), and Luecke (2003).

Especially Kotter's (1996) model has become, since the second half of the 1990s, one of the most known leadership-based approaches to change, and it is still extremely popular among practitioners. Kotter is a Harvard emeritus professor who presented an eight-step model in his work "Leading Change." This book was particularly endorsed by Time Magazine,[1] which defined it in 2012 as one of the 25th most influential business management books along with other extremely famous works in both academic and management circles (e.g., Porter, 1980; Senge, 1990), attesting to its widespread use among managers. Kotter (1996) identified the eight most common errors made by companies when implementing major organizational changes and consequently developed the steps of his model in order to avoid them. The eight most common errors, according to Kotter (1995), are:

- Not establishing a great enough sense of urgency
- Not creating a powerful enough guiding coalition
- Lacking a vision
- Undercommunicating the vision by a factor of ten
- Not removing obstacles to the new vision
- Not systematically planning for and creating short-term wins
- Declaring victory too soon
- Not anchoring changes in the corporation's culture

With reference to recent models like Kotter's (1996, 2012), leadership is generally considered to be central to developing and communicating the vision of the desired future and generating commitment to change among individuals in an organization.

Table 4.1 compares the steps, stages, or approaches of leadership-based models. As we can see, there are often some similarities between these models.

Although most of these models offer a linear and sequential process for implementing change, other authors prefer to adopt a nonlinear, emergent, and processual approach while still providing methodologies to facilitate the organizational transition. Some examples are Dawson's (2019) processual approach or the ADKAR (Hiatt, 2006), which indicates a series of requirements to be met for change to occur effectively. Other significant differences in these theoretical methods for implementing change concern the approach that characterizes them: some prefer a top-down process, others a bottom-up one (Rosenbaum et al., 2018), some prefer a

[1] https://content.time.com/time/specials/packages/article/0,28804,2086680_2086683_2087679,00.html

Table 4.1 Comparison of the most popular and modern change management models

Beckhard and Harris (1987)	Beer et al. (1990)	Kanter et al. (1992)	Kotter (1996, 2012)	Luecke (2003)
Determination of the degree of choice about whether to change and establishment of what needs to be changed	Mobilization of commitment to change through joint diagnosis of business problems	Analysis of the organization and its need for change	Establishment of a sense of urgency	Mobilization of energy and commitment through joint identification of business problems and their solutions
Definition of goals and vision of the desired end state compared to the present state	Development of a shared vision on how to organize and manage for competitiveness	Creation of a shared vision and a common direction	Creation of a guiding coalition	Development of a shared vision of how to organize and manage for competitiveness
Determination and planning of a strategy for change	Fostering consensus for the new vision and competence to enact it	Separation from the past	Development of a vision and a strategy	Identification of the leadership
Management and reduction of resistances during the transition state and reviewing the effort	Spread of revitalization to all departments without pushing it from the top	Creation of a strong sense of urgency	Communication of a change vision	Focus on results, not on activities
	Institutionalizing revitalization through formal policies, systems, and structures	Support of the change by a strong leader role	Empowerment of employees for broad-based action	Start of the change at the periphery, then to the other units without pushing it from the top
	Monitoring and adjusting strategies in response to problems in the revitalization	Alignment of a political sponsorship	Generating short-term wins	Institutionalization of success through formal policies, systems, and structures
		Development of an implementation plan	Consolidating gains and producing more change	Monitoring and adjusting strategies in response to problems in the change process

(continued)

Table 4.1 (continued)

Beckhard and Harris (1987)	Beer et al. (1990)	Kanter et al. (1992)	Kotter (1996, 2012)	Luecke (2003)
		Development of enabling structures	Anchoring new approaches in the culture	
		Honest communication of the change and involvement of people		
		Reinforcement and institutionalization of the change		

focalization on the individuals that compose the organization, while others on financial and organizational variables (Beer & Nohria, 2000).

The main criticisms of prescriptive change methodologies are related to the fact that their inventors did not provide scientific evidence to support their thesis on how change managers should deal with organizational transformations (Stouten et al., 2018), even when academics proposed these models. For example, even Kotter's model is not based on any scientific evidence but exclusively on the author's experiences (Appelbaum et al., 2012; Hughes, 2016).

This is probably because, although distinguished academics developed some of these models, these individuals also worked as management consultants (e.g., Beer et al., 1990; Kanter et al., 1992; Kotter, 1996, 2012). Furthermore, some of the most famous models are developed by pure consultants (see Hiatt, 2006; Judson, 1991). Therefore, the works published by these authors are addressed mostly to practitioners and not to researchers, adopting, as experts in the field, a prescriptive and normative approach without providing significant evidence on the validity of their claims. Nevertheless, as it will be shown in Sect. 4.3, Stouten et al. (2018) examined five of the most known change management models, including Kotter's. They showed that several studies conducted by other researchers support a significant number of the prescriptions offered. In fact, even though their framework is based solely on scientific evidence, it shares many similarities with the other models.

Finally, as also pointed out by Stouten et al. (2018), although the content of the change plays an important role in the success or failure dynamics of the process, there is a dearth of organizational change studies that focus on specific kinds of change. Therefore, very few organizational change management studies and organizational development studies focus on the content of change, and no empirical "organizational change" studies, to the best of the author's knowledge, focus specifically on PMS implementation.

4.2.2 Change Models Focusing on Individuals

In the field of change management, literature often mentions individual transition models (Cameron & Green, 2019; Hayes, 2022). These models can usually have two different purposes: they represent the internal and emotional states experienced during significant transitions, and they offer guidance on facilitating these transitions by mitigating or avoiding the most challenging states. Experts in the field of psychology generally developed these models. Their origins are considered distinct from prescriptive models of organizational change, and can be found specifically in the work of Kübler-Ross (1969). Although the model proposed by Kübler-Ross (1969) was designed to represent the emotional stages that people go through when dealing with grief or serious illness, this model has also been widely applied in the field of organizational change management (Cameron & Green, 2019; Hayes, 2022). This is because many scholars agree that radical organizational change requires, as in these situations, letting go of the past state and accepting the new reality, facing a new situation characterized by new difficulties, and a significant change in habits and behaviors (Bridges, 1986). In particular, the Kübler-Ross (1969) model is composed of five emotional conditions: shock & denial, anger, bargaining, depression, and acceptance. The curve (Fig. 4.2) represents how the mood and energy trend of individuals swing over time when experiencing the five different phases of grief. It's important to underscore that, although these emotions experienced during change are presented sequentially, they do not necessarily occur in this order. Some people may, in fact, skip some of these stages. Or some conditions or events may lead back to emotions already experienced.

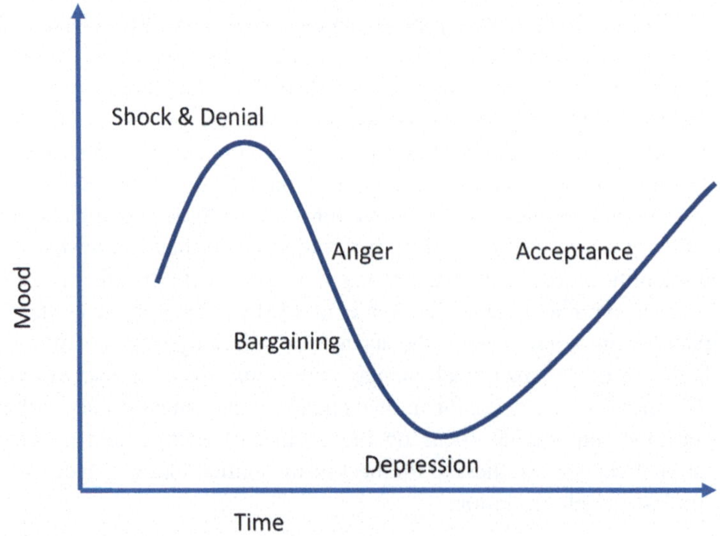

Fig. 4.2 Kübler-Ross's change curve. Based on Kübler-Ross E. (1969). *On Death and Dying*. New York, NY: Scribner

This model begins with the "*shock & denial*" phase, in which an individual is confronted with a new condition or "environmental change" that involves an individual transition. The interaction with this new situation or reality creates *shock*, which causes the individual to *deny* the existence of the change. This individual emotional stage may be followed by a phase of anger as the individual realizes that the new condition is not only real, but is destined to be permanent. *Anger* may be specifically directed at those who are "at fault" for the new situation, or it may be blind, assigning blame to people who have no responsibility or role in the change. The *anger* phase may then be followed by a bargaining phase, during which the individual attempts to negotiate compromise terms to avoid or mitigate the new situation, hoping to avoid having to completely change habits and behaviors to adapt to the new condition. If *bargaining* fails, instead of *acceptance* of change, there may be either a return to the anger phase or a continuation of the *depression* phase. In the latter phase, mood and work performance are generally low. This phase should finally be followed by adequate support in order to reach the *acceptance* phase.

Kübler-Ross's (1969) model has also been taken up, expanded and adapted for explicit application to business reality (Adams et al., 1976; Conner & Patterson, 1982; Hayes, 2022; Parker & Lewis, 1981).

Figure 4.3 provides an overview of the modifications made by Adams et al. (1976) and Parker and Lewis (1981) to adapt the model for use in organizational settings.

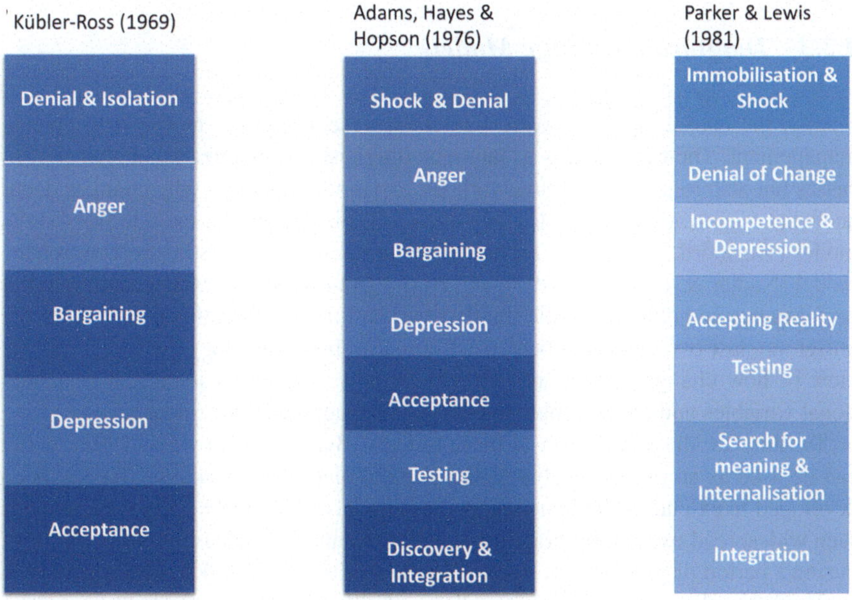

Fig. 4.3 Comparison of the models of Kübler-Ross (1969), Adams et al. (1976), and Parker and Lewis (1981)

Specifically, it was Adams et al. (1976) who first revised the "Change Curve." Their updated model aimed to explain the individual phases and emotions experienced during not only dramatic losses but also more generally radical changes in people's lives. In particular, they added a phase of experimentation after acceptance, where individuals begin to test new ways of functioning and operating to better cope with the new situation. Following this phase, they included another phase dedicated to the full integration of the change. According to the authors, this new version of the model could be applied in organizational settings, such as when an individual experiences a job change.

Parker and Lewis (1981) proposed another revision of the work of Kübler-Ross (1969), and Adams et al. (1976), explicitly designed for application only within organizations. Their expansion was motivated by the observation that it was common for people who received a promotion or experienced a job change to go through a series of emotional phases that affected their work performance. Their study was based on their assumption that even fundamentally positive or desired changes can be difficult for people to cope with. This is because the overly positive view of the desired future failed to account for the new problems and difficulties that would inevitably arise. According to these authors, understanding the stages and emotions experienced during individual transitions is fundamental to providing individuals with adequate support in coping with change and to reducing the duration of low performance periods such as "immobilization & shock" or "incompetence & depression."

4.2.3 Diagnostic Change Models

Finally, the causal and diagnostic models represent another approach to change management. Their function is to facilitate diagnosis in organizational change processes but also to provide a framework for explaining how and why changes occur and what organizational variables they impact. Typical examples include Weisbord's model (Weisbord, 1976), the 7S model (Waterman et al., 1980), the congruence model (Nadler & Tushman, 1997), and Burke and Litwin's (1992) causal model of performance and change. While the first two had more "operational" use from the outset, the last two have also been used in research because they provide a holistic view of how change occurs and, ultimately, how changes in identified organizational variables and the external environment impact firm performance.

To illustrate the application of these models, Burke and Litwin's (1992) model can be used as an example. This model is particularly representative, having been developed to extend and enhance preceding models, such as the 7S model, and has seen widespread use among practitioners. For instance, it was used within the BBC during a period of great transformation in the 1990s (Felix, 2000).

The two authors developed this model explicitly to guide the production of organizational diagnosis, which, as mentioned before, is the starting point of many change management approaches, and to better explain the dynamics of organizational change.

According to Burke and Litwin (1992), a change in any of the variables composing the diagnostic model implies alterations or effects in the others. In addition to organizational variables, however, it is noted that the external environment can also be found represented within the framework, unlike other models such as the 7S model. This is because the authors believe that companies are open systems and, therefore, must adapt to changes that occur in the environment in which they operate (Bertini, 1990). However, according to this model, it is also the company itself that has the ability to influence what happens in its operating environment. In any case, Burke and Litwin (1992) propose that organizational transformations arise mainly because of changes in the environment and not because of internal factors or leadership's initiative. In other words, although they acknowledge that leaders have a fundamental role in the success of organizational changes, they assert that organizational mutations occur mainly because of external forces.

The factors included in their model are divided into two categories. There are transformational factors in which "alteration is likely caused by interaction with environmental forces (both within and without) and will require entirely new behavior sets from organizational members" (Burke & Litwin, 1992, p. 529). Then, there are transactional factors in which changes are achieved through relatively short-term reciprocity among individuals and working groups. The transformational factors are the *external environment*, *leadership*, *mission and strategy*, and *organizational culture*. The transactional factors are *management practices*, *structure*, *systems*, *work unit climate*, *motivation*, *individual needs and values*, *tasks*, and *individuals' skills*.

One significant difference between the two is that transformational factors can produce transformational and radical changes, while the latter are likely to produce the less radical and more incremental ones.

4.3 Introduction to the Framework by Stouten et al. (2018)

As outlined in the introduction, this research aims to conduct an exploratory study to provide empirical evidence that supports or denies the importance of elements deemed essential by change management theories. It aims to deepen our understanding of the reasons behind the failure or success of performance measurement implementation projects. Moreover, it seeks to expand upon the existing body of knowledge regarding the factors that obstruct or facilitate the implementation of management accounting tools and PMS, as explored in prior studies such as the one from Bourne et al. (2002), Kasurinen (2002), Bourne (2005), De Waal and Counet (2009), Munir et al. (2013), and Lueg and Vu (2015).

The primary reference for this research is the work of Stouten et al. (2018). These authors provide an extensive review of the literature related to change management, seeking to understand whether the prescriptions and approaches suggested by the most popular change management models are actually supported by the scientific literature as well. Their review validates only some aspects of these models, indicating that certain recommended practices and factors are either unsupported or only partially confirmed by research findings. Therefore, Stouten et al. (2018) concluded their study with a framework of ten prescriptions or "steps" supported by research and empirical evidence for managing change. This framework is particularly significant for this research as it provides the basis for extrapolating the enabling and hindering factors extensively discussed in the field of organizational change.

The following section analyzes Stouten et al.'s (2018) framework, outlining the associated enabling and hindering factors. These critical success factors will then be commented on in light of what has been stated in the literature about the implementation of PMS.

4.3.1 The Framework

The Stouten et al. (2018) change model consists of ten different prescriptions. Unlike other change management models (e.g., Kotter, 2012), not all of the given prescriptions need to be followed step by step, following a linear sequence of activities to be performed. Rather, this framework collects a set of suggestions, which are commented on and supported by the various literature references identified through the authors' literature review. However, it is implied or is otherwise evident that certain recommendations are more applicable to the initial stages of a change process, while others are relevant to the later stages.

Table 4.2 provides a description of Stouten et al.'s (2018) ten steps and their expected advantages and benefits. Each of these steps has been given an abbreviated name for ease of identification and recall. The steps are then analyzed in order to find similarities or differences from the other models of organizational change outlined earlier.

The first step in the Stouten et al. (2018) model involves conducting a *diagnosis* of the current situation in which the company finds itself. This step is rather "classic," as it is commonly present in both older (Kolb & Frohman, 1970; Lippitt et al., 1958) and more recent change management models (Beer et al., 1990; Kanter et al., 1992; Luecke, 2003). One of the few models to leave out this stage is Kotter's (1996, 2012) model, which seems to start at an immediately later step, already devoted to creating a sense of urgency and need to change. Stouten et al. (2018) noted that the usefulness of this approach is supported by research in the field of change management (Armenakis et al., 1993; Armenakis & Harris, 2009), as well as in the decision-making one (Nutt, 1999).

The second step, the *change readiness assessment*, still relates to the diagnosis of the current situation of the company but introduces the increasingly acknowledged concept of *change readiness* in the organizational change literature (Armenakis et al., 1993; Armenakis & Harris, 2002; Holt et al., 2007; Jones et al., 2005; Rafferty et al., 2013; Weiner, 2009). Nevertheless, it is a concept generally ignored by other

Table 4.2 Description and advantages of following each step of the Stouten et al. (2018) framework

Nr.	Step	Description	Advantages
1	Get facts regarding the nature of the problem(s)—diagnosis step #1 (*organizational diagnosis*[a])	• Gathering of the information to provide insight into the need for change and about preexisting conditions or constraints that might affect implementation.	• Useful to make change recipients and other stakeholders believe that the reasons for change are legitimate and its direction rational. • Helps to identify discrepancies between current assumptions and facts and to develop new thinking about the organization and the need for change. • Avoids basing change initiatives on poorly understood problems.
2	Assess and address the organization's readiness for change—diagnosis step #2 (*change readiness assessment*)	• Conducting an assessment of the capacity of the organization and its members to take on the demands effective change requires. • The assessment considers the (I) change history, (II) degree of stress already faced by employees, (III) leadership commitment, (IV) individual and collective self-efficacy, (V) discrepancy between present and desired end-state, (VI) awareness regarding the existence of, the sources of, and solutions to the organization's problems, (VII) appropriateness of change for the organization, (VIII) capability of the leadership to manage the change, (IX) personal benefits related to the change, & (X) feeling from the employees that they will receive the needed support from the management and the colleagues.	• Helps assess the feasibility of change and build effective change strategies by identifying barriers and enablers to change.

(continued)

Table 4.2 (continued)

Nr.	Step	Description	Advantages
3	Implement evidence-based change interventions (*evidence-based implementation*)	• Recurring to people inside and outside the organization who are experienced with the problem and can help identify plausible solutions. • Listening to stakeholders, including affected employees and managers, as they are essential sources of information about possible solutions and may be able to test alternatives to see what might work. • Looking for scientific evidence on the likely benefits (and risks) of specific kinds of change and how to effectively implement it. • Choosing interventions that develop change-related skills, offering rewards and incentives to motivate change, and providing opportunities to practice change activities in supportive environments.	• Increases the likelihood of successful change. • Helps create acceptance from stakeholders. • Helps improve the technical content of the change. • Helps people feel motivated and capable of implementing the change.
4	Develop effective change leadership throughout the organization (*leadership development*)	• Training and development of existing leaders in change-related skills with a focus both on how to deal with change themselves and how to effectively manage change from the perspective of their employees. • Supporters of the change should be individual leaders who are trustworthy, supportive, honest, and transparent about the nature of the change and future plans because they can create a psychologically safe environment where there is room for voice, mistakes, and learning.	• Leaders play a central role in change as they can serve as change agents and role models. • Effective change leaders are able to support people during the transition and motivate them to change. • Employees are more motivated and feel the support of a capable leadership.

(continued)

Table 4.2 (continued)

Nr.	Step	Description	Advantages
5	Develop and communicate a compelling change vision (*change communication*)	• Developing a vision of the desired future end state and its communication to internal and external stakeholders. • Vision must reflect goals that can be broadly shared. • Information from stakeholder groups (e.g., employees, managers, and clients) can be gathered to help identify motivating features. • Research also supports the value of a vision communication process based on repetition, the use of multiple channels and reliable and convincing evidence to convey a logical structure.	• Shared goals and positive beliefs about the reasons for change that align with the vision improve the likelihood of successful change implementation. • Explanations that help change recipients understand the reasons for the change can enhance their positive reactions. However, where stakeholders incur losses from the change (e.g., job loss), it is less clear how to create a shared vision.
6	Work with social networks and tap their influence (*social networks exploitation*)	• Working with social networks and create and exploit relational ties.	• The effectiveness of change agents depends not only on the individual's skills but also on their network relationships. Creating relational boundaries with potentially influential organizational members who support the change can be an important way to coopt fence-sitters who remain resistant. • Individuals in highly cohesive teams are likely to be more influenced by appeals directed to the team and by change efforts that engage the team as a whole than by efforts disconnected from their team.

(continued)

Table 4.2 (continued)

Nr.	Step	Description	Advantages
7	Use enabling practices to support implementation (*implementation support*)	• Using a number of enabling processes to support change interventions. These are the use of goal setting, the creation of learning opportunities, the involvement of employees, the creation of transitional structures, and the use of fair procedures in decision-making.	• Goal setting can make people realize change and understand its scope and scale, address conflicting goals, and avoid a lack of managerial accountability or change. • Providing room for learning and skill development helps prompt greater change motivation. • Participation favors information sharing and obtaining feedback. • Fairness and treating people respectfully can reduce resistance to change. • A high level of organizational identification can facilitate acceptance of change, as long as the change process is perceived as fair and provides visible benefits for the organization, even when there are disadvantages or no visible benefits for the single individual. • Transitional structures help oversee the change and special projects, rules, or trials that can be used to modify and expand the change as needed.
8	Promote micro-processes and experimentation (*experimentation*)	• romoting small-scale or micro-processes to allow change recipients to provide feedback and make local adjustments to broader change plans based on their own experience.	• It supports learning by doing and allows adaptation of local elements in the organization. • It encourages the achievement of "small wins" that inform change recipients of their potential and provide evidence of the benefits that can be achieved. • It favors bottom-up change proposals from employees themselves. • If leaders respond to these proposals, they favor the feeling of fair treatment.

(continued)

Table 4.2 (continued)

Nr.	Step	Description	Advantages
9	Assess change progress and outcomes over time (*progress assessment*)	• Conducting periodic assessments to determine whether the planned change is producing anticipated activities, experiences, and outcomes.	• It provides feedback to gain an understanding of the change's effects and make improvements. • It supports learning and change implementation. • It may help keep people committed to the change.
10	Institutionalize the change to sustain its effectiveness (*change institutionalization*)	• Sustaining change by integrating it into the larger systems of the organization, including its culture, standard practices and management systems. • Ensuring continuity of commitment and support by the leadership. • Using enabling structures helps maintain new practices and improve their efficiency and effectiveness.	• It helps make change sustainable over time, even when people in the company change.

[a]Parentheses include a name assigned by the author to more easily recall each of the ten steps

prescriptive change management models since they tend to focus more on the "negative" resistance to change instead of the more "positive" *readiness to change*.

Armenakis et al. (1993, p. 681), who were the first to propose the theory about *change readiness*, originally defined *change readiness* as the "beliefs, attitudes, and intentions regarding the extent to which changes are needed and the organization's capacity to undertake those changes successfully." Over the years, this theory has evolved and become a more multidimensional concept as it has been further developed by its original authors and others (Armenakis & Harris, 2002; Holt et al., 2007; Rafferty et al., 2013).

Initially, there were only two dimensions considered, and they concerned the discrepancy between the current situation and the desired situation, which is necessary to develop a need for change, and self-efficacy, i.e., individuals' perception that they and their organization have the capability to introduce change (Armenakis et al., 1993). *Change readiness* was then expanded by taking into account additional elements such as principal support, i.e., the perception that individuals will receive or can seek help from their superiors, and valence, i.e., the perception of the benefits and drawbacks related to the change for the single individuals belonging to the company (Armenakis & Harris, 2002). The concept was further broadened to include both organizational and individual variables (Rafferty et al., 2013), which are detailed in the description of the second step in Table 4.2.

The third step of the change model (*evidence-based implementation*) by Stouten et al. (2018) underscores a point previously discussed: the literature on change management and related models often lacks substantial guidance on the content of change. This model seeks to acknowledge this gap by suggesting that the chosen interventions should be consistent with the issues the company aims to address.[2] While not providing technical suggestions as most of the change models, Stouten et al. (2018) give some steps aimed at supporting the identification of the most congenial solutions to the problem.

The *leadership development*[3] (fourth) step devoted to identifying and developing change leadership is in line with what has been claimed in other models (e.g., Kanter et al., 1992; Kotter, 1996; Luecke, 2003). The absence of support from leadership or the lack of skills related to communication and change management are, in fact, frequently reported in the literature as elements that can hinder the success of change processes (Hiatt, 2006), while the presence of leaders with change-related[4] skills is suggested to be an enabling factor (Hayes, 2022). Therefore, Stouten et al. (2018) advise not taking these capabilities for granted and trying to bring on board project leaders with knowledge and skills that complement each other.

The *change communication* (fifth) step, devoted to developing and communicating a change vision, is present in many modern models (Luecke, 2003; Kotter, 1996; Kanter et al., 1992). However, unlike these models, they do not provide guidelines on what the content of the vision should be due to the presence of conflicting evidence about this topic in the scientific field. They limit themselves to suggesting that stakeholder expectations should be taken into account and that communication should reduce misunderstandings, which are at the root of many cases of resistance. They also suggest repeating communication through various channels and providing evidence to support the development and maintenance of the need for change. These latter suggestions are also in line with what is recommended in other change management models (Hiatt, 2006; Kotter, 1996).

The *social networks exploitation* (sixth) step shares some similarities with other models. For instance, Kotter (1996) suggests composing a guiding coalition to support change, consisting of managers from different areas of the organization to exert more significant influence on employees from the various organizational units to adopt the change. Hiatt (2006), on the other hand, does not explicitly talk about social networks or guiding coalition building but suggests that the type of relationships existing in the company can influence the effectiveness of the change process. He also recognizes that some individuals may be better suited than others for change communication because of their credibility or role in the company. This step also

[2] This also turns out to be coherent with what has been said in the PMS literature, which suggests that tools and related techniques should be chosen based on actual business needs (Bourne et al., 2000, 2002; Hudson et al., 2001).

[3] The importance of the role of leadership is also emphasized in numerous papers related to PMS (Franco & Bourne, 2003; Kasurinen, 2002; Taylor & Taylor, 2013), as seen in the related literature review chapter.

[4] One example is the ability, which a leader may have, to be able to adopt a transactional or transformational leadership style when needed and depending on the situation in order to motivate people toward change (Hayes, 2022).

considers the role of the change agent, who is a facilitator of change and individual transitions. This subject is often found in the organizational change literature, making its first appearance as early as Lippitt et al.'s (1958) model. Initially, this role was seen as external, typically a consultant with expertise in behavioral psychology and organizational knowledge. In more recent years, however, it has been recognized that this role can also be played by figures within the company, such as managers and employees (Hayes, 2022). The kind of support these individuals give is generally both emotional and psychological and sometimes technical. Change agents are usually not seen as change managers, as they are not held accountable to the change project itself. Their task is precisely to facilitate the change, not to act or be directly accountable with respect to its implementation. That said, it is still possible that the role of change agent is also held by a change leader or by figures with important managerial responsibilities.

The *implementation support* (seventh) step is only partly shared with the other change management models. Stouten et al. (2018) advise that the enabling structures and practices should be related to goal setting, learning, employee participation, fairness and justice, and transitional structures. While many models generally consider these aspects relevant (Hiatt, 2006; Kotter, 1996; Kanter et al., 1992; Bridges, 1991; Beer et al., 1990), fewer proposals explicitly consider transitional structures, and fairness and justice. Bridges (1991) is an exception as he argues that providing temporary and transitional structures may help with the implementation of the change. Hiatt (2006), Kotter (1996), Kanter et al. (1992), Bridges (1991), and Beer et al. (1990) all suggest that treating employees respectfully favors the acceptance of the change. However, unlike Stouten et al. (2018), they don't consider all the different aspects of organizational justice, i.e., procedural, distributive, informational, and interpersonal.[5] The concepts expressed in the reflections of the authors of these models seem to only partially address this aspect, as they consider the importance of making people feel involved in the project, communicating the change, and treating employees with respect.

The eighth step, "*experimentation*," is acknowledged in various prescriptive change management models. Bridges (1991), Hiatt (2006), and Schein (1996) emphasize the importance of allowing people to experiment with new work methods in a safe environment and creating a psychologically safe setting in which people do not feel judged if they make a mistake. Additionally, individual change management models like Adams et al. (1976) and Parker and Lewis (1981)

[5] Hayes (2022) provides an extensive explanation of these four types of *organizational justice*. In particular, he affirms that *distributive justice* depends on the perception of how the disadvantages and benefits associated with change are shared among stakeholders. *Procedural justice* concerns the individual perception in relation to the level of involvement granted to them in the implementation process and decision-making processes; it also depends on having granted them the opportunity to express their opinions, concerns or ask for clarifications in relation to the project. *Informational justice* depends on the perceived accessibility given to subjects in relation to information relevant to understanding the reasons for changing and using certain procedures rather than others and their implications. *Interpersonal justice* concerns the perception of having been treated respectfully and without injury to one's dignity.

recognize a "testing phase" as crucial, noting that unsuccessful testing can lead to frustration or denial of the need for change. Stouten et al. (2018) also advocate the importance of achieving small wins rather than quick wins, as Kotter (1996) model suggests. Both approaches recognize the usefulness of achieving desired effects associated with change during implementation. However, the former emphasizes that it is useful to focus on gradually achieving predetermined goals relative to specific areas of the company and then propagating the change progressively to the other areas without necessarily trying to impose short-term timelines. Kotter (1996), on the other hand, focuses heavily on the time frame in which results should be achieved, arguing that if positive effects are not seen regularly every 3–6 months maximum, momentum could be lost, and the project could stall. The reason for this substantial difference is that research has yielded discordant results with regard to the achievement of quick wins (Van Buren & Safferstone, 2009) because while they may reinforce a sense of the usefulness of change, trying to achieve positive results in the short-term could prevent the achievement of far more ambitious results in a longer time frame.

The *progress assessment* (ninth) step, devoted to assessing the change progress, is also considered in many change models. Kotter (1996) suggests achieving regularly "quick" visible and not ambiguous wins to prove that the project is giving the expected results. Lippitt et al. (1958) and Beer et al. (1990) suggest the importance of tracking and communicating the change's progress, as not everyone involved in the change project may be aware that their efforts are producing the expected results. Stouten et al. (2018), as well as the authors of these other models, argue that the achievement of visible and not ambiguous progress not only reinforces the change effort but also helps identify the need for corrective actions if expectations are not being met.

The *change institutionalization* (tenth) step aligns with assertions made in other change management models. For example, Kanter et al. (1992) devote a whole stage to the institutionalization of the change, while Kotter (1996)'s model conclusive phase is about anchoring the new approaches in the organizational culture.[6] Lewin (1947) devotes the final stage of his model to making change sustainable over time.

4.3.2 The Enabling and Hindering Factors in Stouten et al. (2018) Framework

Table 4.3 collects the enabling and hindering factors that emerge from the steps, comments, and recommendations given in each of them by Stouten et al. (2018).

The next section proceeds to analyze these factors in the context of extant research related to the implementation of PMS.

[6] Interestingly, also research related to management accounting change and PMS seems to confirm both the need to "institutionalize change" (Burns & Scapens, 2000) and to integrate new ways of working into organizational culture (Bititci et al., 2006).

4.3.3 *Analysis of the Enabling and Hindering Factors in the Light of PMS Literature*

The analysis now begins by examining the enabling and hindering factors identified in the ten prescriptions. However, it is premised that certain factors recur across multiple steps; in such instances, repetitive commentary on these factors will be avoided.

4.3.3.1 Organizational Diagnosis (First Step)

The first enabling factor discernible in the *organizational diagnosis* step is the "*assessment of the company's situation, problems and opportunities*." Although not explicitly referenced in the majority of publications on PMS design and implementation, this factor is implicitly deemed essential. It is commonly advocated that PMS should be adapted and tailored to the specific needs of the business (Melnyk et al., 2014; Sousa & Aspinwall, 2010). As previously discussed, it is believed that such systems should be developed to meet knowledge and control needs, although the literature does not usually frame this need in terms of a problem to be solved or an opportunity to be seized through the introduction of the change. However, there is little discussion of the potential usefulness of conducting a business diagnosis to build commitment and convince organizational members of the need to implement a PMS. This aspect is often deemed critical in the change management literature (Armenakis & Harris, 2009; Beer et al., 1990; Kanter et al., 1992; Luecke, 2003).

The second enabling factor (*stakeholders believe in the project*) is also reasonably considered. In this regard, the PMS literature indicates that recognizing perceived benefits associated with a change fosters acceptance among internal stakeholders (Bourne et al., 2002; Bourne et al., 2003b; Cavalluzzo & Ittner, 2004; De Waal, 2003; Munir et al., 2013). The perception of benefits associated with this change promotes its credibility and makes it seem rational and legitimate. Conversely, the perception of disadvantages associated with the change can serve as a significant hindering factor, generating resistance to change.

With respect to the third factor (*information gathered from multiple sources*), the PMS literature provides limited guidance on developing a business diagnosis and the type of information to develop a need for change and implement PMS. Typically, the focus is on involving individuals from different organizational levels, as they can contribute additional data, perspectives, and suggestions for improving the system (Sousa & Aspinwall, 2010). There is also usually a focus on information systems and the type of data they can provide, as they form the backbone on which the dashboards of indicators that make up the performance measurement system are built (Bourne et al., 2000). The change management literature also suggests that gathering information from multiple parties can help not only to improve the content of change but also give the opportunity to observe certain problems and opportunities from different angles, as well as give more information about the actual readiness of the organization for change. On the latter aspect, it is also fair to report that Bititci et al. (2006) suggest conducting an analysis of management style and organizational culture to understand the level of readiness in adopting PMS in order to increase the odds of successful implementation and to assess whether the company is actually capable of implementing it.

Concerning the hindering factors, both the first (*reasons for change poorly understood*) and the second (*stakeholders don't believe in the change*) are acknowledged by the PMS literature. Disagreement or misunderstanding with respect to the implications or usefulness of the PMS for the company, and what the goals of the change should be, are generally described as significant hindering elements (Kasurinen, 2002; Wouters & Wilderom, 2008). In many cases, it has already been mentioned that the failure of these projects is related to the unsuitability of the tool for the type of company, thus denoting a lack of understanding of what the actual business needs are (Sgrò et al., 2020; Hudson et al., 2001).

4.3.3.2 Change Readiness Assessment (Second Step)

Moving into the second step, the associated enabling and hindering factors are intrinsically linked to the concept of *change readiness*, a topic previously discussed in this chapter. While *change readiness* has been extensively explored in numerous articles and studies, the literature on PMS is relatively less vocal on this subject. Nevertheless, certain components of this multidimensional concept are indeed considered within PMS contexts. To begin with, Stouten et al. (2018) suggest that *organizational history* decisively influences both the likelihood of success of change initiatives and how they should be conducted. They state that if a company has successfully undertaken similar past changes, the possibility of success is higher, and managers, in their communication of change, can foster the acceptance of individuals by reminding them of what happened in the past. Conversely, if similar changes have not been successfully implemented in the past, the likelihood of success decreases. This is mostly because individuals may be less likely to believe in the new change project. As a result, managers need to make a greater effort to clearly differentiate the current change from past failures and highlight why it is more likely to succeed. In any case, the impact of *organizational history* is usually not considered in the literature on PMS. Rather, some studies highlight how a *change-adverse organizational culture*, sedimented over the years, can hinder the implementation of these systems (Bititci et al., 2004; Franco & Bourne, 2003; Madsen & Stenheim, 2014).

A further element considered is the *degree of stress* already experienced by employees and managers within an organization. Indeed, it has been shown that in the presence of a high level of *stress*, people are less receptive both to the need to introduce changes and to accept them (Linden et al., 2005; Meuris & Leana, 2015). These attitudes seem even more likely if these changes are associated with the perception that is necessary to work harder or expend effort in order to implement them.

Table 4.3 Enabling and hindering factors identified in each step of Stouten et al. (2018) framework

Nr.	Step	Success/enabling factors	Hindering factors
1	Organizational diagnosis	1. Presence of an assessment of the company's condition, problems to solve and opportunities to catch, constraints and enablers of change 2. Stakeholders believe that the reasons for change are legitimate and its direction rational (i.e., awareness of the need for change) 3. Information for the assessment is gathered through multiple sources	1. The reasons for change and the problems affecting the organization are poorly understood 2. Stakeholders don't believe in the change process 3. The assessment is not based on multiple information sources (e.g., one subject's perceptions, using only one information channel, etc.)
2	Change readiness assessment	1. Organizational history is characterized by previous similar successful change processes 2. Change recipients are not stressed 3. Leadership commitment is present 4. Leadership has the capability to manage the change and support individuals 5. There are perceived benefits associated with the change for the individuals who compose the organization 6. Individuals and groups believe that they have the knowledge and skills to implement the change (self-efficacy) 7. Individuals feel that they'll receive the needed support from the leadership and the colleagues 8. Individuals feel a discrepancy between present and desired end-state 9. There is an awareness regarding the existence of, the sources of, and solutions to the organization's problems 10. Individuals feel that the change is appropriate for the organization	1. There are previous similar unsuccessful changes or experiences of unfair change processes 2. The degree of stress that change recipients currently face is high 3. The change is perceived as detrimental to the interests of the stakeholders 4. Individuals feel they would not be able to manage or cope with the change 5. Individuals don't feel the support from the others 6. Leadership is not committed 7. Leadership does not provide support to individuals 8. Individuals don't understand the reasons for change 9. Individuals don't feel that the change is appropriate for the organization

(continued)

Table 4.3 (continued)

Nr.	Step	Success/enabling factors	Hindering factors
3	Evidence-based implementation	1. The change intervention is appropriate for the organization, taking into account the problems to be solved and the opportunities to be seized 2. The change intervention is implemented with the support of internal or external individuals who already have experience with that kind of change 3. The change intervention is supported by other studies that provide a method for implementing it 4. Individuals possess change-related skills 5. Rewards are offered to those who adopt the desired behaviors 6. There is intervention compliance, especially when the change success depends on fully implementing key aspects of a targeted change	1. The change intervention is not appropriate to address the company's problems and opportunities 2. The change intervention is managed and supported by individuals who don't have the right skills or knowledge 3. The actions and activities of the change interventions are not coherent with the change project
4	Leadership development	1. Leadership continuously supports the change during its implementation and does not lose commitment 2. Leadership has change-related skills 3. Leadership is shared by individuals who have complementary roles and competencies 4. Leadership has an idea of what may be the barriers to change and is prepared to address them 5. Employees trust the leadership	1. There is no leadership (laissez-faire leadership) 2. Leadership loses commitment 3. Leadership does not provide support to company members 4. Leadership is composed of only one individual or is shared by individuals who have the same competencies and/or roles 5. Leadership is not prepared to deal with the issues related to the change implementation
5	Change communication	1. A compelling vision/change message is developed and communicated 2. The change message reflects a goal that is broadly shared 3. The vision favors positive beliefs about the reasons for change 4. The change message is repeated multiple times and using different communication channels 5. The change message provides evidence about the need for change	1. The change message is under communicated 2. The vision does not reflect a broadly shared goal 3. The vision favors negative beliefs about the reasons for change 4. The change message is supported by little or no evidence

(continued)

Table 4.3 (continued)

Nr.	Step	Success/enabling factors	Hindering factors
6	Social networks exploitation	1. The change agent has relational ties with the change recipients and people who have an influence on the members of the organization or the team they belong to 2. The change agent is perceived as trustworthy	1. The change agent has no relationship with the most influential stakeholders 2. The change agent is not perceived as trustworthy, reliable, or capable
7	Implementation support	1. Set goals are also related to the development of new competencies and achievement of targets 2. There's a psychologically safe environment that allows learning, testing, and experimenting 3. The implementation process enables learning processes 4. Individuals are accountable for their actions 5. Employees participate and are involved in the change process 6. Employees feel to be treated respectfully and equally in the change process (organizational justice) 7. There is a high level of employee identification with the organization, and the change process is perceived as fair (organizational justice) and appropriate for the organization 8. There are transitional structures that allow experiments and local initiatives	1. People don't feel free to express their concerns and feelings because they fear being judged or blamed 2. Individuals feel that they are not being treated respectfully 3. People are not involved or feel that their opinion doesn't count 4. There is no room for learning or improvement 5. People are entrusted with conflicting or unclear goals 6. There is no accountability related to the change 7. There is a low level of employee identification with the organization, and the change does not produce benefits for the single individual
8	Experimentation	1. Individuals are allowed to conduct experiments and pilot tests related to the change 2. Change recipients are allowed to provide feedback and make local adjustments to broader change plans based on their own experience 3. The company achieves small wins	1. Individuals are not allowed to conduct experiments and pilot tests related to the change 2. Change recipients are not allowed to provide feedback or make local adjustments to broader change plans based on their own experience 3. The company does not achieve small wins

(continued)

Table 4.3 (continued)

Nr.	Step	Success/enabling factors	Hindering factors
9	Progress assessment	1. Periodic assessments are conducted to verify the implementation progress and that change is anticipated activities, experiences, and outcomes 2. The metrics used for these periodic assessments are considered reliable and are aimed at measuring information sharing, learning, commitment, competency, and efficacy over time as well as whether implementation of new practices has increased	1. Individuals don't know at what point is the implementation process and whether there's progress 2. Individuals don't know if their efforts are producing the desired outcome or, at least, positive results
10	Change institutionalization	1. The change is integrated into the larger systems of the organization, including its culture and management systems 2. Leadership remains committed to the change, even after its implementation 3. The new practices have become routine 4. Use of enabling structures to maintain the new practices	1. The change is not successfully integrated into everyday routines, systems, and practices and is not anchored to the organizational culture 2. The leadership loses interest in the new practices, systems, and tools

However, the aspect of *stress* is predominantly overlooked in the literature concerning the implementation of PMS. Most of the contributions in the literature concern increased stress on the part of employees and managers related to the use of PMS, with adverse effects on the performance of individuals (Franco-Santos & Otley, 2018; Franco-Santos et al., 2012). One issue that may be similar is the loss of management commitment to the project, as other, seemingly more stringent and perhaps "stressful" priorities may emerge. These situations can cause PMS implementation projects to slow down or fail.

Leadership commitment, as identified in the literature review on PMS implementation, is widely recognized as crucial (Bianchi & Rivenbark, 2013; Bourne et al., 2003b; Kasurinen, 2002; Taylor & Taylor, 2013). The capability of the *leadership* to manage the change and to possess *change-related skills* is partly consistent with what PMS literature claims. The presence of management that has received *training* or had *past experience* with the use of PMS is generally considered an enabling factor (Kasurinen, 2002; Panno, 2020; Van Camp & Braet, 2016). However, change management literature extends beyond skills directly related to the "content" of change, encompassing the skills related to the management of "individual transitions." In particular, this includes interpersonal and social skills that allow managers to offer emotional support and to share *change-related communications* more effectively (Stouten et al., 2018).

The *perception of benefits* associated with change is another enabling factor already considered in PMS literature (Bourne et al., 2002; Castellano & Leto, 2021), and a detailed discussion can be found in the related chapter. Closely linked to this is the *appropriateness* of the system, which is also extensively acknowledged as vital in PMS literature (Sgrò et al., 2020; Bourne et al., 2003a;). In fact, managers will only be able to perceive benefits associated with a certain PMS if they think it is indeed effectively applicable in their organization.

Perception of self-efficacy is another factor that seems to be fairly well considered (De Waal, 2003; Munir et al., 2013), although there has not been much exploration of what elements this self-efficacy depends on. Training is frequently cited as a factor that enhances the implementation of PMS by bolstering individuals' confidence in introducing and utilizing such tools. Change management studies, however, indicate that the *perception of self-efficacy* is multifaceted, influenced by past experiences and psychological conditions, such as an individual's locus of control or learned helplessness[7] (Hayes, 2022).

As reported in the PMS literature and as mentioned in the previous section, typically, one of the elements that originate the process is the need to increase the company's information and control capabilities (Bourne et al., 2003a). Thus, it can be said that for PMS, the enabling element of the perception of a *discrepancy* between a current situation and a desired future one, which is extensively described in the change management literature (Armenakis et al., 1993), primarily concerns dissatisfaction with knowledge and control needs (Bourne et al., 2003b).

Fairly ignored, instead, is the aspect of individual support that leadership can provide to those who will be affected by the change. Generally, the literature focuses mostly on factors such as *leadership support* with respect to the system (Cavalluzzo & Ittner, 2004; Huelsbeck et al., 2011) and *active sponsorship* (Argyris & Kaplan, 1994) as an element that influences its adoption by employees at lower levels of the organization. It is also recognized that a leader already trained in PMS use can act as a facilitator and foster change by sharing their knowledge with employees (Bourne et al., 2003b; Kasurinen, 2002). Yet, in contrast to the literature on change management (Armenakis et al., 1993), there is little emphasis on the emotional support provided by leaders, nor on the importance of giving employees the feeling that they are allowed to ask their supervisors for help when they feel the need.

[7] Locus of control theory posits that individuals differ in whether they attribute the outcomes of events to their own actions or to external forces. People who believe that their own behavior influences outcomes are called "internals," while those who attribute outcomes to external factors such as luck, fate, or external circumstances are called "externals." This theory reflects the extent to which individuals perceive their behavior as influencing life events. The concept of learned helplessness is closely related to locus of control. It is based on the assumption that individuals learn to expect their ability to control outcomes. According to this theory, the experience of repeated failure in similar situations can lead to feelings of discouragement and helplessness when faced with the same type of situation again.

4.3.3.3 Evidence-Based Implementation (Third Step)

The enabling factors traced in the third step of the change process of Stouten et al. (2018) are generally acknowledged within the PMS literature. To begin with, the *presence or introduction* of people in the company *who already have experience or knowledge* with respect to these tools is considered a significant enabling factor (Kasurinen, 2002; Panno, 2020). In addition, as explained in the previous chapter, there are many approaches aimed at providing a method for implementing PMS, and, therefore, their usefulness is rather perceived (e.g., Sousa & Aspinwall, 2010). According to the organizational change literature, the assignment of *rewards* associated with adopting change aims to increase the perceived benefits associated with its introduction for each individual. While PMS implementation research doesn't emphasize this aspect much, the accounting and management control literature covers it extensively. It acknowledges the value of linking rewards to management control systems, though the effectiveness varies in different contexts (Franco-Santos & Otley, 2018; Franco-Santos et al., 2012). Furthermore, *intervention compliance* turns out to be an issue that is considered crucial as well. As discussed in the previous chapter, problems can arise from incomplete system development, insufficient reliability, or inadequate and infrequent use (Huelsbeck et al., 2011; Islam et al., 2018).

4.3.3.4 Leadership Development (Fourth Step)

The fourth step has several elements in common with what has been elaborated in the literature on PMS and management accounting change since leaders are even one of the elements that make up the framework of Kasurinen (2002). The importance of *leadership commitment throughout the implementation process* is a widely discussed element (Bianchi & Rivenbark, 2013; Bourne, 2005; Bourne et al., 2002; De Waal, 2003; Taylor & Taylor, 2013). Although it's not a particularly explored aspect, *trust in leadership* has also been recognized as a success factor for implementation in a few studies (Tuan, 2012).

In relation to leadership characteristics and styles, not much has been said about which ones should make the implementation process more manageable. One exception comes from Jansen (2011), who reported how the adoption of both a *transactional* and *transformational*[8] leadership styles has greatly facilitated individuals' acceptance of change in management control systems and a significant reduction in resistance. Although not covered in Stouten et al.'s (2018) framework, the topic of *transformational* leadership and *transactional* leadership is widely addressed by

[8] Transactional leadership, as the name suggests, is about rewarding desired behaviors by providing rewards or incentives. Such a "transaction" could be monetary or simply consists of recognition of what has been done. Transformational leadership, on the other hand, is based on motivating individuals through the adoption of specific actions, attitudes, and behaviors by the leader to inspire individuals to do better.

change management studies (Eisenbach et al., 1999). In addition, the involvement of managers from different levels of the organization is also contemplated by PMS literature because it is assumed that they can provide complementary valuable knowledge for the development of the system as well as being able to strengthen PMS sponsorship in their individual areas of authority (Argyris & Kaplan, 1994; Bourne et al., 2003b).

4.3.3.5 Change Communication (Fifth Step)

As mentioned in the previous section, the importance of leadership in PMS implementation processes is already recognized. Also acknowledged is its role in communicating and developing a vision of the future (Ansari & Bell, 2009; Kasurinen, 2002) in order to align people's behavior toward the acceptance and use of the new system. However, research in this area has not focused much on identifying the most effective communication approaches for PMS implementation, or whether, for example, using multiple channels and repeating the change message actually increases the likelihood of success and reduces misunderstandings. The change management literature offers numerous strategies for improving the effectiveness of communication. For example, researchers in this field suggest that face-to-face communication is often the most effective channel, as it facilitates understanding and reduces misunderstandings (Hiatt, 2006). However, it is also the most time-consuming, necessitating the development of communication strategies that consider these trade-offs (Hayes, 2022).

One study in the field of management accounting change that offers some communication strategies is provided by Argyris and Kaplan (1994). These authors present some suggestions on the content of communications and stress the importance of providing evidence, perhaps gathered through other experiences or scientific articles, which shows the usefulness of the new system.

4.3.3.6 Social Networks Exploitation (Sixth Step)

Since the role of the *change agent* is essentially ignored in the literature on PMS, it is natural that little consideration is given in this field of research to the characteristics or relational ties these individuals should have to foster implementation processes. Therefore, further comparisons with the PMS literature will not be pursued.

4.3.3.7 Implementation Support (Seventh Step)

Regarding the topic of *goal setting* and *accountability*, there exists a substantial body of literature discussing the use of PMS for assigning targets and holding individuals accountable for their achievement (Ferreira & Otley, 2009; Franco-Santos et al., 2012). Moreover, the PMS literature offers at least some insights into creating a *psychologically safe environment* for *testing* new methodologies, even though this is not an explicitly addressed topic. In fact, the nature of the implementation process is often characterized as experimental and trial and error due to the inherent challenges in identifying useful and adequate indicators right away (Andon et al., 2007; Sharma et al., 2016; Wouters & Wilderom, 2008), which implies testing. Some studies also suggest that a blame culture, often viewed as antithetical to creating a *psychologically safe environment*, can inhibit the full realization of PMS's potential and hinder associated learning processes (Gao, 2015; Goh, 2012). More in general, there are also some reported cases where this type of culture fostered resistance to change and blocked the implementation process (Nudurupati et al., 2007).

With respect to *organizational justice*, several studies in the PMS and management accounting fields have considered its effects, particularly focusing on how PMS usage and design affect its perceptions by the employees (e.g., Burney et al., 2009; Parker & Kohlmeyer III, 2005; Rowland & Hall, 2012). However, this concept is not usually addressed when focusing specifically on the implementation process of PMS. Moreover, also the components of *organizational justice*, i.e., *procedural*, *informational*, *distributive*, and *interpersonal justice*, are generally not explicitly explored in the context of PMS.

The employee's level of *identification with the organization*, a factor highlighted for its significance in fostering change acceptance (Stouten et al., 2018), is another aspect largely overlooked in PMS literature. When employees identify strongly with their organization, the change management literature suggests that they are more likely to accept to changes that benefit the organization, even if they require effort on their part or do not have a direct perceived individual benefit (Hayes, 2022).

Participation and *involvement* are generally recognized as critical in the literature related to PMS, both for the contributions managers from different areas can provide during the design phase to improve the system and for their role in fostering acceptance of change. Both PMS and change management literature agree that a participatory approach in project implementation generates a sense of ownership, which facilitates commitment (De Waal, 2003; Rowland & Hall, 2012).

4.3.3.8 Experimentation (Eighth Step)

The eighth step is devoted to experimenting with new practices and it is at least partially supported in the PMS literature. As previously discussed, *experimentation* is often considered an integral aspect of the design and refinement of PMS (Wouters & Wilderom, 2008). Thus, it can be hypothesized that allowing management and system users to *experiment* freely with new indicators may be a factor that fosters change, enables system improvement, and generates learning processes.

Instead, while the concept of *small* or *quick wins* is frequently emphasized in the change management literature, it is not extensively addressed within the literature on PMS. Although the implementation of PMS is often a gradual process, with new indicators and measures being incrementally introduced across various organizational areas (Bourne et al., 2000), there is a lack of empirical research explicitly examining the impact of achieving positive results during the implementation phase on the overall success of these initiatives. In contrast, the change management literature underscores the significance of achieving wins in sustaining momentum, persuading skeptics, and providing tangible evidence of the benefits of the change (Hayes, 2022; Stouten et al., 2018; Kotter, 1996, 2012).

4.3.3.9 Progress Assessment (Ninth Step)

The critical factors that emerge from the ninth step emphasize the importance of *tracking the progress* achieved to understand if corrective actions must be taken and whether the change is yielding the desired results. The primary goal is to verify that change is taking place, with individuals engaging in the desired behaviors and achieving appropriate levels of performance (Kanter et al., 1992). This aligns with the prescriptive approaches in PMS literature, which advocate for regular reviews of the implementation process and system effectiveness, particularly to refine the design and ensure the introduction of a PMS that aligns with business needs (e.g., Sousa & Aspinwall, 2010). However, these evaluations are predominantly focused on the adequacy of the system design rather than on assessing how the people within the organization are utilizing the system.

Research on PMS implementation typically deems the process successful when the system is regularly and extensively used within the company, thereby supporting decision-making and control processes (Franco-Santos et al., 2012). It can, therefore, be hypothesized that verifying the actual usage of the system could be beneficial. If it is found that the system is underutilized, appropriate corrective measures could be implemented to promote and encourage its adoption.

4.3.3.10 Change Institutionalization (Tenth Step)

The factors that favor the initiative's success identifiable in this step are overall confirmed by what has been reported in both the PMS and management accounting change literature. As mentioned in the previous chapter, it was noted that in order to introduce a PMS successfully, it is often essential for the management to regularly use it and develop a new mindset, new knowledge, and a new type of *organizational culture* (Bititci et al., 2006). *Organizational culture* is considered in the literature related to management accounting change based on institutionalist theories (Busco et al., 2005) since *organizational culture* itself has often been conceptualized as an institutionalized phenomenon (Schein, 2010). According to management accounting change literature, change is only realized when new activities and practices related to the control system become routine in the company, meaning they are integrated into daily operations (Burns & Scapens, 2000). When these new practices evolve into routines, they become integrated into the *organizational culture*.

The literature on PMS is not explicit in relation to *enabling structures* that can promote the durability of change. However, there are some recognized practices that reinforce change and encourage the adoption of the system, such as *assigning targets* to managers related to factors that they can effectively influence (Castellano, 2012).

4.3.3.11 The Less Explored Critical Success Factors

After reviewing the factors outlined in the model and comparing them to the existing literature on PMS implementation, it is apparent that the following factors have not been particularly explored:

- Production of a *diagnosis* on the basis of which to identify an issue to be solved or on an opportunity to be caught that requires the implementation of the tool
- Level of *change readiness*
- Achievement of *small* or *quick wins* during the implementation process
- *Perceived fairness* of the change process
- *Enablement* of *testing* and *experimentation* activities also with the support of transitional structures and/or the use of a prototype of the tool
- level of employees' *identification with the organization*

Starting with the first factor, the literature on PMS suggests it is useful to assess the company's current situation, information and control needs, and readiness in terms of organizational culture and knowledge for the system's introduction. Thus, this diagnosis is not aimed at developing *awareness of the need for change* by identifying problems and opportunities but assumes that there is already a recognized need to implement a PMS. In other words, this *diagnosis* is only intended to assist in the design and implementation of the system, but not to develop the need to specifically implement a PMS.

Instead, the issue of *change readiness* is completely ignored, and only part of its components is considered important to the success of PMS implementation initiatives.

The same holds true for the value of achieving *small* or *quick wins* throughout the implementation process. Although not widely recognized by PMS literature, their importance is supported by both prescriptive models and research related to organizational change.

The issue of *fairness* or *organizational justice*, on the other hand, turns out to be considered targets are assigned or management's use of the system (e.g., Burney et al., 2009; Rowland & Hall, 2012).

In relation to *testing* and *experimentation* of the system, it has already been mentioned that it is considered essential to refine and improve the way in which the PMS is designed, finding the most suitable indicator dashboards to be used (e.g., Wouters & Wilderom, 2008). Less has been said about the usefulness of creating transitional structures and a psychologically safe environment, in which to try out and become familiar with the system, for generating commitment, acceptance, mitigating resistance, and reducing people's sense of inability to use it. However, a similar issue considered in the literature might be the negative effect that a blame culture can have on the implementation and use of such aspects (Gao, 2015; Goh, 2012). The presence of such an organizational culture can make individuals in the company feel scrutinized and judged, and this could reasonably prevent the creation of a psychologically safe environment.

Finally, there appears to be a notable absence of discussion regarding the impact that a high level of *organizational identification* (Stouten et al., 2018) by management and employees might have on the acceptance of a PMS. This could represent a significant success factor, particularly in instances where the PMS is perceived to benefit the organization more than individual employees. As previously outlined, one specific form of resistance associated with PMS usage is the opposition to increased measurement (Nudurupati et al., 2011), given that not all individuals are inclined to subject their performance to more detailed scrutiny. This raises the question of whether strong identification with the organization could motivate individuals to accept personal disadvantages, such as having their performance measured more accurately, if there are important perceived benefits to the organization of which they are a part.

References

Adams, J., Hayes, J., & Hopson, B. (1976). *Transition: Understanding and managing personal change*. Allanheld, Osmun & Co.

Andon, P., Baxter, J., & Chua, W. F. (2007). Accounting change as relational drifting: A field study of experiments with performance measurement. *Management Accounting Research, 18*, 273–308.

Ansari, S., & Bell, J. (2009). Five easy pieces: A case study of cost management as organizational change. *Journal of Accounting and Organizational Change, 5*(2), 139–167.

Appelbaum, S. H., Habashy, S., & Malo, J. (2012). Back to the future: Revisiting Kotter's 1996 change model. *Journal of Management Development, 31*, 764–782.

Argyris, C., & Kaplan, R. S. (1994). Implementing new knowledge: The case of activity-based costing. *Accounting Horizons, 8*(3), 83–105.

Armenakis, A. A., & Bedeian, A. G. (1999). Organizational change: A review of theory and research in the 1990s. *Journal of Management, 25*(3), 293–315.

Armenakis, A. A., & Harris, S. G. (2002). Crafting a change message to create transformational readiness. *Journal of Organizational Change Management, 15*, 169–183.

Armenakis, A., & Harris, S. G. (2009). Reflections: Our journey in organizational change research and practice. *Journal of Change Management, 9*, 127–142.

Armenakis, A. A., Harris, S. G., & Mossholder, K. W. (1993). Creating readiness for organizational change. *Human Relations, 46*, 681–703.

Bartunek, J. M., Rousseau, D. M., Rudolph, J. W., & DePalma, J. A. (2006). On the receiving end: Sensemaking, emotion, and assessments of an organizational change initiated by others. *Journal of Applied Behavioral Science, 42*, 182–206.

Beckhard, R. (1975). Strategies for large system change. *Sloan Management Review, 16*(2), 43–55.

Beckhard, R., & Harris, R. T. (1987). *Organizational transitions: Managing complex change* (2nd ed.). Addison Wesley OD Series.

Beer, M., Eisenstat, R. A., & Spector, B. (1990). Why change programs don't produce change. *Harvard Business Review, 68*(6), 158–166.

Beer, M., & Nohria, N. (2000). Cracking the code of change. *Harvard Business Review, 78*, 133–141.

Bertini, U. (1990). *Il Sistema d'Azienda*. Giappichelli.

Bianchi, C., & Rivenbark, W. C. (2013). Alla ricerca dei fattori rilevanti nell'adozione dei sistemi di gestione della performance nelle amministrazioni pubbliche territoriali. L'analisi di due casi di studio. *Azienda Pubblica, 1*, 35–59.

Bititci, U. S., Mendibil, K., Nudurupati, S., Turner, T., & Garengo, P. (2004). The interplay between performance measurement, organizational culture and management styles. *Measuring Business Excellence, 8*(3), 28–41.

Bititci, U. S., Mendibil, K., Nudurupati, S., Turner, T., & Garengo, P. (2006). Dynamics of performance measurement and organizational culture. *International Journal of Operations and Production Management, 26*, 1325–1350.

Bordia, P., Restubog, S. L. D., Jimmieson, N. L., & Irmer, B. E. (2011). Haunted by the past: Effects of poor change management history on employee attitudes and turnover. *Group & Organization Management, 36*, 191–222.

Bourne, M. (2005). Researching performance measurement system implementation: The dynamics of success and failure. *Production Planning & Control, 16*(2), 101–113.

Bourne, M., Mills, J., Wilcox, M., Neely, A., & Platts, K. (2000). Designing, implementing and updating performance measurement systems. *International Journal of Operations and Production Management, 20*(7), 754–771.

Bourne, M., Neely, A., Mills, J., & Platts, K. (2003a). Implementing performance measurement systems: A literature review. *International Journal of Business Performance Management, 5*(1), 1–24.

Bourne, M., Neely, A., Mills, J., & Platts, K. (2003b). Why some performance measurement initiatives fail: Lessons from the change management literature. *International Journal of Business Performance Management, 5*(2–3), 245–269.

Bourne, M., Neely, A., Platts, K., & Mills, J. (2002). The success and failure of performance measurement initiatives—Perceptions of participating managers. *International Journal of Operations & Production Management, 22*(11), 1288–1310.

Bridges, W. (1986). Managing organizational transitions. *Organizational Dynamics, 15*, 24–33.

Bridges, W. (1991). *Transitions: Making sense of life's changes*. Addison-Wesley.

Buchanan, D., Fitzgerald, L., Ketley, D., Gollop, R., Jones, J. L., Lamont, S. S., & Whitby, E. (2005). No going back: A review of the literature on sustaining organizational change. *International Journal of Management Reviews, 7*(3), 189–205.

Bullock, R. J., & Batten, D. (1985). It's just a phase we're going through: A review and synthesis of OD phase analysis. *Group & Organization Studies, 10*(4), 383–412.

Burke, W. W. (2023). *Organization change: Theory and practice* (6th ed.). Columbia University, Sage.

Burke, W., & Litwin, G. (1992). A causal model of organizational performance and change. *Journal of Management, 18*, 523–545.

Burnes, B. (2004). Kurt Lewin and the planned approach to change: A re-appraisal. *Journal of Management Studies, 41*(6), 977–1002.

Burnes, B., & Bargal, D. (2017). Kurt Lewin: 70 years on. *Journal of Change Management, 17*(2), 91–100.

Burney, L. L., Henley, C. A., & Widener, S. K. (2009). A path model examining the relations among strategic performance measurement system characteristics, organizational justice, and extra- and in-role performance. *Accounting, Organizations and Society, 34*(3–4), 305–321.

Burns, J., & Scapens, R. W. (2000). Conceptualizing management accounting change: An institutional framework. *Management Accounting Research, 11*, 3–25.

Busco, C., Riccaboni, A., & Scapens, R. W. (2005). Accounting, learning and cultural. *Accounting, the Social and the Political: Classics, Contemporary and Beyond*, 285.

Cady, S. H., Jacobs, J., Koller, R., & Spalding, J. (2014). The change formula: Myth, legend, or lore. *OD Practitioner, 46*(3), 32–39.

Cameron, E., & Green, M. (2019). *Making sense of change management: A complete guide to the models, tools, and techniques of organizational change* (6th ed.). Kogan.

Castellano, N. G. (2012). *La misurazione delle performance per le piccole imprese Strumenti di misurazione e processi di controllo* (pp. 1–127). G. Giappichelli Editore.

Castellano, N., & Leto, L. (2021). Implementazione di Sistemi di Misurazione delle Performance nelle PMI: elementi di analisi nella prospettiva del cambiamento organizzativo. *Management Control, 1*, 129–150.

Cavalluzzo, K. S., & Ittner, C. D. (2004). Implementing performance measurement innovations: Evidence from government. *Accounting, Organizations and Society, 29*(3–4), 243–267.

Choi, M. (2011). Employees' attitudes toward organizational change: A literature review. *Human Resource Management, 50*(4), 479–500.

Conner, D. R., & Patterson, R. W. (1982). Building commitment to organizational change. *Training & Development Journal, 36*(4), 18–30.

Cummings, S., Bridgman, T., & Brown, K. G. (2016). Unfreezing change as three steps: Rethinking Kurt Lewin's legacy for change management. *Human Relations, 69*, 33–60.

Dannemiller, K. D., & Jacobs, R. W. (1992). Changing the way organizations change: A revolution of common sense. *Journal of Applied Behavioral Science, 28*(4), 480–498.

Dawson, P. (2019). *Reshaping change: A processual perspective* (2nd ed.). Routledge.

De Waal, A. (2003). Behavioral factors important for the successful implementation and use of performance management systems. *Management Decision, 41*(8), 688–697.

De Waal, A. A., & Counet, H. (2009). Lessons learned from performance management systems implementations. *International Journal of Productivity and Performance Management, 58*(4), 367–390.

Eisenbach, R., Watson, K., & Pillai, R. (1999). Transformational leadership in the context of organizational change. *Journal of Organizational Change Management, 12*(2), 80–89.

Felix, E. (2000). Creating radical change: Producer choice at the BBC. *Journal of Change Management, 1*(1), 5–21. https://doi.org/10.1080/714042453

Ferreira, A., & Otley, D. (2009). The design and use of performance management systems: An extended framework for analysis. *Management Accounting Research, 20*(4), 263–282.

Franco, M., & Bourne, M. (2003). Factors that play a role in managing through measures. *Management Decision, 41*, 698–710.

Franco-Santos, M., & Otley, D. (2018). Reviewing and theorizing the unintended consequences of performance management systems. *International Journal of Management Reviews, 20*(3), 696–730.

Franco-Santos, M., Lucianetti, L., & Bourne, M. (2012). Contemporary performance measurement systems: A review of their consequences and a framework for research. *Management Accounting Research, 23*(2), 79–119.

Gao, J. (2015). Performance measurement and management in the public sector: Some lessons from research evidence. *Public Administration and Development, 35*(2), 86–96.

Goh, S. C. (2012). Making performance measurement systems more effective in public sector organizations. *Measuring Business Excellence, 16*(1), 31–42.

Greiner, L. E. (1998). Evolution and revolution as organizations grow. *Harvard Business Review, 76*(3), 55–64.

Hayes, J. (2022). *The theory and practice of change management* (6th ed.). Palgrave Macmillan.

Hiatt, J. M. (2006). *ADKAR: A model for change in business, government and our community: How to implement successful change in our personal lives and professional careers*. Prosci Research.

Holt, D. T., Armenakis, A. A., Feild, H. S., & Harris, S. G. (2007). Readiness for organizational change: The systematic development of a scale. *The Journal of Applied Behavioral Science, 43*(2), 232–255.

Hudson, M., Lean, J., & Smart, P. A. (2001). Improving control through effective performance measurement in SMEs. *Production Planning & Control, 12*(8), 804–813.

Huelsbeck, D. P., Merchant, K. A., & Sandino, T. (2011). On testing business models. *The Accounting Review, 86*(5), 1631–1654.

Hughes, M. (2016). Leading changes: Why transformation explanations fail. *Leadership, 12*(4), 449–469.

Hunsucker, J. L., & Loos, D. (1989). Transition management: An analysis of strategic considerations for effective implementation. *Engineering Management International, 5*, 167–178.

Islam, S., Adler, R., & Northcott, D. (2018). Managerial attitudes towards the incompleteness of performance measurement systems. *Qualitative Research in Accounting and Management, 15*(1), 84–103.

Jansen, E. P. (2011). The effect of leadership style on the information receivers' reaction to management accounting change. *Management Accounting Research, 22*(2), 105–124.

Jones, R. A., Jimmieson, N. L., & Griffiths, A. (2005). The impact of organizational culture and reshaping capabilities on change implementation success: The mediating role of readiness for change. *Journal of Management Studies, 42*(2), 361–386.

Judson, A. (1991). *Changing behavior in organizations: Minimizing resistance to change*. Basil Blackwell.

Kanter, R. M., Stein, B. A., & Jick, T. D. (1992). *Challenge of organizational change: How companies experience it and leaders guide it*. The Free Press, MacMillan Inc.

Kasurinen, T. (2002). Exploring management accounting change: The case of a balanced scorecard implementation. *Management Accounting Research, 13*, 323–343.

Kolb, D. A., & Frohman, A. L. (1970). *Organizational development through planned change: A development model*. Massachusetts Institute of Technology.

Kotter, J. P. (1995). Why transformation efforts fail. *Harvard Business Review, 73*(2), 59–67.

Kotter, J. (1996). *Leading Change*. Harvard Business Review Press.

Kotter, J. P. (2012). Accelerate. *Harvard Business Review, 90*(11), 45–58.

Kübler-Ross, E. (1969). *On death and dying*. Scribner.

Lewin, K. (1946). Action research and minority problems. *Journal of Social Issues, 2*, 34–46.

Lewin, K. (1947). Frontiers in group dynamics. *Human Relations, 1*, 5–41.

Lewin, K. (1951). *Field theory in social science*. Harper.

Linden, D. V. D., Keijsers, G. P., Eling, P., & Schaijk, R. V. (2005). Work stress and attentional difficulties: An initial study on burnout and cognitive failures. *Work & Stress, 19*, 23–36.

Lippitt, R., Watson, J., & Westley, B. (1958). *The dynamics of planned change*. Harcourt, Brace and World.

Luecke, R. (2003). *Managing change and transition* (Vol. 3). Harvard Business Press.

Lueg, R., & Vu, L. (2015). Success factors in balanced scorecard implementations: A literature review. *Management Revue, 26*(4), 306–327.

Madsen, D. Ø., & Stenheim, T. (2014). Perceived problems associated with the implementation of the balanced scorecard: Evidence from Scandinavia. *Problems and Perspectives in Management, 12*(1), 121–131.

Melnyk, S., Bitici, U., Platts, K., Tobias, J., & Anderson, B. (2014). Is performance measurement and management fit for the future? *Management Accounting Research, 25*(2), 173–186.

Meuris, J., & Leana, C. R. (2015). The high cost of low wages: Economic scarcity effects in organizations. *Research in Organizational Behavior, 35*, 143–158.

Miller, D., & Friesen, P. H. (1984). A longitudinal study of the corporate life cycle. *Management Science, 30*, 1161–1183.

Munir, R., Baird, K., & Perera, S. (2013). Performance measurement system change in an emerging economy bank. *Accounting, Auditing and Accountability Journal, 26*(2), 196–233.

Nadler, D., & Tushman, M. (1997). *Competing by design: The power of organizational architecture*. Oxford University Press.

Nudurupati, S., Arshad, T., & Turner, T. (2007). Performance measurement in the construction industry: An action case investigating manufacturing methodologies. *Computers in Industry, 58*, 667–676.

Nudurupati, S. S., Bititci, U. S., Kumar, V., & Chan, F. T. S. (2011). State of the art literature review on performance measurement. *Computers and Industrial Engineering, 60*(2), 279–290.
Nutt, P. C. (1999). Surprising but true: Half the decisions in organizations fail. *Academy of Management Executive, 13*, 75–90.
Panno, A. (2020). Performance measurement and management in small companies of the service sector; evidence from a sample of Italian hotels. *Measuring Business Excellence, 24*(2), 133–160.
Pardo Del Val, M., & Martínez Fuentes, C. (2003). Resistance to change: A literature review and empirical study. *Management Decision, 41*(2), 148–155.
Parker, R. J., & Kohlmeyer, J. M., III. (2005). Organizational justice and turnover in public accounting firms: A research note. *Accounting, Organizations and Society, 30*, 357–369.
Parker, C., & Lewis, R. (1981). Beyond the Peter principle—Managing successful transitions. *Journal of European Industrial Training, 5*(6), 17–21.
Porter, M. E. (1980). *Competitive strategies*. The Free Press.
Rafferty, A. E., Jimmieson, N. L., & Armenakis, A. A. (2013). Change readiness: A multilevel review. *Journal of Management, 39*(1), 110–135.
Rosenbaum, D., More, E., & Steane, P. (2018). Planned organisational change management: Forward to the past? An exploratory literature review. *Journal of Organizational Change Management, 31*(2), 286–303.
Rowland, C. A., & Hall, R. D. (2012). Organizational justice and performance: Is appraisal fair? *EuroMed Journal of Business, 7*(3), 280–293.
Schein, E. H. (1996). Kurt Lewin's change theory in the field and in the classroom: Notes toward a model of managed learning. *Systems Practice, 9*(1), 27–47.
Schein, E. H. (2010). *Organizational culture and leadership* (4th ed.). Jossey-Bass.
Senge, P. M. (1990). *The fifth discipline: The art and practice of the learning organization*. Doubleday.
Sgrò, F., Palazzi, F., Ciambotti, M., & Gelsomini, L. (2020). Factors promoting and hindering the adoption of management accounting tools. Evidence from Italian manufacturing SMEs. *Management Control, 1 suppl.*, 19–38.
Sharma, N. P., Sharma, T., & Agarwal, M. N. (2016). Measuring employee perception of performance management system effectiveness: Conceptualization and scale development. *Employee Relations, 38*(2), 224–247.
Sousa, S., & Aspinwall, E. (2010). Development of a performance measurement framework for SMEs. *Total Quality Management and Business Excellence, 21*(5), 475–501.
Stouten, J., Rousseau, D. M., & De Cremer, D. (2018). Successful organizational change: Integrating the management practice and scholarly literatures. *Academy of Management Annals, 12*(2), 752–788.
Taylor, A., & Taylor, M. (2013). Antecedents of effective performance measurement system implementation: An empirical study of UK manufacturing firms. *International Journal of Production Research, 51*(18), 1–14.
Tuan, L. T. (2012). From unbalanced to balanced: Performance measures in a Vietnamese hospital. *Leadership in Health Services, 25*(4), 288–305.
Van Buren, M. E., & Safferstone, T. (2009). The quick wins paradox. *Harvard Business Review, 116*, 54–61.
Van Camp, J., & Braet, J. (2016). Taxonomizing performance measurement systems' failures. *International Journal of Productivity and Performance Management, 65*(5), 672–693.
Van de Ven, A. H., & Poole, M. S. (1995). Explaining development and change in organizations. *Academy of Management Review, 20*, 510–540.
Waterman, R., Peters, T. J., & Phillips, J. R. (1980). Structure is not organization. *Business Horizons, 23*(3), 14–26.
Weick, K., & Quinn, R. (1999). Organizational change and development. *Annual Review of Psychology, 50*, 361–386.

Weiner, B. J. (2009). A theory of organizational readiness for change. *Implementation Science, 4*(1), 67. 1–9.
Weisbord, M. R. (1976). Organizational diagnosis: Six places to look for trouble with or without a theory. *Group Organization Management, 1*, 430–447.
Whelan-Berry, K. S., & Somerville, K. A. (2010). Linking change drivers and the organizational change process: A review and synthesis. *Journal of Change Management, 10*(2), 175–193.
Wouters, M., & Wilderom, C. (2008). Developing performance-measurement systems as enabling formalization: A longitudinal field study of a logistics department. *Accounting, Organizations and Society, 33*(4–5), 488–516.

Chapter 5
Implementing Performance Measurement Systems: A Management Accounting Change Case Study Through the Lens of Change Management

Drawing on the framework of Stouten et al. (2018), this chapter examines the implementation of a performance management system (PMS) in a medium-sized Italian company operating in the physics research equipment sector. Using a retrospective case study approach based on semi-structured interviews and document analysis, the chapter explores the challenges and dynamics of introducing a PMS.

The chapter highlights key success factors such as leadership commitment, transparent communication, and learning and the usefulness of employing change management theories to better understand management accounting change processes. In particular, Stouten et al.'s (2018) framework supported the identification of key psychological and organizational factors that influence the implementation process. However, the study also found that relying solely on Stouten et al. (2018) was not adequate to capture all the aspects of PMS implementation, which led to the inclusion of Bourne et al.'s (2000) model to better address the technical challenges faced during the design, implementation, and use phases of the system.

The findings suggest that successful management accounting change requires careful management and balancing of both technical and human-centered aspects.

5.1 Methodology of the Case Study

5.1.1 Research Design

This research employs a qualitative methodology, relying on data gathered through semi-structured interviews to develop a single retrospective case study. Consistent with prior studies in the field of management accounting change and PMS implementation, a direct analysis of a company that has recently implemented a PMS is considered advantageous. Since the phenomenon of organizational change is

L. Leto, *Integrating Change Management and Management Accounting Change*, SIDREA Series in Accounting and Business Administration,
https://doi.org/10.1007/978-3-031-84387-7_5

non-static, one of the most effective analytical approaches for examining the dynamic process of change is probably the longitudinal case study (Macchia, 2000). This is because it allows to examine the whole process of organizational change before, during, and after its realization. For this case study, however, the data collection through interviews occurred post-implementation of the PMS. Although a longitudinal case study could provide a more comprehensive observation of the phenomenon, the choice of a retrospective case study, where the implementation of a PMS had already taken place, allowed for more efficient and quicker collection of interviews. In any case, the case study methodology remains generally ideal for studying a phenomenon in its entirety (Chiucchi, 2012; Yin, 2003). This is supported by the presence of many retrospective studies (Berg & Madsen, 2020) and single case studies (Cullen et al., 2013; Kasurinen, 2002) in the management accounting research, suggesting that its usefulness is well-recognized also in this field.

The subject of the study, CAEN, is a medium-sized Italian company that has experienced significant and steady growth over the last two decades. This growth, together with increasing competitiveness, led the company to implement, adopt and regularly use a management control system that includes both financial and qualitative and nonfinancial variables. The case is also interesting because of the peculiarity of the sector in which the company operates: the company specializes in the production of equipment for carrying out experiments to support scientific research in the field of physics, and its customers are therefore researchers and research institutes. To the author's knowledge, there are very few case studies of companies operating in the same industry as CAEN. Moreover, since it is more generally a company in which creativity[1] is an essential component for its success, it is to be expected that there may be specific difficulties in relation to system design and identification of the most suitable performance indicators (Giovannoni & Maraghini, 2013).

Semi-structured interviews were chosen as the primary data collection method, as they are considered effective to study the process of organizational change, especially given the human-centric nature of the issues examined. This is because they make it possible to gather perceptions, concerns, opinions, and thoughts related to the phenomenon under analysis. This was complemented by the direct observation of several examples of the system's dashboards to better understand their level of detail and application within the company.

5.1.2 Data Collection

The main source for the development of this retrospective case study consists of interviews conducted with the management of the organization. These interviews were complemented by an analysis of documents available on the company's

[1]The company bases much of its success on the creativity of developers in the R&D area. The company competes on the basis of its ability to develop new tools that meet its customers' needs better than others.

website and observations of some dashboards of indicators used at CAEN. Finally, some insights were gained from an informal and fortuitous meeting with one of the company's now-retired founders. The interviews followed a semi-structured format, guided by predetermined guidelines to ensure all major issues relevant to the research were covered. Great freedom was given to each respondent to answer each question, enabling the exploration of relevant insights not initially anticipated in the interview guidelines.[2] As a result, each interview had a different course, shaped by the emergent themes and key points highlighted by the interviewees, which allowed for a broader view of the phenomenon under analysis. Prior to conducting these interviews, a literature review on PMS and management accounting change was undertaken to identify the main topics for discussion. In regard to the change management literature, there was prior familiarity with the main theories and models, as well as the framework proposed by Stouten et al. (2018).[3] This knowledge about the change management theories aided in the formulation of the interview guidelines.[4] In any case, the decision to employ Stouten et al. (2018) framework for supporting the analysis of the phenomenon was made after having already conducted half of the interviews.

The interviews lasted an average of 1 h and were supplemented by a focus group lasting about 2 h. Three of these interviews and the focus group were conducted in person at the company, while the remaining interviews were organized online via Microsoft Teams and Google Meet. Interviewees included the (I) President/General Director, (II) Chief Supply Chain Officer (CSCO), (III) Sales Manager, (IV) Chief Financial Officer (CFO), and (V) Chief Technology Officer (CTO).

All interviews were conducted and subsequently recorded and transcribed by the author of this study. The focus group additionally included the involvement of another researcher, who provided support in the management of the discussions, topics, and interactions. Analysis of the interview transcripts involved a coding process, enabling the application of Stouten et al.'s (2018) framework in the case analysis. However, it was determined that solely relying on Stouten et al.'s framework did not sufficiently capture the complexities of the PMS implementation process. As a result, Bourne et al. (2000) framework focused specifically on the design, implementation, and use of PMS, was also employed to favor a better understanding of the phenomenon.[5]

[2] For example, the role the ISO 9001 adoption project played in the company's growth and development of management control systems was an element not considered until the administration of the interviews.

[3] Stouten et al. (2018) framework was chosen both because it is recent and because it is based exclusively on scientific evidence, unlike other distinguished models. In any case, the model presents remarkable similarities with other less recent and more emblazoned ones such as that of Kotter (1996) or that of Kanter et al. (1992). Thus, the questions were still aimed at investigating the importance of organizational change issues for the implementation of the PMS.

[4] An example of these can be found in the appendix at the end of the manuscript.

[5] In the following section dedicated to data analysis, it will be explained in greater detail why it has proved necessary to resort to further theoretical frameworks.

5.1.3 Data Analysis

In order to emphasize the dynamic nature of the implementation process, the results of this study were reported to reflect the various stages of PMS implementation within the studied organization. The model by Stouten et al. (2018), although designed to be broadly applicable to diverse types of organizational changes, from the introduction of new technologies to structural and cultural changes, was found insufficient for providing a complete view of the phenomenon and key events that characterize the PMS implementation process. This situation arose because the exclusive application of Stouten et al.'s (2018) framework led to the omission of more technical aspects of the implementation process. In other words, it did not allow to consider aspects related to the design and use of the specific tool in the business environment. Furthermore, the element of "timing" within this framework predominantly addressed the group and individual transitions within the company rather than including the technical timelines and milestones of the implementation. To give greater clarity and completeness in the exposition and analysis of the results, it was, therefore, decided to use, along with the framework of Stouten et al. (2018), the framework of Bourne et al. (2000).[6] However, it became necessary in the view of the author to even expand and refine Bourne et al.'s (2000) framework by incorporating aspects from Stouten et al. (2018).

It is noted that the stages defined in Bourne et al. (2000) framework are design, implementation, and use. According to the authors, these three phases will occur again when the company decides to upgrade the system. Despite acknowledging the usefulness of the model, the author realized that these phases still did not fully represent the process of PMS adoption. In fact, the organizational change literature and various change management models suggest that the change process begins before the development or design of the new system, technology, or tool (Hayes, 2022). Stouten et al.'s (2018) framework initiates the change process with a phase devoted to the assessment of the situation the company finds itself in and the development of a need to change. By taking inspiration from Stouten et al. (2018), it is possible to affirm that the implementation process starts prior to the actual design phase, as management must gain the awareness of the need to introduce the new system before deciding to design, implement, and use it.

The analysis of the case study seemed to confirm that this first stage is actually propaedeutic in order to start the process reported in the Bourne et al. (2000) framework. It is, therefore, suggested that the addition of a fourth phase, necessary to initiate the design phase, is more representative of these processes and helps us better understand the dynamics that lead to PMS implementation. Therefore, in the following analysis, this additional first phase, called "predesign," which is closely

[6] This framework is the one already employed in the literature review chapter since it is a non-static framework that gives a representation of what are the phases that constitute the implementation of PMS.

related to developing awareness of the need for change among the individuals within the company, is also considered.

In summary, this study uses both an extended version of Bourne et al.'s (2000) framework and Stouten et al.'s (2018) framework to study the PMS implementation process. Each framework contributes to understanding the process flow and the dynamic nature of the phenomenon, aspects that are sometimes less emphasized in other frameworks (e.g., Kasurinen, 2002). Furthermore, the Stouten et al. (2018) framework helps to identify the enabling and hindering factors of change and to assess their impact on the change project. Employing these two frameworks concurrently seems to favor a more holistic analysis of the PMS implementation process, accounting for the timing, effects, and roles of various factors across different implementation phases.

The initial stage of analyzing the interview data involved a thorough examination of the transcripts prepared in Microsoft Word™. Within each transcript, segments pertinent to the study were highlighted, identifying along the way the citations that could be traced back to the enabling and hindering factors[7] identified in the framework of Stouten et al. (2018). Subsequently, these coded data were systematically transferred to a Microsoft Excel™ file. An individual Excel sheet was created for each of the ten steps of the change management framework, in which enabling or hindering factors pertinent to each step were identified. Quotations relevant to each factor were then reported on the respective Excel sheets. Using Bourne et al.'s (2000) framework, the specific timing of these factors within the PMS implementation process was identified, determining the implementation stage in which they occurred.

5.2 The Case Study

5.2.1 Description of the Case Company

CAEN was founded in Viareggio (Tuscany, Italy) in 1979 by a group of senior engineers and physics researchers from the Istituto Nazionale di Fisica Nucleare (INFN), which is the Italian National Institute of Nuclear Physics. In particular, the founders, who were engaged in research activities within INFN, identified a critical issue frustrating many of their own colleagues: the challenge of developing and acquiring the necessary equipment for conducting physics research. From this shared need, the founders saw a business opportunity. They decided to establish a company dedicated to the development and production of the tools that physics researchers can use in conducting their experiments.

[7] These factors can be found in the previous chapter when presenting the analysis of the hindering and enabling factors traceable in Stouten et al. (2018) framework. Some examples include the *assessment/diagnosis of problems and opportunities*, *leadership commitment*, and *change readiness*.

Initially, three individuals, who were all deeply invested in this shared vision and business project, founded the company and subsequently resigned from their positions at INFN. Despite their departure, they maintained contacts within this institution, which facilitated the creation of an immediate and consistent customer base for the new organization. Over the years, CAEN has experienced steady growth, leading to the establishment of offices abroad and the acquisition of several smaller companies in the same sector. Recently, the company has undergone substantial expansion, growing from a workforce of approximately 60–70 employees to over 100 in the past 6–7 years. Although the company has continued to expand over the years, it faces a fair amount of competition. The industry remains rather a niche, and the competitors are not numerous. Since the market is relatively small, there is some significant competition in the ability to meet customer needs in terms of product and after-sales service. Competition based on price and cost reduction, on the other hand, does not seem to be particularly important, as researchers and institutes are primarily interested in having adequate and reliable tools to carry out their research. Competition based on costs occurs only in some specific tenders, which are seldom announced. Moreover, in these cases, competition can include, but is actually not limited to, bids based on the lowest price. After all, the company always uses production costs as a base to determine the price at which it sells its products, without taking account of market prices. According to the company's management, there are Chinese companies that offer some products similar to CAEN's at lower prices, but they usually fail to be a true menace to the company.

The organization's final target clients are national or international institutions operating in different parts of the world. Because of that, CAEN currently has some offices in the United States, Europe, and China. The company has a product list on its website, from which institutes or individual researchers can identify products of interest to them that are already in production at CAEN. In addition, CAEN frequently receives requests for custom products not currently in production, necessitating assessments of feasibility and profitability. In other words, decisions regarding such requests involve balancing financial viability with the strategic importance of maintaining customer relationships. In this case, the company has to make convenience assessments to determine whether or not it is profitable to meet these specific requests. Occasionally, management may decide to decline certain requests or unprofitable orders in order to maintain relationships with key customers that are deemed essential to the business.

Although these cost-benefit analyses are performed regularly, some product lines that the company decides to introduce do not always prove to be profitable. There are instances where the company decides to produce certain tools based on management's initial assessment of their potential success, only to later find that they have limited popularity and demand. Conversely, some strategic decisions to invest in new products have led to favorable outcomes. Particularly advantageous have proved those instances where the investment actually ends up aligning with the research trends of other institutes or researchers:

> There are, as always, pros and cons: Having an answer always ready with the toy the researcher wants is a great added value for the customer. I always say that we make toys for scientists. *It's clear that providing them with any kind of toy at a reasonable price may not always be convenient for the company.* Typically, you also have to deal with the fact that you can only make very few of these objects, and this is a burden that affects you financially because of all the investment you have to make to develop them. CFO

In addition, CAEN participates in tenders for institute-wide research projects in competition with other competitors. The selection criteria in these tenders typically include several key factors: the expected time to complete the orders, the cost of the orders, the certifications held by the competing companies (such as ISO 9001, 14001, etc.), and the reputation of the companies.

CAEN's organizational structure is functionally oriented, with clearly defined departments each handling specialized tasks. There is a research and development (R&D) department, which is focused on designing new products that not only meet current customer demands but also anticipate future market trends. This department comprises designers and developers with expertise in engineering and physics. The head of the R&D department oversees the progress of work and assesses the feasibility of orders conveyed by the sales managers.

The production department is responsible for the actual manufacturing of already accepted customer orders. Its key functions include ensuring that production adheres to predetermined timelines and budget constraints.

The purchasing department is responsible for sourcing the materials and components needed for production and managing supplier relationships. Given that many subparts of CAEN products are externally sourced, the company heavily depends on a range of subcontractors. The purchasing department's duty is to acquire these components efficiently, focusing on minimizing time and cost. For example, the company's heavy reliance on semiconductors in recent years has made it particularly vulnerable to supply disruptions, such as the recent crisis in Taiwan.

The organization then has an administrative department responsible for accounting and financial matters, including the use of economic and financial planning tools such as budgets.

In this context, the sales department plays a crucial role in maintaining customer relationships, with sales managers typically assigned to specific countries. In some cases, however, some managers are assigned exclusively to individual institutions that frequently place large orders, treating these key customers almost as separate markets or "countries" because of their significant purchasing volume. A notable example of these "country-like" institutions is CERN (European Organization for Nuclear Research). In some markets, such as China, Japan, or South America, CAEN relies on agents or distributors to facilitate customer relations and act as liaisons for the sales manager responsible for the regions.

A distinctive characteristic of CAEN since its inception is that the managers of various departments, with the exception of some within the administration and finance area, typically do not possess a background or degree in economics. Sales managers at CAEN often have significant technical expertise, usually being graduates in engineering or physics. This "technical" background enables them to effectively understand the complex needs of their customers, who are often highly demanding. This know-how also facilitates efficient communication between the sales team and the production and R&D managers, ensuring that customer requests are accurately conveyed and assessed for feasibility.

> We don't have pure salespeople; all salespeople have technical and scientific backgrounds. I, for example, am an electronic engineer, and I also do, let's say, the sales manager. Sales manager

After all, the founders themselves were not subjects with much experience in the business world. It is true, however, that from the very beginning they have been very forward-thinking and willing to learn new approaches and adopt new solutions and ways to grow the business.[8] This mindset is still embodied today by the company's current top management, which no longer includes the original founding partners.

> We have always tried to identify and point out gaps and problems in order to improve (…) This is something that also characterized the way the founders acted and that we have internalized. CFO

> We do things every day to make our business grow, and we are succeeding. (…) Macroscopically, if you look at the results achieved, it has been a continuous growth in profits. President

At the research and development department level, designers generally hold degrees in engineering, physics, and (in some rare cases) computer science.

The company's management views these designers not only as technically skilled subjects, but also as inherently creative individuals, likening them in some ways to artists. This perspective underscores the blend of scientific expertise and creativity that characterizes the R&D department's approach to product development.

> Designers, as well as researchers, are artists and do not like to be harnessed. They want to be free to exercise their creativity and develop more and more innovative products. Since theirs is an intellectual job, it weighs heavily on intellectual honesty. It weighs a lot on the inner involvement of people who have their own ethics and their own personal concept of justice. We have so many employees who are almost "freelancers" who carry out an ideological mission related to their highly intellectual background. CTO

Partly due to this, the R&D unit has always been one of the most challenging areas to implement new control systems. Another significant challenge is the inherent unpredictability of the results of the developed prototypes. This uncertainty complicates accurate cost and benefit estimation, making it difficult to establish effective control systems. Estimating costs becomes particularly complex because the results

---

[8] This element also emerged from the informal and unscheduled meeting with one of the company's founding partners who, although retired, continues to visit the company frequently. The individual expressed a sense of pride in the company's growth and articulated a consistent focus on aspects of business management and competitive strategy to foster this expansion. During the management transition, he also ensured that the "spirit and mindset" of the founding partners remained present in the company.

of experimental prototype development are not always guaranteed to be marketable. Additionally, development timelines are often subject to variations, leading to further cost fluctuations. Fundamentally, the inherent unpredictability of R&D processes and the resistance of R&D personnel to measurement pose significant challenges to establishing consistent and reliable control systems.

> We used to say we need 100 [Euros], but then maybe we end up needing 300. It's hard to predict. The project is finished when it's finished, not when the designer makes a shapeless thing that's fine for him but useless for the client, who would never even hold it with his own hands. CTO

Yet, to remain competitive and meet customers' needs, the company must make significant investments in both R&D and inventory management. Innovation is a key driver in this industry; therefore, the company must continually offer cutting-edge products. A lack of innovation may constitute a risk of losing customers to competitors, who might provide more advanced alternatives.

> Those who do physics experiments are always on the cutting edge and conceive the coolest tools. Sometimes we are asked things that leave us speechless. But if we gave in to all their demands, we would disappear. We work in a challenging field. President

At the same time, these research tools often have a rather long life span, which could be around 10 years or more. Therefore, the company has to incur significant warehouse expenses in order to maintain spare parts and make repairs for products that may have been out of production for years but are still in use among researchers at a certain institution. These inventory costs are compounded by the difficulty of using the same raw materials and components across different and newer product lines. For this reason, it is quite common for specific product lines to require unique materials and components that are not interchangeable with others, resulting in increased complexity and inventory management costs.

> It's not like you can wave a magic wand and increase margins by selling new products that are much cheaper. As soon as there is a demand for a new type of product, there is an immediate push on the marketing side to try to understand how the market might take to this type of development and whether there are similar needs. The new production lines bring with them an overall increase in structural costs and financial assets related to inventory. It is impossible to sell overnight at double the margin of the past. We have a lot of products that are very different from each other, and even the sub-parts can be different. We have aerospace, and then we have synchrotron electronics, and then spectroscopy. We have a large inventory that we have always tried to understand, scratch and analyze, but we have finally given up and achieved peace of mind. President

The company has built a strong reputation and brand identity, known for its quality and reliability, which are critical success factor for its target market.

> There is the virtuous incentive to sell a lot of products and take advantage of economies of scale, but there is a much bigger incentive to make things of value. In the end, volumes are difficult to increase because we operate in a niche. If we didn't have this added value of the brand, we wouldn't have satisfactory margins. President

5.2.2 *Brief Description of the Implementation of the Management Control System*

According to the head of the administration and finance department, the first step in the development of a management control system was the launch of the project to implement ISO 9001 certification. In order to obtain this kind of certificate, the company needed to trace better the performance at the R&D, production, and delivery levels to satisfy the minimum quality standards required by ISO 9001. The necessary training to obtain this certification also made it easier for managers to identify the areas and elements that needed to be monitored. In fact, the first non-economic-financial indicators were closely related to technical aspects (e.g., number of defective products, delivery times, repair times, etc.) and the concept of quality. Therefore, it seems that the adoption of ISO 9001 standards has been instrumental in raising management awareness of the need to monitor certain elements that significantly influence customer satisfaction and the strategic success of the company.

> At the level of our experience, what allowed us to win was the training we received from ISO 9000. It gave us a mental shape. CFO

Fifteen years ago, certifications such as ISO 9001, although they were not a formal requirement for participation in tenders, they were increasingly recognized as essential, and management was becoming aware that they could significantly contribute to CAEN's success in bidding. It was during this period that the impetus for adopting a new system, guided by these certification standards, originated from an external consultant. As the CTO said, "*A consultant with whom we had worked in the past came and offered to help with the transition and tried to encourage CAEN in this endeavor*." One of CAEN's founding partners also initially supported the initiative to adopt the new quality standards and certification. This individual was an early advocate of the value of such standards, recognizing their potential not only to improve the company's management and performance, but also to enhance its reputation among potential customers. This acknowledgement of the need to change marked the beginning of a strategic shift toward integrating quality certification into the company's operations.

> There was one of the three founding partners who was kind of pulling the strings and took this quality aspect to heart. Then the CFO came providing a further essential push. CTO

To facilitate the quality standards integration project, CAEN brought on board a new employee with an engineering background, in addition to the existing consultant, who provided substantial support in terms of expertise and the development of an action plan. The key individuals driving this initiative at the beginning were the founding partner who initially supported the project, the external consultant, and the newly hired engineer, who would eventually take on leadership roles within the company's IT function.

> I began this project with this partner when I was new to the company. The partner, who had considerable influence at the time, was persistent and very involved in the company. The consultant also demonstrated remarkable tenacity. CTO

Although the company initially lacked the knowledge and know-how, some managers rather perceived from the beginning the need to obtain ISO 9001 and, consequently, to develop a management control system based on the analysis of financial and nonfinancial measures within the company. This push for change, as highlighted by the CFO, was primarily motivated by the need to resolve existing challenges in the company's production and delivery processes.

> The need to address existing operational challenges at CAEN was widely recognized within the company. As stated by the CTO, there had been prolonged discussions over the years aimed at identifying a solution that would be both effective and acceptable to all the individuals of the company: "Let's say we did it because we had to do it. We knew about these problems, management had been discussing them for several years, and we were trying to get to an achievable improvement. (...) When we said let's start doing something, there was constant complaining and arguments among colleagues. There was very little willingness to accept change." CTO

The implementation of ISO 9001 standards and a management control system in CAEN coincided with significant structural changes within the organization. A notable development during this period was the strategic decision to segment the market geographically and allocate the responsibility for each area or country to individual sales managers. This represented a significant transformation in the company's market approach and operational organization:

> We decided to introduce a system to track sales, and from there, we then decided to develop a real budget. This system was able to determine the orders acquired from year to year in various countries. Later the company itself evolved to create sales offices for various countries. Now, there are individuals these offices who are responsible for sales performance or maintaining relationships with the distributor in a certain country. CFO

Within a few years, the company moved from a sales-focused management control system to a PMS that is still closely linked to the budget tool. This new system allowed for the tracking of all business expenses and included a number of nonfinancial indicators that allow for a comprehensive assessment of the company's performance. Despite the help of an external consultant, the company faced the challenge of developing new skills, especially since many managers, including those in administration and finance, had no formal business or management training. As a consequence, the process of setting metrics and achieving targets was iterative and experimental, further complicated by the difficulty in aligning individual targets with the broader organizational objectives.

Initially, the proposal to implement a control system was not received enthusiastically by everyone. At the highest hierarchical levels, some R&D and production managers thought that the system could not be effectively implemented and used in the company, or at least in their specific areas. Designers-researchers also resisted because they feared the PMS would limit their freedom of action and creativity. Last but not least, there was a fear that the introduction of the new control systems and ISO 9001 would lead to increased costs. As a result, the initial stages of the development of the management control system were approached cautiously, and participation across the organization was initially limited. This approach was adopted to mitigate the risk of resistance or rejection from both management and employees.

Despite this situation, the broader Italian context was actually favorable for the adoption ISO 9001, due to significant government incentives aimed at encouraging companies to implement this certification. CAEN benefited from these incentives, which facilitated the integration of ISO 9001 and the PMS needed to monitor quality requirements. This system was later further expanded and improved through a fine-tuning process.

In any case, the project to implement a management control system and obtain ISO 9001 certification gained real momentum with the arrival of a new partner-owner, who assumed the role of CFO. Finally, with the continued support of the original project sponsors and the CFO, the system was gradually rolled out across the organization.

However, as indicated by the CTO, there were still doubts regarding the tool's adoption at the onset of the process:

> There were some unhealthy ideas in the beginning, especially from designers. On their side, they proposed to have two companies: the one that does research does whatever they like, and the other one that does the manufacturing and sales introduces the new system. CTO

The increasing availability of detailed data gradually changed the perspective of management and employees, who began to see the value of the initiative. The recognition of benefits linked to the organizational change seems to have played a crucial role in not only ensuring the successful completion of the project but also in fostering its subsequent evolution and expansion:

> It allowed us to manage production costs and calculate bills of materials in a decent way, whereas before, it was not possible. It allowed us to create a real link between the administrative side and production. We started with the loose bridle, but from there, many things started, and more evolved dashboards for different areas were born. CTO

According to the management, without the introduction of the management control system, among other things, obtaining ISO 9001 certification would not have been possible because there was no system in place to monitor and manage performance to meet quality requirements. This same certification, only a short time later, enabled the company to win a major tender with CERN. At that point, all opposition and obvious resistance to the system was finally extinguished. As the President explains in the following quote, using the COVID vaccine as a metaphor, the presence of nonambiguous and visible benefits was actually the element that finally dispelled all skepticism regarding the implementation and use of the system:

> As the vaccine gave the evidence that it works, this thing allowed us to move forward. Due to this, CAEN 2.0 was born, and from there on, there were even further small improvements. It allowed us to convince the most skeptical. Without the results related to the pandemic, there would be many more vaccine skeptics. Instead, there is evidence. The company quickly made a big leap forward. President

This is also supported by the CTO, who acknowledges the benefits of the system:

> We would not have successfully pursued certain initiatives and challenges without this system. Sometimes, it allowed us to go through them just with ease. It makes you have a certain organization, a certain internal structure. CTO

The new dashboards of indicators of the PMS were being introduced simultaneously for all managers in the same area, but the rate of adoption differed from manager to manager. Although the usefulness of the system has been gradually recognized, its actual adoption by individuals did not happen as quickly. To this day, some managers, especially the oldest ones, use the system very little and only when they are forced to. In contrast, several individuals already use the system abundantly, and it has become part of their routine.

To make this transition even easier, the company is continuing to hire new, young, inexperienced staff so they can embrace and learn how to use the new system more easily.

It may be interesting to mention that there are also some areas where the system has been adopted more quickly. In fact, CAEN purchased during this period of continuing transition a small company in the United States that became "CAEN Technologies" after the acquisition. This small business directly handles sales for the U.S. and Canadian markets, as well as providing service and repairs. This subsidiary already possessed relatively advanced control tools, even more than the ones CAEN wanted to adopt, and a rather developed CRM system. In this case, the adoption of the systems promoted by CAEN took place without any particular problems.

5.2.3 Brief Description of the Company's Management Control System

The management control system at CAEN comprises several key components:

- Organizational structure
- Budget & cost accounting system
- Dashboards of nonfinancial indicators through the use of ERP systems
- Clan control
- Targets
- Reward system
- Values

The management control system employed by CAEN aligns with the criteria outlined by Franco-Santos et al. (2012) for contemporary PMS. This system integrates both economic-financial and noneconomic indicators and plays a central role in the company's strategic decision-making processes. Notably, the system extends beyond diagnostic purposes, being actively utilized to drive and incentivize the achievement of targets. These targets are not set at an individual level but are rather established for teams, organizational units, or the company as a whole.

5.2.3.1 Organizational Structure and Job Description

The company has a well-defined organizational structure with clear roles assigned to each individual. Job descriptions at CAEN allow individuals within the company to know which actions and behaviors are authorized or prohibited for each company member. While this aspect of "organizational" control is not the central focus of this research, it merits acknowledgement due to its influence on guiding employees' permitted actions and conduct within the company.

5.2.3.2 Budget & Cost Accounting System

With particular reference to the tools used in the company, one of the primary control tools is the budget.

> Everyone prepares their budget and gives their "share" to the administration. The budget is then reassembled by the administration into a budget plan, which is then reviewed on a monthly basis. CTO

CAEN employs a forecasting tool that covers all the major business areas, although the unique nature of R&D often makes it difficult to estimate costs. On the other hand, budget components covering other areas can be calculated with considerable accuracy. At the production level, the company relies on well-defined and reliable bills of materials. The cost accounting system in place allows for the calculation of contribution margins by product and market lines, an essential element for assessing the viability of specific product lines. Over time, this system has become more advanced to offer detailed breakdowns of various cost components.

The budgeting approach used by CAEN can be characterized as an "evolved" rolling budget. This budget is reviewed monthly and updated quarterly, with a constant time horizon of one and a half years. Regular adjustments are made to the forecasts and corrective actions are taken when necessary to ensure that the budget remains in line with operational aspects. Each business area uses several secondary dashboards, which then contribute to composing the overall corporate budget. Individual managers are responsible for compiling financial data and budgets for their respective areas, which then feed into the overall corporate budget managed at the administration level.

5.2.3.3 Dashboards of Nonfinancial Indicators Through the Use of ERP Systems

Along with the budget, CAEN integrates across its various organizational units a range of technical and nonfinancial indicators to support decision-making processes. The nonfinancial indicators used in the company are generally aimed at evaluating customer satisfaction, which remains a critical success factor for the company. Some examples are the number of defective products, delivery times, repair times, number of support and repair requests, the time required to make an offer to the customer, the number of orders, time to give a response to a specific request made by a customer,[9] the number of cyber-attacks suffered and the number of computer and machinery malfunctions.

The company has not deemed it necessary to develop specific indicators based on customer interviews or questionnaires to measure customer satisfaction levels. This is because the company's customers look specifically at certain elements that the organization can directly monitor, such as the ability of the product to meet their specific requests, its durability, the price of the products, and the delivery and repair time. In addition, CAEN keeps track of the reasons for lost bids, which helps the company understand customer preferences and identify areas for improvement.

The company manages the various information and indicators by resorting to an enterprise resource planning (ERP) system. This system enables managers from different departments to access and extract the specific indicators that are most relevant to their operational needs. At the sales manager level, a customer relationship management (CRM) system is employed. This system provides individual sales managers with all useful information to guide their actions and is directly linked to the management control system used at the administrative level. In particular, sales managers have access to a series of dashboards with indicators that regularly monitor customer satisfaction through proxy measures, track revenue generated, and detail production and delivery costs. The latter are regularly studied in order to define the most suitable selling price. Sales managers' dashboards are also structured to track which orders or requests the company can actually fulfill, which can be partially fulfilled, and which cannot be fulfilled. Regarding unfulfilled orders, the company not only identifies the reasons for nonfulfillment, but also monitors the activities of competitors, particularly if these missed opportunities are being exploited by rival companies.

The senior management regularly organizes meetings to discuss the achieved results and understand the company's direction and ways to enhance organizational performance. The effectiveness of the current choices is also evaluated, and corrective action is taken if necessary.

At the level of production, different software is used in order to keep track of the production times, the number of defective products, the production costs, and the capability to effectively fulfill the orders that come from the marketing and commercial units. The company is currently considering further development of the system in order to include indicators also related to sustainability. This shift is driven by the growing importance of obtaining ISO 14001 certification in the tenders CAEN participates in. The inclusion of sustainability measures would require the analysis of various production-related elements that have not been previously monitored, marking a significant expansion in the company's performance measurement scope.

[9] As said, sometimes the company finds itself having specific requests from customers and, therefore, having to make assessments of convenience and feasibility with respect the products requested by the customer.

5.2.3.4 Clan Control

CAEN exercises a distinct approach to control at the individual employee level. While targets related to timelines, compliance with quality standards, and adherence to some cost constraints are established, the company refrains from close monitoring of each employee's specific actions. This is particularly evident in the case of designers and developers, where management has opted for a more lenient form of control. Given the unique and variable nature of product development, setting specific targets and strict timelines for designers proves challenging, with considerable variability in costs as well. The management believes that too tight control of individuals' actions, in addition to not being willingly accepted by the researchers-developers in the company, could actually end up affecting their freedom of action and, thus, creativity. After several discussions about the possibility of implementing a system to better monitor the actions of employees, management decided to maintain loose control. In this case, what the president said in the following quote seems significant:

> We don't ask to clock out. We ask just to give notice if you are not in the company as a matter of insurance if you get into a car accident. Nobody checks you if you take three breaks or stay 20 minutes or 40 minutes at the bar. President

In implementing the new system and setting targets at the corporate and organizational unit levels, management has always tried to avoid authoritarian and punitive approaches. Even when a problem emerges in terms of performance, management has attempted to avoid having to take direct action against the individual employee or manager. To do this, the founding partners sought to imprint a "clan" control among employees, in which employees themselves try to point out mistakes and critical issues to their colleagues, and gently nudge them to do things differently if necessary. As the CFO explains: "*If a colleague is not doing his or her job well, the coworker tells him or her directly by quietly calling him or her back*" CFO.

5.2.3.5 Targets

In addition to dashboards composed of financial and nonfinancial indicators, the company sets specific target standards to be achieved.

The targets assigned to each organizational unit have been deliberately chosen to make each unit manager feel that their own contribution is critical to the realization of the bigger picture, while avoiding setting targets that are overly challenging and difficult to achieve. At the same time, where there are gaps and problems, management has tried to always act with a view to continuous improvement, providing constructive criticism when strictly necessary. One of the effects of this target system, according to management, has been to make everyone in the company more aware of the levers available to them and the company as a whole to achieve desired results.

> We have always taken a motivating approach. At the management level, we have been committed to making everyone understand that everyone makes a contribution (...). CFO

5.2.3.6 Reward System

When it comes to using incentives and awarding bonuses, there are different approaches depending on whether external parties or the company's own employees are involved. As mentioned above, the company often uses intermediaries to sell its products in certain geographic areas. Exclusive dealers, with whom the company has a close relationship, were required to use the same CRM system mentioned earlier that is used by internal sales managers. This allows the company to closely analyze the performance of external parties, which is rewarded by giving dealers an additional percentage of money based on sales performance, customer growth, and customer retention. Most of CAEN's external retailers are nonexclusive and deal with products from various sectors outside the company's specific sector. Consequently, the level of control over these external retailers is comparatively lower. Despite this reduced control, CAEN maintains a system of incentives for these retailers based primarily on the volume of sales they generate.

On the other hand, the incentive system is less defined at the internal staff level. Although there is the possibility of evaluating the performance of individual managers, the top management prefers to maintain an evaluation that is more qualitative and subjective and not based solely on the use of numbers. In fact, it may sometimes happen that the top management feels that certain individuals have performed well even when not all targets have been met, reserving the possibility of awarding rewards anyway. Then, there are cases where an objective assessment is complicated, at least with the information systems currently available to the company. For example, since sales managers operating abroad rely on intermediaries to sell to end customers, it would be difficult to hold these internal CAEN managers directly accountable for the level of sales achieved. Since sales managers do not have full control over the variables used to evaluate their performance, top management has decided to use more subjective evaluation methods that are still informed by the numerical values achieved.

Finally, the company's management prefers, where possible, to give shared rather than individual awards, always trying to generate a sense of community and belonging. Nevertheless, there were occasions when, due to unsatisfactory performance, the company was unable to provide rewards even when staff had worked well. In these circumstances, top management engages in transparent communication activities to make employees understand the problem. The company always pledges to cover the "unearned" rewards later, once the crisis situation has been resolved. According to management, it is because of the strong sense of belonging and identification with the organization that there have never been any protests to how the awards are given. In fact, even in times of difficulty when management did not give bonuses, there has never been a case of someone complaining that they had done a good job and still deserved an award.

> At the production level, we can look by order book who did better or worse, but in the last two or three years, we still managed to secure uniform rewards. The results have been good. Some have excelled more and some less, but no one has done badly, and that has made things easier. They all seem quite happy with our approach. CSCO

5.2.3.7 Values

Although the company is made up of "creatives," one element that has played in favor of the implementation of the system, according to management, is the type of organizational culture prevalent in the organization. As noted in the section about the description of the company, the organization has been growing and performance-driven since its inception, creating fertile ground for the introduction of a PMS. The company has always tried to make everyone feel like part of one big family by giving rewards at the team or organization level and by organizing regular social events to try to increase the level of involvement. In addition, management has always believed in sharing all available information and acting transparently. In order to communicate the company's values and goals, management has tried to follow a leadership-by-example style, giving the impression that the values communicated are actually lived and embodied firsthand by the company's leaders.

> There is a certain attention and sensitivity from us due to being part of a certain ecosystem. CSCO

5.3 Unpacking the Process of Change: Examining the Dynamics of PMS Implementation Through the Lens of Change Management

This section introduces the enabling and hindering factors identifiable in CAEN's case study, utilizing the Stouten et al. (2018) framework. These factors are then examined in more detail in the subsequent sections to analyze the specific case of CAEN's implementation. Here, they are presented in a general manner to better highlight their key aspects and facilitate their identification in other similar situations and case studies. By way of example, the face-to-face communication factor identified in the CAEN case study was changed to effective communication.[10]

In essence, this section provides practitioners with a checklist of factors that may be important to consider—to promote or to avoid—as they affect the PMS implementation process. Moreover, it provides a lens for supporting the analysis of the case study in the following sections, where the PMS adoption process of CAEN is divided into the phases of predesign, design, implementation, and use (Bourne et al., 2000; Nudurupati et al., 2009).

Tables 5.1 and 5.2 are organized to show the enabling and hindering factors that played a role in the process of change and implementation of PMS. Along with the

[10] In fact, face-to-face communication has often been described as the most effective form of communication by psychology studies, as it makes it the most difficult for misunderstandings to be generated by allowing direct interaction (e.g., the ability to see the expressions and reactions of the recipient of the message) and feedback (Hayes, 2022). However, it is the most time-consuming and least efficient, and therefore not applicable in every situation, organization, and context.

factor, the stage at which it occurs or becomes relevant in the Stouten et al. (2018) model is indicated. Finally, it is indicated when the factor occurred or when it played a role in the implementation dynamics in this specific case study. For the latter, the Bourne et al. (2000) model was used, which, as explained in the methodology section, was extended by increasing the number of stages from 3 to 4 (predesign, design, implementation, and use).

As shown in Table 5.1, the first essential factor or "step" is to develop an *awareness of the need for change*, i.e., *the need to implement the PMS* (Stouten et al., 2018). According to change management literature, this element is crucial for initiating the planned change process, without which it cannot even commence. In the specific case of CAEN, this *awareness* did not emerge from a *structured diagnostic process*, as typically recommended by change management studies. Nevertheless, it is evident that regardless of whether this *awareness* arises from a structured or informal process, the critical aspect remains the *perception that the current situation is neither convenient nor sustainable*. This *awareness* can also be reinforced and disseminated throughout the organization with the support of external parties, such as consultants or individuals with credibility and influence within the company. In the case of CAEN, the intervention of an external consultant, along with the support of a founding partner and the new CFO—individuals with significant influence—was crucial in promoting the PMS implementation project and the *awareness of the need for change*.

Related to the *development of the need for change* is the *belief that the reasons for change are legitimate*, as the introduction of change seems justified when individuals perceive the presence of opportunities to be seized or problems to be solved (Stouten et al., 2018). However, this *awareness* does not necessarily justify a specific type of change, but may foster a more general need to change something in the way the company operates. In the CAEN case, the perception of some individuals that the PMS was *not appropriate* ended up creating *resistance* and *slowing down* the change process. Therefore, to create the *belief that the reasons for change are legitimate*, it is necessary not only to *develop a need for change*, but also to ensure that the chosen direction is perceived as *appropriate*. Efforts, such as in the case of CAEN, should be made to convince the most skeptical by increasing *communication* about the change and demonstrating the *benefits* expected and achieved by implementing the system.

Ongoing *leadership commitment* (Kotter, 1996) is another key element, widely recognized in the PMS literature, that played an essential role in the case of CAEN. The *continuous leadership support* of the project and those affected by the change during the implementation and use of the system contributed significantly to the success of the initiative. This element aligns with the evidence brought by change management literature and PMS studies, as the *loss or absence of commitment* inevitably leads to a *loss of momentum* and, more generally, a decline in interest in the project.

In the case study, an external consultant who acted as a *change agent*, also appears to have played an important role. This individual shared his knowledge of PMS and ISO 9001 and made a concerted effort to raise *awareness of the need for*

Table 5.1 General summary of the enabling factors that can be identified in the different phases that make up the extended framework of Bourne et al. (2000) and the Stouten et al. (2018) framework

Enabling factors	Stouten et al. (2018) step	Bourne et al. (2000) phase
Awareness of the need for change	Organizational diagnosis (first step)	Predesign
Belief that the reasons for change are legitimate	Organizational diagnosis (first step)	Predesign/design/implementation
Presence of visible evidence from multiple sources of the need for change	Organizational diagnosis (first step)	Predesign/design
Leadership commitment	Change readiness assessment (second step)/leadership development (fourth step)/change institutionalization (tenth step)	Design/implementation/use
Support of a change agent perceived as reliable	Social networks exploitation (sixth step)	Predesign/design/implementation
The company partially had the know-how related to change	Change readiness assessment (second step)	Design/implementation/use
Involvement and participation in the change process	Implementation support (seventh step)	Design/implementation
The leadership and promoters of change actively support the system during its implementation and use	Leadership development (fourth step)/change institutionalization (tenth step)	Implementation/use
The implementation process enabled/allowed learning processes	Change interventions implementation (third step)/implementation support (seventh step)/experimentation (eighth step)/progress assessment (ninth step)	Implementation/use
Keeping track of the change progress	Progress assessment (ninth step)	Implementation
Effective communication of the change content and implications	Change communication (fifth step)	Implementation
The individuals responsible for the project had complementary skills	Leadership/development (fourth step)	Design/implementation/use
Achievement of small wins/presence of visible benefits gradually obtained with the gradual adoption of the tool	Experimentation (eighth step)/progress assessment (ninth step)	Implementation/use
Organizational identification	Implementation support (eighth step)	Design/implementation/use
Organizational justice and respectful treatment of the employees	Implementation support (eighth step)	Design/implementation/use
Cultural change	Change institutionalization (tenth step)	Implementation/use

Table 5.2 General summary of the hindering factors that can be identified in the different phases that make up the extended framework of Bourne et al. (2000) and the Stouten et al. (2018) framework

Hindering factors	Stouten et al. (2018) step	Bourne et al. (2000) phase
Individuals feel the change is not appropriate for the organization	Change readiness assessment (second step)	Design/ implementation/use
The individuals don't have the necessary knowledge to implement the change	Change readiness assessment (second step)	Design/ implementation/use
Issues in routinization/adoption/ diffusion/spread of the system by a part/all of the individuals	Progress assessment (ninth step)/ change institutionalization (tenth step)	Implementation/use

change. The use of external consultants who are experts in both human factors management and the implementation of the specific change is often reported in the literature (Stouten et al., 2018) and could be evaluated especially when specific knowledge is lacking in the company.

The CAEN case also shows that a general *lack of knowledge* about management control practices delayed the implementation and use of the PMS. In fact, this required the administration of training, the independent study of some topics, and the adoption of a *learning-by-doing* and *trial-and-error* approach to system development, all of which contributed to the length of the implementation. However, the presence of at least some individuals with *adequate knowledge* and *expertise* provided critical support for the continuation of the project. In addition, as some individuals acquired new knowledge, there was an emphasis on sharing that knowledge with others, as exemplified by the CFO's approach. In CAEN case, the coalition of subjects that undertook the change process was composed of subjects with *different skills and areas of expertise*, which was even more conducive to creating synergies, sharing knowledge, and solving problems more effectively. Thus, the creation of change teams with diverse expertise (Kotter, 1996) could be another enabling factor for the success of PMS implementation initiatives.

Another factor that contributed to the success of the initiative in this case was the creation of a *psychologically safe environment* (Schein, 1996). Management consistently avoided a punitive approach, allowing the implementation and use of the system to proceed at a pace that allowed individuals to adjust to the new reality. This approach facilitated the development of the system through *trial-and-error*, allowing for *learning processes* among employees. In other words, the case seems to confirm the importance of *encouraging learning processes* while avoiding judgmental and punitive approaches.

A key focus throughout the implementation was also to maintain *transparent and recurring communication* about the impact and necessity of the change (Hiatt, 2006). This *transparency* made it easier to understand the *benefits* of the change, which helped drive adoption. Change management literature has consistently emphasized this aspect, offering numerous communication strategies and approaches (Hayes, 2022). In this case, the small size of the company allowed for extensive use of face-to-face interactions and live meetings, which many studies have shown to be most effective in reducing misunderstandings. However, it may be more beneficial to use different channels depending on the needs of the organization. Especially in larger organizations there is usually a need to consider the trade-off between the effectiveness and efficiency of different communication channels (Hayes, 2022). Generally, face-to-face communication is the most effective channel, but it is also the most time-consuming. Emails, on the other hand, are highly efficient as one email can be prepared and sent to all employees in the company. Yet, emails are more indirect and can more easily lead to misinterpretations, making them less effective overall. In light of this, a communication strategy suitable for a large company might involve, for example, using more effective channels, such as face-to-face dialogue, only with the most influential stakeholders. Other systems, such as email or video calls, can be used instead for broader but less in-depth communication with employees.

Another factor that appears to be important is the *involvement* of employees in the change process. In fact, allowing them to make decisions and contribute to the change seems to promote *acceptance* and *ownership*. Through meetings, CAEN has always tried to allow each individual to express themselves freely and to make decisions together, as much as possible, without imposing them from above. This element seems to have helped to promote acceptance and support the implementation process.

Essential to maintaining *momentum* and generating *acceptance* by the most reluctant people appears to be also the achievement of so-called "*small wins*." Such "*small wins*" consist of the achievement of *visible* and *unambiguous benefits* that can be directly attributed to the change. Therefore, it is important to *track the progress* of the change process and *share the results* with the members of the organization. In this way, it seems possible to create an awareness of each individual's *contribution* to the change, as well as the goals that have been achieved. CAEN has sought to regularly engage those affected by the change to discuss what has been achieved and what needs to be done to continue the implementation of the PMS and performance improvement. This made it possible to share and demonstrate the positive results achieved and related to the change project introduced, which helped the members of the organization to feel involved and believe in the initiative.

While change usually involves additional effort or even some kind of individual loss, the ability to foster a strong sense of *identification with the organization* can help generate acceptance of change, at least when it benefits the organization. In the case of CAEN, once skepticism about the lack of benefit to the organization was allayed, the change was accepted. In fact, the primary concerns were more about potentially harming the organization's creativity and flexibility, which are factors underlying the company's strategic success. In this case, the acceptance can be attributed to the climate of *strong participation* and *identification* with the company, which encourages employees to make greater efforts for the success of CAEN.

Finally, *cultural change*—specifically, a shift in the *values* and *mindset* that drive the organization—appears to be another essential factor. As discussed in earlier chapters, for a PMS implementation project to succeed, the tool must be consistently used and integrated into the company's routine. This integration essentially means that the system has become an integral part of not only the company's day-to-day operations, but also its *culture* and *mindset*. At CAEN, management not only uses the PMS regularly, but also bases its decisions on it. In addition, many of the company's employees have become absolutely dependent on the data generated by the system, to the point where employees "panic" when they are unable to access the dashboards.

In general, *cultural change* is particularly important to make the *change sustainable*, which is an essential element for the success of change initiatives, according to both change management and management accounting change literature. The latter devotes considerable attention to analyzing the factors that lead to the initiation, institutionalization, and routinization of new management accounting practices. Stouten et al.'s (2018) change management model, like other change models (e.g., Kotter, 1996), even devotes an entire step to make change sustainable over time. This is not surprising, given that from the earliest days of the discipline of change management, the problem of sustaining change after it is introduced has been central. Lewin himself (1947), in his model of change, identified a refreezing phase aimed at making the achieved change permanent. Much quoted with respect to Lewin's studies is the following passage:

> a change toward a higher level of group performance is frequently short lived; after a 'shot in the arm,' group life soon returns to its previous level. This indicates that it does not suffice to define the objective of a planned change in group performance as the reaching of a different level. Permanency of the new level, or permanency for a desired period, should be included in the objective. (Lewin, 1947, pp. 34–35)

However, in the case under analysis, other factors seem to have played an important role in making the change not only happen, but last. To begin with, the introduction of the new system was accompanied by a *learning process* that enabled the subjects to become more familiar with it and to be able to use it more regularly. *Learning* is generally a factor that creates a "loyalty" of the subjects toward the tool, who, having expended effort in order to be able to learn how to use it, are not inclined to adopt a different one or to go back, thwarting their efforts (Hayes, 2022). Moreover, the *learning process* itself generally allows for a greater understanding of the tool and, consequently, of the potential *benefits* associated with its use.

In addition, the *sustainability of change* at CAEN seem to have been greatly favored by the achievement of *clear, unambiguous benefits* directly attributable to the change. Following this implementation, these *benefits* further fostered a sense of loyalty towards the newly established system. This loyalty was apparent in the interviews with executives, who highlighted the system's critical contribution to the company's success and its significant role in corporate operations and work routines. The following sections will break down the PMS implementation process at CAEN into stages (Bourne et al., 2000) and present the specific factors that influenced it at each stage.

5.3.1 Predesign

Table 5.3 lists the factors that played a role in the predesign[11] phase and were identified with the support of the frameworks of Stouten et al. (2018) and Bourne et al. (2000). As can be seen in Table 5.3, some factors appear in more than one phase of Bourne et al.'s (2000) framework. However, when they appear in more than one stage, these factors are discussed only once to avoid redundancy, at the stage where they appear to have played a more significant role.

In the case study examined, it can be argued that the change process started, as the change management literature and Stouten et al. (2018) framework suggest, before the actual start of the system design phase. The development of an *awareness of the need for change* proved to be, in fact, a prerequisite of paramount importance at this stage. The decision to implement PMS was based on the fact that part of the company's management strongly felt the presence of problems affecting the production and product delivery processes:

> Its introduction did not have an end in itself. Whenever a problem arose with a product that halted the production line—whether due to a missing component, an assembler's error, or a design flaw that failed to meet testing specifications—production came to a complete stop. This caused delays in delivery to customers, leading to dissatisfaction and damage to our reputation, as well as delays in billing. Additionally, the entire company had to work to resolve the issue. We received numerous customer complaints that required immediate attention and resolution. CFO

Unlike what the main prescriptive models of change management and the Stouten et al. (2018) framework suggest, however, there was no real formalized *organizational diagnosis* to assess the company's situation. Indeed, the change management literature suggests that conducting an assessment of the current condition of the company is essential to start a planned organizational change. This is because it is

Table 5.3 Enabling and hindering factors identified in the predesign phase

Factor	Stouten et al. (2018) step	Bourne et al. (2000) phase
Awareness of general issues affecting the organization	Organizational diagnosis (first step)	Predesign
Awareness of specific problems at the top management level (unsatisfied need for better managerial control)	Organizational diagnosis (first step)	Predesign
Belief that the reasons for the change were legitimate	Organizational diagnosis (first step)	Predesign/design/implementation
Presence of visible evidence from multiple sources of the need for change	Organizational diagnosis (first step)	Predesign/design
Support from an expert external consultant in raising awareness and developing the system	Social networks exploitation (sixth step)	Predesign/design/implementation

[11] This kind of table was also used for each of the following subsections, for each step that characterized the implementation process.

generally acknowledged that identifying problems or opportunities to be seized motivates management and employees to embrace change and helps identify the type of change most likely to meet real business needs. In this case, the company's problems were already well-known and obvious to everyone without the need of a *business diagnosis*, fostering a collective awareness of the need for change to address these issues. The Stouten et al. (2018) model does not consider the possibility of developing a need for change without conducting a *business diagnosis*. Still, this is likely because it takes a general perspective that is not specifically tailored to specific contexts or firm sizes. In general, as with most change management models, the proposed approaches are largely derived from empirical analyses conducted in larger organizations. Moreover, the model is aimed at providing prescriptions to support practitioners, which are not necessarily useful in every situation. Since CAEN is a small company, it appears that the management could have an idea of the performance of the various business areas even without the conduction of specific *business assessments*, as explained by the CTO:

> We knew about these problems, and the management had been debating this for several years, and we were trying to reach an achievable improvement. CTO

In any case, even in the absence of this formalized moment, the development of *awareness* of the presence of issues and of the *need for change* has proven essential. As the CTO mentions:

> Let's say we did it because we had to do it. CTO

This awareness fostered a general inclination towards introducing a change, particularly as the company's management has consistently been committed to continuous improvement in business performance.

In addition, it was also recognized that the existing management control tools at CAEN were inadequate, failing to fulfill the company's evolving control needs. This realization increased the urgency for change and, in particular, for the development of more effective management tools:

> Previously, navigating the economic and financial aspects was often based on intuition and gut feeling, which sometimes led to unexpected and potentially unpleasant surprises at the bottom line of the balance sheet. CFO

Prior to the introduction of the system, as the following quote from the president shows, there was, in fact, no use of the PMS to monitor performance and guide the company:

> There was a disconnection between the operating budget and everyday life. President

All these problems seem to have contributed together in producing change, as explained by the CFO:

> This gave rise to the need to set up control tools that then ended up inside the "infamous" dashboards of quality indicators that would allow the company's performance to be better kept under control. CFO

In other words, CAEN's decision to implement an effective PMS was influenced not only by general issues affecting the company, such as long production and delivery times, but also by more specific control needs. *Multiple sources* reported *evidence* of the existence of these problems, furthermore spreading and reinforcing the *awareness of the need for change*.

5.3.2 Design

As the CTO claimed, the project started when

> A long-time CAEN consultant had come, proposing and trying to stimulate CAEN toward this venture. CTO

This individual was one of the subjects who drove the change and was the most supportive of the initiative, even though there was already a significant *awareness of the need for change*. In particular, this consultant proposed to assist CAEN in achieving ISO 9001 certification, marking the beginning of the PMS implementation process. Because of the *awareness* of the problems that plagued the company, a part of management was very receptive to what the consultant proposed. In fact, to obtain ISO 9001 certification, the company needed to improve performance monitoring and management across R&D, production, and delivery to meet essential quality standards, which it was actually failing to achieve (Table 5.4).

In order to achieve ISO 9001 requirements, training was administered to all the management to clarify the key areas requiring close monitoring and the actions to be taken to improve performance. According to the management, the implementation of ISO 9001 standards truly proved essential, among other things, in enhancing management's understanding of performance measurement and management:

> At the level of our experience, what allowed us to win was the training we received from ISO 9000. It gave us a mental shape. This mental shape that I acquired allowed me to ask myself questions when I found myself overnight dealing with economic-financial and strategic aspects even though I had studied law at the university and attended liceo scientifico.[12] CFO

In the early stages, the system was developed through the work of a very small team of people: the consultant, one of the founding partners, and a newly hired engineer. The consultant proved to be particularly persistent in raising awareness of the need for change, sharing his knowledge and acting as a key *change agent*.

In any case, there wasn't initially a high level of participation and involvement.

> I began this project with this partner when I was new to the company. The partner, who had considerable influence at the time, was persistent and very involved in the company. The consultant also demonstrated remarkable tenacity. CTO

[12] *This term is difficult to translate into English. It's a kind of high school present in Italy that focuses on scientific subjects.*

Table 5.4 Enabling and hindering factors identified in the design phase

Factor	Stouten et al. (2018) step	Bourne et al. (2000) phase
Leadership commitment	Change readiness assessment (second step)/leadership development (fourth step)/ change institutionalization (tenth step)	Design/implementation/use
Support of knowledgeable people (consultant, new hire) to manage the new situation	Change readiness assessment (second step)	Design/implementation/use
Missing consensus on change appropriateness	Change readiness assessment (second step)	Design/implementation/use
Lack of knowledge regarding MCS and PMS	Change readiness assessment (second step)	Design/implementation/use
Administration of training	Change readiness assessment (second step)	Design/implementation/use

This is because although everyone shared the need to solve the problems that plagued the production and customer delivery processes, not all people agreed on the *appropriateness* of the chosen change. The extended discussions at CAEN over finding a universally accepted solution to its operational challenges adversely impacted the company's level of *change readiness* (Stouten et al., 2018). The protracted nature of these debates, spanning several years, contributed to a delay in the change process, since it was not an easy task to achieve a consensus among stakeholders about the best course of action to be taken (Kasurinen, 2002). When the idea of starting the project of implementing a PMS finally prevailed, there was still no support from everyone, as can be seen from what the CTO said:

> Obviously, in the adoption of the system, there were many creaks and some skepticism. When we said, let's start doing something there was constant complaining and arguments among colleagues. There was very little willingness to accept the change. CTO

Developers and managers from the R&D and production departments felt that the introduction of a PMS was not feasible in a company composed mainly of creatives and researchers, who usually do not want their freedom of action restricted or controlled.

> Management was struggling to come to a commonly accepted solution, and there was much discussion. (...) Skepticism was related to the fact that the company was made up of creative people and the feeling that control systems could not effectively be employed into their [managers'] areas of responsibility. CTO

In other words, the concern of the CAEN developers-researchers was related to the perception that the proposed changes would be directly detrimental to their work, but also to the company as a whole:

> Designers, as well as researchers, are artists and do not like to be harnessed. They want to be free to exercise their creativity and develop more and more innovative products. Since theirs is an intellectual job, it weighs heavily on intellectual honesty. (…) The researcher, by definition, in my opinion, is not a neat person. He is a bit of an artist, so the idea of the

> quality of meeting specifications of time schedules and so on was not well regarded. They also feared increased costs and difficulties in communicating between different parts of the company. CTO

The perception of more disadvantages than benefits related to organizational change is often a precursor to strong resistance, either passive or active, and can potentially lead to the failure of change initiatives (Bridges, 1991; Hayes, 2022; Stouten et al., 2018). In this case, the lack of perceived benefits among some employees hindered the specific change initiative related to the PMS implementation. Although the Italian government provided funding to get ISO 9001 certified, it did little to overcome this resistance. As a consequence of these perplexities, it was decided to keep the ongoing development of the PMS low-profile for the time being. As the CTO explains, "*This was kept somewhat under wraps at first. It was not a highly publicized aspect or the flagship of the company. We got off to a slow start*" CTO.

Indeed, there was no communication or sponsorship at the beginning of the design effort to avoid too much discussion and criticism.

According to the CTO, the slowdown related to *resistance to change* was significant:

> In this way, it took several years, without being able to get the system in place and certified. (…) Everyone is happy in theory to have accounts, data, and processes a little better sorted and organized, but it's a long way from here to implementation. CTO

Resistance to change sometimes took the form of active counterproposals. These counterproposals often lacked credibility or presented significant challenges in terms of practical implementation, reflecting the researchers' apprehension about the proposed changes within the organization. As the CTO claimed:

> There were some unhealthy ideas in the beginning, especially from designers-researchers. On their side, they proposed to have two companies: the one that does research does whatever they like, and the other one that does the manufacturing and sales introduces the new system. But in the end, it was never questioned to abandon it. CTO

Finally, besides the skepticism from the researchers-developers, it was also pretty challenging to design the system per-se. In fact, a significant problem for monitoring and goal setting was that projects and products developed within the company were often highly unpredictable gambles that did not always yield the desired results. Therefore, estimating the timing and costs of new product development remained sometimes very difficult.

5.3.3 *Implementation*

The implementation process started before the design phase was fully completed. This is in line with what is advised by Bourne et al. (2000), who recognize that in the implementation of these types of tools, the phases tend to overlap. This was evident also at CAEN, where the PMS was introduced progressively across different business areas. Consequently, while some dashboards were still in the developmental-design stage, others were already operational, facilitating a gradual *learning* curve for management in their utilization. The implementation process advanced at a modest pace until the arrival of a new CFO, who was also a member of the ownership group, marking a turning point in the project's *momentum* (Table 5.5).

> Four to five years went by without completing the project, but with the arrival of **** [CFO], within a year we had the system and also the certification. CTO

This subject was convinced early on of the project's usefulness and importance, showing a strong *commitment* towards the new system throughout the implementation process.

> The CFO has taken the initiative to heart since her arrival. CTO

At this point, the company's leadership decided to change its approach:

> In addition to setting up the indicators and whatnot, it was making sure that everyone acquired and understood the goals and issues. CFO

The arrival of the new CFO proved to be essential in moving the implementation project out of its impasse. Throughout the process, from the initial design to the final stages, the new CFO demonstrated a strong *commitment* to the project and decided to adopt a *leadership by example* approach, explicitly using the system and embodying new values that were previously absent in the company. These values related to putting customer satisfaction and product and service quality first, and monitoring and managing performance with dashboards to achieve these strategic goals.

The presence and proactive approach of the CFO led to a shift in the project's visibility within the company. In contrast to the earlier phase of partial concealment, there was a concerted effort to encourage employee involvement through regular meetings, which significantly increased the *momentum* and *transparency* of the implementation process. In particular, a great deal of effort went into *communicating* and convincing members of the organization of the value of the change. Much effort was put into making it clear to everyone the implications of the change and the reasons for choosing both ISO 9001 and PMS implementation:

> As the project got underway, we had weekly meetings where we discussed what needed to be done to improve the performance of our processes. We discussed problems and the improvements we were able to obtain through the management of the performance. This means pursuing quality. CTO

The meetings held during the implementation of the PMS served multiple purposes. To begin with, these meetings aimed to foster involvement among team members and facilitate the sharing of knowledge. Secondly, they were used as a platform to monitor the progress of the PMS implementation. As the system took shape, these gatherings became instrumental in identifying new targets and indicators that would constitute the various components of the system's dashboards. Therefore, the meetings were not only a medium for collaboration and learning but also a critical tool for tracking development and refining the system's structure.

Table 5.5 Enabling and hindering factors identified in the implementation phase

Factor	Stouten et al. (2018) step	Bourne et al. (2000) phase
CFO acted as a leader and supporter of the project	Leadership development (fourth step)/ change institutionalization (tenth step)	Design/implementation/ use
The leadership's active support during the implementation and use	Leadership development (fourth step)/ change institutionalization (tenth step)	Implementation/use
The implementation process enabled/allowed learning processes	Change interventions implementation (third step)/implementation support (seventh step)/experimentation (eighth step)/progress assessment (ninth step)	Implementation/use
Keeping track of the change progress	Progress assessment (ninth step)	Implementation
Face-to-face communication about the change through meetings	Change communication (fifth step)	Implementation
The individuals responsible for the project had complementary skills	Leadership/development (fourth step)	Design/implementation/ use
Involvement and participation in the change process	Implementation support (seventh step)	Design/implementation
Lack of knowledge about MCS and PMS	Change readiness assessment (second step)	Design/implementation/ use

> We had and still have frequent meetings with all interested parties to at least share the status of the work. Everyone is kept informed about our plans and progress. Whether mistakes have been made by taking a wrong fork in the road or whether we need to get back on the right track. We've made a habit of these periodic meetings, which are more about managing performance than just measuring and reviewing indicators and plans (…). We try to figure out how to continuously review and observe how the project is progressing. We make everyone aware of the status and any deviations. CTO

In this way, the individuals composing the company became *aware of the progress* that the change process was achieving and that it was actually becoming more and more concrete.

This element seems to have facilitated change by allowing individuals to better *understand the progress* of the work and their contribution to achieving the desired results. As the following quote from the CFO illustrates, there has been and continues to be an effort on the part of management to clarify how each individual contributes to the success of projects and the company:

> We have a commitment to making everyone understand that everyone makes a contribution, like a cog in the clock. If one does not work, that insignificant little cog will wobble everything. Everyone has understood the importance of their activity overall, everyone is motivated to improve and monitor the performance of the others. CFO

As a *leader*, the CFO contributed maintaining the *momentum* and pushing the company toward the set direction. As the quote below from the president confirms, with this person's input, management has accepted and embraced a set of previously not employed indicators to make decisions and guide its behavior and actions.

> With the new CFO management has been able to come together around indicators that everyone agrees on and everyone is clear about the goals and direction. President

Nevertheless, management was not experienced in the implementation of PMS and management control systems. Therefore, in conjunction with developing and implementing the PMS, the process of *learning* played a key role. The *learning* process, strongly supported by the external consultant, was an integral part of the initiative, with meetings to *review progress* and *participation* in system development emerging as key *learning* opportunities.

The CFO put also lot of effort into making sure that people felt involved and informed about the state of the company at all times:

> Sometimes everything is fine. Sometimes, I have to go down to the lower levels to say that we are making too little money, and you find out the problem. (...) There were years when I went downstairs and I said guys do what you want, but this year, we're not gonna make it. And we got everybody involved by explaining to everybody what the problem was. CFO

Moreover, the CFO proactively engaged in self-education to deepen his understanding of management control and the quality concepts set in ISO 9001. This independent study involved consulting relevant literature and participating in training courses. Due to this, the CFO played a central role in imparting knowledge gained through ISO 9001 certification training:

> When I learned something, I transferred it to others as well. CFO

The process of *learning* and disseminating knowledge as it was acquired emerged as an essential element for the successful implementation and facilitation of change at CAEN. However, the initial *lack of knowledge* actually led to a delay. This was primarily because, alongside developing the PMS, the management was simultaneously required to acquire new skills and insights to actually start using the system to monitoring and managing performance. The system's progression was characterized by a "learning-by-doing" approach. This required top management to *experiment* to determine the most effective indicators that would both guide the actions of subordinates and improve the quality of decision-making processes:

> Especially in the beginning, however, it wasn't easy. We realized that if, for example, you give a salesperson a goal to make 3 million orders or turnover, that person starts giving discounts to everyone, and so reaches the result, and I have to give him the bonus anyway, but by doing so, we don't achieve the overall profit goal at all. We had to experiment with several indicators before we understood the most useful ones for our goals. CFO

During the implementation phase, the guiding coalition promoting the change grew in size and remained essential to the initiative's success. Each member brought a unique contribution to the project, leveraging their specific areas of knowledge. Notably, the change team now included the CFO, who, as an owner, wielded considerable influence in the company. In addition, she was actively acquiring the necessary management accounting skills. Then there was the consultant, who brought special experience and training in quality management, particularly in meeting the requirements for ISO 9001 certification. Additionally, there was the founding member with a research background in physics and the ability to understand the company's production processes and goals. Completing the team there was an engineer who, although lacking direct experience in developing performance measurement and control systems, had valuable skills in software development and computer languages. This combination of complementary skills and expertise played a critical role in managing the technical complexities and bringing the project to completion:

> The consultant was more knowledgeable about the technical aspects rather than the strictly technological/IT aspects. (…) Then the new CFO came, bringing a different level of influence. (…) We were essentially a team where everyone had their specific responsibilities (…) Personally, I tried to manage the [IT] infrastructure to provide the tools necessary to keep everything running and working smoothly.—CTO

This division of roles among actors with *different and complementary skills* further facilitated implementation. For example, the CFO's main role was to design the system and identify the most effective indicators to perform the control activity, while the strictly IT aspect was mostly left in the hands of the engineer who later became the CTO.

During the implementation process, incentive systems focused on individual performance were not used to encourage the use of the PMS for monitoring, managing, and improving performance. The change management literature suggests that it is useful to assign goals and incentives that drive the adoption of behaviors consistent with the organization's desired future state (Stouten et al., 2018). In this case, since individual goals were not assigned and only overall company performance improvement was more rewarded, individuals were indirectly motivated to use the PMS. This approach was generally preferred because of the organizational areas characterized by the use of creativity and high rate of the unpredictability of projects. The President of CAEN believes that in such an organizational context, enforcing detailed control over individual actions is not only challenging but also potentially counterproductive:

> The fact is, we don't control how they manage their time. We work in a company of brains. The important thing is to give ourselves attainable goals at all levels. President

Certainly, with the implementation of the new dashboards, it was possible to get a more accurate picture of business performance and to identify with some degree of accuracy where the company was performing better and where it was struggling. However, management generally preferred to reward everyone in the company equally when company performance was satisfactory to avoid envy and the perception of unequal treatment. To sum up, while the change management literature suggests directly rewarding people who engage in desired behaviors,[13] in this case, the

[13] This can also translate into achieving certain levels of performance or numerical targets as reported by both Stouten et al.'s (2018) model and Hayes' (2022).

rewards were provided when performance improvement at the level of the organization and not for engaging in specific actions. Thus, it can be argued that, although in a somewhat indirect form, the incentive approach was anyway used to motivate staff to do better and, therefore, to regularly use dashboards to monitor and manage performance:

> We then gave rewards aimed toward performance improvement. The rewards were generally given to everybody in the company and were not related to the individual's performance. (...) A reward is given for overall improvement of the company's performance. The company has moved from words to deeds at the top management level, and when there have been good budget results, there have been rewards for everyone. CFO

This is not surprising given that CAEN's overarching focus on improving business performance has been a key driver behind the implementation of organizational changes, including the PMS. This general orientation towards performance improvement seems to have not only facilitated the acceptance of change but also encouraged individual employees to actively engage with the PMS and its indicator dashboards.

While individual awards and specific targets were not assigned, clear goals at the company and team levels were communicated in meetings. These goals focused on achieving and retaining certain quality standards and performance targets. However, the approach to setting these targets was not authoritarian or "military" in nature. Instead, there was a concerted effort to foster a sense of shared ownership and collective responsibility for the change among various team members.

> It was determined to give motivating targets, without adopting a military or punitive approach […] we try to make the colleague be the conduit, preventing the boss from making the calls. There is much attention to how things are communicated. If a colleague is not doing his or her job well, the coworker tells him or her directly by quietly calling him or her back. We avoid the boss calling back. This approach comes from the mindset of the founding partners, and management has internalized this approach and made it their own. (…) There was a commitment to making everyone understand that everyone contributes. CFO

This approach to motivating people to do better led to an attempt to provide rewards even when significant efforts, no matter how obvious, did not result in better financial or nonfinancial performance. This seems confirmed by this quote below from the president.

> Even if the numerical goal is not achieved, if we feel that the organization has acted and worked well, we still give the rewards to push to continue to do better. We worked on common results and goals. President

Leadership realized that while they could push for adoption of the new system, they needed to *involve* individuals in the implementation process to achieve satisfactory adoption and use. In fact, management at CAEN held a firm conviction that the success of change initiatives hinged on individual acceptance of the change. As highlighted in the following citation, the management team endeavored to promote a sense of *ownership of the change* process among employees to foster this acceptance.

> I always went in as gently as I could and tried to share the decisions and make a joint decision, or at least make it seem like it was their decision, and then put it into action. CTO

This was achieved by emphasizing collaborative decision-making, which favored the creation of an environment where individuals felt that decisions were made collectively and shared. Such an approach was aimed at ensuring that employees perceived themselves as active participants in the change process rather than mere recipients of top-down directives.

This approach appears effective, as *participation* and *involvement* are generally considered important factors in the Stouten et al. (2018) and PMS implementation literature (Bourne et al., 2002), both to improve the system and to promote acceptance. As the following citation shows, being the company not particularly big, it was easy to involve everybody and ensure that communications about the project and the implications of the change reached everyone:

> The climate was quite participatory. We were not more than 50–60 people, so everyone knew everything, and therefore everyone was very involved. President

This participatory climate is still present today, allowing information to travel with ease and create involvement in the various projects the company decides to initiate:

> There is a climate of participation and involvement. CFO

Despite the CFO also being an owner and thereby possessing the authority to unilaterally impose changes, the adoption of an inclusive approach was instrumental. This method proved particularly effective in garnering acceptance of the change among more hesitant managers and those within the "creative" sectors of the company:

> Slowly, it was understood by everyone that quality is needed if you do it right with a capital Q. (…) Everyone understood that it is necessary to have a certain organization, a certain internal structure. Both from an organizational and managerial point of view. CTO

5.3.4 Use

The implementation of the PMS at CAEN has been an overall success, as the system is now regularly used in top management decision-making processes. In addition, the dashboards that are part of the PMS are actively used by middle managers in both production and sales. However, the frequency and regularity of PMS use varies among middle managers, indicating that the process of *routinizing* the use of the system across all operational areas is still partially ongoing. In other words, some parts of the organization are still in the process of adopting the PMS:

> The problem is not at all IT-related as one might think; by now, these tools are extremely intuitive and user-friendly. What I realized is that it is really a problem of working method and mindset. It is no coincidence that those people who have a little more difficulty are often, let's say… a little more âgé. (…) Before, there was no such system, so it is still dif-

> ficult for some to make it an everyday thing. (…) Obviously, new hires adopt it easily because they are young people with little experience or habits to change. Sales manager

Some of the company's managers, who are generally older and have spent their entire careers there, have usually no experience in other organizations and with the use of PMS. This professional background has fostered certain routines, mindsets, and approaches to work that are not consistent with regular use of the PMS. As a result, these managers use the system only for diagnostic purposes or, in some cases, avoid using it at all unless absolutely necessary. This reluctance significantly hinders the full adoption of the PMS and can potentially impact the effective management of performance in some areas (Table 5.6). However, this situation is not really a permanent obstacle to the initiative, as new employees who are able to learn the system are gradually being introduced in the company.

In any case, as the PMS implementation progressed and the system became operational, the company began to realize *tangible benefits and advantages* from the change. ISO 9001 certification itself, which would not have been possible for the company to obtain without implementing at least part of the system, was gained before the implementation process was even fully completed:

> It's one of those roads that once you start down, it's hard to leave. Partly because you've done the work, and partly because you can actually see the benefits. (…) Some benefits were apparent, and we received funding from the Italian government for adopting the certification. (...) Once you start on such a virtuous path, it's difficult to turn back—it guides you well. (...) Over time, the 'artists' within the company began to see the advantages. (…) I believe everyone gradually realized that it wasn't about rigidifying the company, but about finding a healthy balance between laissez-faire and control, explained the CTO.

> As the vaccine gave the evidence that it works, this thing allowed us to move forward. Due to this, CAEN 2.0 was born, and from there on, there were even further small improvements. It allowed us to convince the most skeptical. Without the results related to the pandemic, there would be many more vaccine skeptics. Instead, there is evidence. The company quickly made a big leap forward. President

Achieving these "*small wins*" seems to have been essential to maintaining *momentum*, but also to convincing those individuals who were skeptical and management to continue using the PMS. This factor seems to have been essential in ensuring that the project was completed and the system further developed and expanded. The presence of visible benefits over time seems to have had a positive impact on the *sustainability of the change*, as management remains quite convinced of the benefits and the need to continue using the PMS on a regular basis.

Another related factor that appears to have encouraged change at CAEN is the strong sense of *organizational identification* among the company's members. According to change management theories, individuals' sense of *identification* and belonging to the organization has a significant impact on their commitment and acceptance of organizational change. In the case of CAEN, resistance to the PMS implementation seemed diminished when employees recognized the *benefits* of the change for the organization as a whole, rather than for individuals. Moreover, the additional workload associated with developing, learning, and adopting the PMS

Table 5.6 Enabling and hindering factors identified in the use phase

Factor	Stouten et al. (2018) step	Bourne et al. (2000) phase
Delay in routinization/adoption/ diffusion/spread of the system	Progress assessment (ninth step)/change institutionalization (tenth step)	Implementation/use
Achievement of small wins/presence of visible benefits gradually obtained with the gradual adoption of the tool	Experimentation (eighth step)/ progress assessment (ninth step)	Implementation/use
Organizational identification	Implementation support (eighth step)	Design/ implementation/use
Integration of change into organizational values and mindset	Change institutionalization (tenth step)	Implementation/use

did not emerge as a resistance factor in this case, although it is often cited as such in the organizational change literature.

To sum up, it seems confirmed that employees may accept changes that don't directly benefit them if they *identify strongly with the organization* and the changes *benefit* the organization.

This presence of a strong sense of *organizational identification* seems supported by the good inter-firm relationships highlighted by the CFO.

> We have good inter-company relations, increasingly innovative products, and a higher margin. CFO

Moreover, to keep a strong sense of inclusion and belonging, even during the crisis years, management usually tried to make individuals aware of the issues that had led to unsatisfactory results, even when those issues were not dependent on their actions.

> There have been years when I've come down and said, guys do what you want, but this year we can't make it. We explained the problems to everybody. We also had to put people on leave, but we gave them back what they didn't get in the following years because it wasn't their fault. CFO

To foster a sense of belonging, management still aligns individual goals with the company's goals by providing incentives based on the company's overall performance:

> We try to incentivize people to work for the organization, let them know that if they work well and the organization is profitable, they also gain. President

In an effort to strengthen the sense of *identification*, the company has also tried to create moments of togetherness outside of work:

> Before Covid, there were fixed events like the CAEN summer party where the company bore all the costs. Not only the company workers came, but also families and children, to familiarize and laugh about the work. It was so good that even customers asked to attend. We also had a monthly date. On the last Fridays of each month, CAEN paid the costs at the café for everyone to be together. (…) As we grow, we try to maintain good inter-company relations and maintain a good perception outside the company by customers. President

In addition, the company continues to promote a focus on performance improvement, which remains one of the organization's core values[14]:

> There is this general climate of wanting to do well for the company, wanting to contribute. This creates an environment that is particularly conducive to change. CTO

In the current practical application of the PMS, adjustments and *experimentation* with indicators at the level of individual organizational units are permitted. This flexibility allows for the creation of personalized dashboards through the use of a software, supplying specific informational needs. To support this experimentation, targeted training was provided after the implementation of the system, particularly in areas like the production department, improving employees' proficiencies in utilizing the available data to develop meaningful indicators.

> We can create numerous types of reports that can help us to monitor our performance. We are doing a BI course to try to pull out the information we need in a way that is easy to understand and intelligible to everyone. That way, we will be able to make even better use of the system we have. (…) Consultants have come in to figure out what key information we want to pull out. They will set up a baseline for us where we can pull out dashboards that we might need at any given time. CSCO

This element made it possible to improve proficiency in using the system and facilitated the durability of the introduced change. Moreover, theories related to organizational change suggest that as the ability to master a new tool, system, or technology increases, individuals become more committed and loyal to it.

In relation to the initiative's success, some factors suggested in the concluding phase of the framework by Stouten et al. (2018) and related to making change lasting over time seem to have played an important role.

Particularly prominent among these is *integrating* the new system and related approaches with *organizational culture* and main business processes. In fact, not only is the system regularly used by management to make decisions, but there has been a visible change in mentality. The system has effectively become part of top management *routine*, and when meetings are convened, the results achieved and how performance can be managed or improved are always discussed:

> We transformed this company. From a business run in an improvised way by technicians who had no idea of how to run a business to a more entrepreneurial way where performance targets and management control became everyone's bread and butter. (…) This evolution has brought awareness to all people about what levers are at our disposal, always balancing on the other side a whole series of factors that are essential for business continuity. CFO

Moreover, some employees have become so accustomed to using the system that its eventual and possible abandonment would generate difficulties at this point, as the quote below from the CTO points out:

> Now, many people panic if the indicators are gone. Everyone wants to see them. Sales managers, for example, are always very interested in their indicators because, through them, they can see if they are doing well and what should be improved. I also think that

[14] It is an element that comes directly from the mindset of the original founders of the organization and has therefore been passed down over time, even as managers and employees have changed.

> everyone gradually understood that it was not a matter of stiffening the company but of finding a healthy compromise between laissez-faire and control. Some indicators, such as those related to incoming orders, are almost always of interest to everyone. It is an element that stirs great interest. The sales manager is typically always there to update the data on the screen day by day. CTO

This shows how strong the system is now linked to *organizational* mindset and *values*. As the use of the new systems has become part of the company's *routine* and processes, it is very unlikely at this point that there will be a return to the initial situation.

In conclusion, it can be understood that these latter factors seem to play an important role in relation specifically to the sustainability of change, which is a topic commonly addressed by change management literature since its inception.

5.4 Discussion

The discussion section is organized to provide an overview of the study's contributions. First, the theoretical contributions of the study are outlined. This first section aims to enrich the existing body of knowledge with new insights and perspectives derived from the study's findings. Subsequently, the focus shifts to the empirical contributions, contextualizing the study's results within the existing literature on PMS implementation. This segment links the study's findings to the broader empirical research in the field. Finally, the discussion also includes some practical considerations that underpin the actionable insights from the study, aiming to bridge the gap between theory and practice and provide useful guidance for practitioners.

In light of what has been presented in the results section, the use of Stouten et al.'s (2018) framework has been fruitful. The framework allowed for the identification of the organizational and individual factors that influenced the change process, while maintaining a processual rather than static perspective. This shows that change management frameworks, like the one proposed by Stouten et al. (2018), seem appropriate to support the analysis of the dynamics of a PMS implementation process. The extended version of Bourne et al.'s (2000) framework, on the other hand, proved to be instrumental in delineating the different phases of the PMS implementation in CAEN. It allowed to establish the timing of occurrence and impact of the enabling and hindering factors identified by Stouten et al. (2018) and it allowed the tracking of technical elements integral to the process, which are not considered in the adopted change management framework. The latter addresses, in fact, generic change processes, but not the specific phenomenon of PMS implementation. In other words, Bourne et al. (2000) expanded framework was useful to also consider the specificities related to this type of organizational change.

Moreover, this research supports the importance of adding the "predesign" phase to the original work of Bourne et al. (2000), which in the case studied was of paramount importance in preparing the ground for the implementation of the PMS. Without this phase, Bourne et al.'s (2000) framework does not seem to be able to fully represent the dynamics of implementation and the factors that enable or hinder this process.

As already stressed in previous chapters, another contribution of this study is related to the adoption of a different perspective compared to the majority of management accounting change literature, which mostly leans on sociological theories such as institutionalism and neo-institutionalism (Alsharari et al., 2015; Burns & Scapens, 2000). Contrary to this trend, this work is rooted in organizational change and psychological theories that adopt the perspective of planned organizational change (Bourne et al., 2000; Stouten et al., 2018), while also emphasizing the active role of individuals in these processes. This approach appears fruitful since it transfers the focus towards individual actions and behaviors, offering a different lens through which to examine and understand the process of planned management accounting change. Individuals are seen here as active participants who directly shape the change process and influence its outcomes, whether successful or not (Burke, 2023), rather than being passively influenced by a range of institutional factors and forces. In other words, individuals can be key agents of change, making deliberate decisions that significantly influence the whole process.

In our case of analysis, the actions of certain individuals indeed seem to have played an important role in producing the change and favoring its realization. The initiation and progression of the implementation process at CAEN can be attributed to the arrival and involvement of specific key individuals, namely the consultant, the newly hired engineer and the CFO. The very development of *awareness of the need for change*, essential to the change management literature (Stouten et al., 2018) and necessary to initiate PMS implementation in the studied company, related to specific agents of change. According to the managers interviewed, there were issues that affected the entire company, but awareness developed at the "micro-level" of individuals and then spread throughout the organization (Stouten et al., 2018). Additionally, the adoption of the system is still uneven within the company, which, as mentioned, is due to the different individual characteristics of each member of the organization. In fact, some individuals have been more willing and ready to adopt the new tool, while others have not yet begun to use it regularly.

To sum up, the present study suggests the application of change management theories and approaches to support the analysis of the dynamics of management accounting change and increase the chances of successful PMS implementation. This study also supports the importance of reconsidering the influence of "micro-level" factors, and of considering individuals as active agents of change, in order to provide a different understanding of the dynamics that lead to the success and failure of these processes. In doing so, it may be valuable to consider recent advances in change management and organizational change research (e.g., Buchanan et al., 2005; Stouten et al., 2018). This would be particularly interesting given the significant gap—about two decades—since these disciplines last intersected significantly with PMS implementation research (Bourne et al., 2003). Since change management is a very practice-oriented strand of study, it may also be possible to generate some new prescriptions that are useful for practitioners. In any case, this approach would represent a departure from traditional management accounting change approaches (e.g., Brignall & Modell, 2000; Burns & Scapens, 2000), which are rooted in institutionalist theories. In fact, these approaches focus primarily on the "meso-level" of organizational units and the broader "macro-level" of the environment in which the company operates rather than the "micro-level" of the individuals.

From a more empirical perspective, this study also highlighted the presence of factors[15] that are not explored in the PMS literature, but are addressed in the change management literature and may influence the change process. Among these, one that could gain more attention in the area of PMS implementation and management accounting change is the concept of *change readiness*. This concept has been developed in the field of change management and has been gaining more and more relevance and attention over the years. Still, despite the significant evolution and expansion of this concept in the field of organizational change research (Rafferty et al., 2013; Weiner, 2009) since its initial conceptualization by Armenakis et al. (1993), its implications for PMS implementation and management accounting change processes remain largely unexplored. The lack of consideration of this concept in these fields suggests a gap in the literature. Taking into account *change readiness* could be valuable in understanding, managing, and facilitating this specific type of change.

The present study has only acknowledged and shown the importance of some components of *change readiness*, while others remain fundamentally unexplored, as noted in the results section. Future management accounting change studies should continue to explore this concept, as some key components may deserve further consideration. To begin with, this further investigation might include examining the effect of *organizational history* (Bordia et al., 2011; Rafferty & Restubog, 2017) on individuals' perceptions concerning the likelihood of success or failure in implementing management control and PMS. The influence of *organizational history* (Bordia et al., 2011; Rafferty & Restubog, 2017) on the success of these initiatives remains currently indeterminate, as there were no previous instances of similar change efforts in the company analyzed. Yet, it could be hypothesized that companies that have successfully implemented and updated their PMS may find it easier to repeat the process. In cases where this type of change has not been successful, there may be more resistance, disinterest, and skepticism. Similarly, the impact of workplace stress (Linden et al., 2005; Meuris & Leana, 2015) on individuals' receptiveness to change could not be conclusively determined. This is because interviews suggest that the members of the organization have not experienced significant stress, maintained a consistently relaxed environment, and promote a culture of collaboration.

---

[15] At the end of Chap. 3, the least explored factors identified through the literature review were respectively: (1) production of a diagnosis on the basis of which to identify an issue to be solved or on an opportunity to be caught that requires the implementation of the tool, (2) level of change readiness, (3) achievement of small or quick wins during the implementation process, (4) perceived fairness of the change process, (5) enabling of testing and experimentation activities including with the support of transition facilities and/or the use of a prototype of the tool, and (6) level of employee identification with the organization.

Instead, a factor found in this study and that negatively impacts *change readiness* (Armenakis et al., 1993; Rafferty et al., 2013) is related to the lack of adequate knowledge within the organization to implement the specific change. *Learning* took place in the field, and the system was developed through trial and error, which made implementation longer. The individuals' perception that the change would adversely impact their freedom, and subsequently, the company's overall performance, also significantly hindered organizational *change readiness*. Not only was the change seen by some as inappropriate and difficult to implement in the given context, but there was also concern that its implementation might limit the creativity of the R&D department.

Contrary to the recommendations of Stouten et al. (2018) and other change management models (Beer et al., 1990; Luecke, 2003), the initial phase of this case study did not include a *formal business diagnosis* to identify the specific challenges or opportunities facing the company. Nevertheless, there was widespread awareness among the management and a good portion of employees of significant problems that required solutions. This observation suggests that, while the structured approach to *business diagnosis* recommended by Stouten et al. (2018) seems valuable, it may not be essential for initiating a change process, particularly in smaller organizations. In such settings, there tends to be a more immediate and holistic awareness of the company's overall performance and the key issues impacting various organizational units (Castellano, 2012). Therefore, it is possible to argue that this inherent awareness can serve as a sufficient basis for recognizing the need for change, even without a *formalized diagnostic process*. In any case, in the absence of a valid reason to introduce such tools, a planned PMS implementation, as proposed in the framework of Bourne et al. (2000), seems difficult to achieve or even to start. In particular, it is advanced that in the case study, the awareness of existing problems within the organization generally stimulated the initiation of change. Concurrently, management's recognition of deficiencies in financial performance measurement pushed explicitly the development of a more sophisticated management control system (Kasurinen, 2002). The development of this awareness had a significant impact on *change readiness*, as there was a *discrepancy between the current state and the desired state of things* (Armenakis et al., 1993).

Finally, another element that appears to be of significant importance was the *leadership commitment* to support the employees, consistently seeking to disseminate knowledge and ensure that they were not isolated in their journey to adopt the system. This perceived support seems to have facilitated the implementation process and favor *change readiness* (Stouten et al., 2018).

One aspect not related to *change readiness*, supported by the study but not particularly considered in the PMS literature, is the achievement of *small wins* during the implementation process and use of the system (Kotter, 2012; Stouten et al., 2018; Van Buren & Safferstone, 2009). These small "victories," while not commonly taken into account in the literature related to PMS implementation or management accounting change, seem to have played an essential role both during and after implementation in the case study. The gradual accumulation of benefits and visible progress during the implementation allowed the project to move forward and overcome the most stubborn resistance, especially in some areas of the company.

Another aspect that has proven to be important in this case but still tends to be ignored is the elements of *fairness* and *organizational justice* (Koivisto et al., 2013). Indeed, the literature on management control and PMS has considered this element and how it affects individual performance and behavior, but mainly in terms of how the system is designed and used and how goals and rewards are assigned (Burney et al., 2009; Groen, 2018; van Veen-Dirks et al., 2021; Voußem et al., 2016). Silent, on the other hand, remains the literature with respect to the effect that the perception of *fairness* can have on the success of implementation initiatives (Hayes, 2022; Stouten et al., 2018). In the case examined, the leadership put significant effort into making people feel they were always treated with respect. There was an attempt to make the employees feel involved and to ensure that everybody understood the implications and progress achieved during the implementation process. Regular meetings were held throughout the company to encourage participation by allowing people to voice their concerns and offer solutions and suggestions. This appears to have created an adequate perception of *procedural justice*. Second, there was also a focus on the aspect of *distributive justice*. In fact, management decided to allocate rewards based on company-wide goals, without linking the reward system to individual targets, while still having a clear idea of each manager's performance. This avoided fostering perceptions of unfair or unequal rewards and outcomes among employees. According to the interviewees, relations have also always remained quite positive and cordial, which has had a positive impact on perceptions of *interpersonal justice*. Finally, even in terms of *informational justice*, as soon as the project properly got underway, there was a focus on keeping everyone informed at all times, both on the progress of the work and the results achieved. According to the organization's management, the adopted approach has contributed to the creation of a positive climate, facilitating the acceptance of the change within the company.

The factor of *organizational identification* also seems to have played a significant role in this case study. Resistance was apparently primarily due to concerns that the change could negatively impact the company's flexibility and creativity. However, as the change demonstrated tangible benefits to the organization, even with the increased workload for individuals, any initial *resistance* appeared to substantially diminish. Resistance to measurement seems to have been substantially mitigated by the perception of company-related benefits, despite the personal disadvantages associated with more effort and control. This seems justified by the presence of a strong sense of belonging to the organization.

This study also seems to suggest the importance of *social networks exploitation*[16] (Stouten et al., 2018), mainly due to the presence of *change agents* such as the consultant who promoted the project and made significant efforts to raise *awareness* of its importance. Some subjects, such as the CFO, could even exert significant influence and use their power as owners of the company.

---

[16] Sixth step of the framework.

Finally, with respect to allowing individuals *to experiment* with the new tool and make local adaptations (Stouten et al., 2018), CAEN gave individual managers the autonomy to develop customized dashboards tailored to their specific needs. At the same time, the organization provided essential training to enhance their ability to efficiently extract and use the data needed for their respective areas of interest. While the precise impact of individual customization of the tool remains not fully clarified, the gathered interviews indicate management's satisfaction with their ability to adapt and utilize the tool according to their specific requirements. Consequently, it is reasonable to suppose that this sense of satisfaction—seemingly connected also to the perceived improvement in performance measurement and management with the PMS—contributed positively to the utilization and fostered a sense of loyalty towards the newly implemented system.

Fundamentally, the findings seem to support the claims of Nudurupati et al. (2009) regarding the usefulness of change management approaches at different stages of the implementation process, despite these authors' lack of empirical evidence. However, this study highlights the importance of change management approaches even during the "predesign" phase, a stage not considered in their division of the implementation process, which traditionally follows Bourne et al.'s (2000) three-phase framework. Consistent with their claims, this study also finds that change management methodologies offer significant benefits during the design phase of a PMS. However, their value becomes more pronounced during the implementation and use phases. This distinction in level of usefulness can be attributed to the varying requirements and challenges at each stage. In the predesign stage, the focus tends to be on identifying a need to introduce the system, which may arise from significant issues a company faces—as was the case with CAEN—or from potential perceived opportunities and benefits. In the design phase, the focus tends to be more technical. Therefore, change management principles provide a moderate level of guidance, given that its focus is on individuals rather than technical aspects. However, as the process progresses to implementation and use, the importance of managing human factors, organizational dynamics, and cultural shifts seems to become increasingly important (Hiatt, 2006). In these later stages, the principles and strategies of change management seem decisive in ensuring that the new systems are effectively integrated into the organization's workflow, embraced by its members, and utilized to their full potential.

In conclusion, from the case study analysis, it emerges that many of the factors and prescriptions provided by Stouten et al. (2018) seem to confirm their relevance and usefulness in fostering the success of PMS implementation processes. This is significant because, although several previous studies (Bourne et al., 2003; Nudurupati et al., 2009) have cited the general usefulness of change management approaches for facilitating PMS implementation, none have provided substantial evidence supporting the recommendations in these models. However, future research should further examine factors such as the influence of *organizational history* (Rafferty & Restubog, 2017) and the role of *stress* (Linden et al., 2005; Meuris & Leana, 1992) in recognizing and accepting the need for change. Nonetheless, this study's results highlight the potential relevance of applying change management theories to analyze and support management accounting change processes.

References

Alsharari, N. M., Dixon, R., & Youssef, M. A. E. A. (2015). Management accounting change: Critical review and a new contextual framework. *Journal of Accounting & Organizational Change, 11*(4), 476–502.

Armenakis, A. A., Harris, S. G., & Mossholder, K. W. (1993). Creating readiness for organizational change. *Human Relations, 46*, 681–703.

Beer, M., Eisenstat, R. A., & Spector, B. (1990). Why change programs don't produce change. *Harvard Business Review, 68*(6), 158–166.

Berg, T., & Madsen, D. Ø. (2020). The evolution of a management control package: A retrospective case study. *Journal of Applied Accounting Research, 21*(4), 763–781.

Bordia, P., Restubog, S. L. D., Jimmieson, N. L., & Irmer, B. E. (2011). Haunted by the past: Effects of poor change management history on employee attitudes and turnover. *Group & Organization Management, 36*, 191–222.

Bourne, M., Mills, J., Wilcox, M., Neely, A., & Platts, K. (2000). Designing, implementing and updating performance measurement systems. *International Journal of Operations and Production Management, 20*(7), 754–771.

Bourne, M., Neely, A., Mills, J., & Platts, K. (2003). Why some performance measurement initiatives fail: Lessons from the change management literature. *International Journal of Business Performance Management, 5*(2–3), 245–269.

Bourne, M., Neely, A., Platts, K., & Mills, J. (2002). The success and failure of performance measurement initiatives—Perceptions of participating managers. *International Journal of Operations & Production Management, 22*(11), 1288–1310.

Bridges, W. (1991). *Transitions: Making sense of life's changes*. Addison-Wesley.

Brignall, S., & Modell, S. (2000). An institutional perspective on performance measurement and management in the 'new public sector'. *Management Accounting Research, 11*(3), 281–306. https://doi.org/10.1006/mare.2000.0136

Buchanan, D., Fitzgerald, L., Ketley, D., Gollop, R., Jones, J. L., Lamont, S. S., & Whitby, E. (2005). No going back: A review of the literature on sustaining organizational change. *International Journal of Management Reviews, 7*(3), 189–205.

Burke, W. W. (2023). *Organization change: Theory and practice* (6th ed.). Columbia University, Sage.

Burney, L. L., Henley, C. A., & Widener, S. K. (2009). A path model examining the relations among strategic performance measurement system characteristics, organizational justice, and extra- and in-role performance. *Accounting, Organizations and Society, 34*(3–4), 305–321.

Burns, J., & Scapens, R. W. (2000). Conceptualizing management accounting change: An institutional framework. *Management Accounting Research, 11*, 3–25.

Castellano, N. (2012). *La misurazione delle performance per le piccole imprese. Strumenti di misurazione e processi di controllo*. Giappichelli Editore.

Chiucchi, M. S. (2012). *Il metodo dello studio di caso nel management accounting*. Giappichelli Editore.

Cullen, J., Tsamenyi, M., Bernon, M., & Gorst, J. (2013). Reverse logistics in the UK retail sector: A case study of the role of management accounting in driving organisational change. *Management Accounting Research, 24*(3), 212–227.

Franco-Santos, M., Lucianetti, L., & Bourne, M. (2012). Contemporary performance measurement systems: A review of their consequences and a framework for research. *Management Accounting Research, 23*(2), 79–119.

Giovannoni, E., & Maraghini, M. P. (2013). The challenges of integrated performance measurement systems: Integrating mechanisms for integrated measures. *Accounting, Auditing and Accountability Journal, 26*(6), 978–1008.

Groen, B. A. C. (2018). A survey study into participation in goal setting, fairness, and goal commitment: Effects of including multiple types of fairness. *Journal of Management Accounting Research, 30*(2), 207–240.

Hayes, J. (2022). *The theory and practice of change management* (6th ed.). Palgrave Macmillan.

Hiatt, J. M. (2006). *ADKAR: A model for change in business, government and our community: How to implement successful change in our personal lives and professional careers.* Prosci Research.

Kanter, R. M., Stein, B. A., & Jick, T. D. (1992). *The challenge of organizational change: How companies experience it and leaders guide it.* The Free Press.

Kasurinen, T. (2002). Exploring management accounting change: The case of a balanced scorecard implementation. *Management Accounting Research, 13*, 323–343.

Koivisto, S., Lipponen, J., & Platow, M. J. (2013). Organizational and supervisory justice effects on experienced threat during change: The moderating role of leader in group representativeness. *Leadership Quarterly, 24*, 595–607.

Kotter, J. P. (1996). *Leading change.* Harvard Business Review Press.

Kotter, J. P. (2012). Accelerate! *Harvard Business Review, 90*(11), 45–58.

Lewin, K. (1947). Frontiers in group dynamics. *Human Relations, 1*, 5–41.

Linden, D. V. D., Keijsers, G. P., Eling, P., & Schaijk, R. V. (2005). Work stress and attentional difficulties: An initial study on burnout and cognitive failures. *Work & Stress, 19*, 23–36.

Luecke, R. (2003). *Managing change and transition* (Vol. 3). Harvard Business Press.

Macchia, S. (2021). Are we ready to change?: A case study of management accounting change (MAC) in an Italian co-operative. *Management Control, Special Issue, 1*, 141–164.

Meuris, J., & Leana, C. R. (2015). The high cost of low wages: Economic scarcity effects in organizations. *Research in Organizational Behavior, 35*, 143–158.

Nudurupati, S. S., Bititci, U. S., Kumar, V., & Chan, F. T. S. (2011). State of the art literature review on performance measurement. *Computers and Industrial Engineering, 60*(2), 279–290.

Rafferty, A. E., Jimmieson, N. L., & Armenakis, A. A. (2013). Change readiness: A multilevel review. *Journal of Management, 39*(1), 110–135.

Rafferty, A. E., & Restubog, S. L. D. (2017). Why do employees' perceptions of their organization's change history matter? The role of change appraisals. *Human Resource Management, 56*, 533–550.

Schein, E. H. (1996). Kurt Lewin's change theory in the field and in the classroom: Notes toward a model of managed learning. *Systems Practice, 9*(1), 27–47.

Stouten, J., Rousseau, D. M., & De Cremer, D. (2018). Successful organizational change: Integrating the management practice and scholarly literatures. *Academy of Management Annals, 12*(2), 752–788.

Van Buren, M. E., & Safferstone, T. (2009). The quick wins paradox. *Harvard Business Review, 87*(1), 54–61.

van Veen-Dirks, P. M., Leliveld, M. C., & Kaufmann, W. (2021). The effect of enabling versus coercive performance measurement systems on procedural fairness and red tape. *Journal of Management Control, 32*(2), 269–294.

Voußem, L., Kramer, S., & Schäffer, U. (2016). Fairness perceptions of annual bonus payments: The effects of subjective performance measures and the achievement of bonus targets. *Management Accounting Research, 30*, 32–46.

Weiner, B. J. (2009). A theory of organizational readiness for change. *Implementation Science, 4*(1), 67. 1–9.

Yin, R. (2003). *Case study research: Design and methods* (3rd ed.). Sage.

Chapter 6
Conclusions

This chapter provides an overview of the key topics discussed in the earlier sections of the book. In particular, this manuscript analyzes the process of management accounting change, specifically the implementation of a performance management system (PMS), through the lens of change management theories, an approach that is less common in the field. While previous research has often relied on sociological frameworks such as institutionalist theory, this study emphasizes individuals as active agents of change and focuses on the psychological aspects of organizational transitions.

The analysis confirmed the usefulness of change management approaches in explaining the dynamics of PMS implementation. These theories helped identify key enabling factors such as leadership commitment, communication, and achieving small wins, as well as hindering factors such as resistance to change and lack of change readiness. The case study provides empirical support for the effectiveness of these models in supporting PMS implementation, as well as a better understanding of the success and failure dynamics of these initiatives.

6.1 Conclusions

In this study, the phenomenon of management accounting change, particularly the implementation of a PMS, was analyzed through the lens of change management studies. This is an element of originality of this work, as most studies related to management accounting change are based on sociological theories (e.g., neo-institutionalism, institutionalism). Instead, this work considers individuals as active agents of change and addresses the psychological implications of transitions and change.

L. Leto, *Integrating Change Management and Management Accounting Change*, SIDREA Series in Accounting and Business Administration,
https://doi.org/10.1007/978-3-031-84387-7_6

So far, the analysis of PMS implementation through the perspective of change management has been suggested only by studies inherent to operations management (Bourne et al., 2003; Nudurupati et al., 2011). However, while these studies suggested the apparent usefulness of change theories in supporting implementation processes and better understanding the dynamics of their success and failure, they did not show any empirical application to support their claims. In light of the literature review and case study analysis, this research seems to confirm the usefulness of such theories for analyzing management accounting change processes and better identifying the factors that influence these initiatives and their impacts.

Concerning the topics covered in the book, the first chapter is devoted to presenting the research problem and the aim of the study. The second chapter provides a brief overview of the main theories, frameworks, and studies that have been developed in the field of management accounting change. What emerges from this chapter is a prevalence in this field of studies based on sociological and institutionalist theories (e.g., Alsharari et al., 2015), and a general focus on the investigation of the dynamics that lead to change in management accounting systems. This chapter helps to illustrate the differences between the approach taken here and that of other management accounting change studies, while also highlighting the criticisms and limitations recognized in relation to the main approaches taken in this field.

The third chapter is, instead, devoted to an examination of PMS and their design, implementation, and use in organizations (Bourne et al., 2018). This chapter begins with a brief history of the development of these systems, explaining why they were created and how they have evolved over time to meet the changing needs of organizations. The chapter then provides an excursus on the major models and theoretical frameworks that have been influential in the field of PMS. The models taken into consideration and commented upon include the tableau de bord (Pezet, 2009), the SMART model (Lynch & Cross, 1991), the intangible assets monitor (Sveiby, 1997), the performance prism (Neely et al., 2002), and the balanced scorecard (Kaplan & Norton, 1996). This section extensively analyzes each model, explaining its main characteristics, the knowledge needs each system aims to fulfill, and its main strengths and weaknesses. Additionally, this segment illustrates the evolutionary trajectory of PMS proposals, highlighting how each successive model sought to address the limitations inherent in traditional systems or improve upon earlier PMS proposals.

In the subsequent section within the third chapter, the study delineates its boundaries. Given the broad range of PMS proposals and the varied interpretations of performance measurement in both corporate and research contexts (Franco-Santos et al., 2007), it was deemed necessary to clearly establish the criteria for what constitutes a PMS in this study. To this end, this book adopts the classification provided by Franco-Santos et al. (2012), who identified four types of PMS based on their components and key uses. In particular, according to them, the defining criteria for a system to be considered a PMS include the incorporation of both financial and nonfinancial measures and their implicit or explicit alignment with the company's strategic objectives. Furthermore, the utilization of these systems might be broad in scope, encompassing not only the support of managerial decisions and the assessment of business performance but also the evaluation of managerial performance and the allocation of incentives.

The section devoted to setting the boundaries of the study is followed by a review of definitions of PMS in the literature (Franco-Santos et al., 2007). In order to obtain the most comprehensive view of PMS, it was decided to consider not only the definitions provided by studies in the field of management accounting, but also those of operations management and strategy. This interdisciplinary perspective appears useful, as PMS, including widely recognized models like the balanced scorecard, have been developed and applied across different fields of study.

The concluding part of the third chapter is dedicated to a literature review on designing, implementing, and using PMS (Bourne et al., 2000). This literature review again incorporates findings from a variety of research streams, including management accounting, human resource management, strategy, marketing, and operations management. The analysis of the literature is organized according to the three phases of the PMS implementation process outlined by Bourne et al. (2000). Therefore, it reports separately on studies that focus on the design, studies that focus on the implementation, and studies that focus on the use of the system.

In the analysis of the literature on PMS design, implementation, and use, different topics have emerged depending on the phase they focus on. The studies that examine the design phase seem to primarily concentrate on technical considerations, presenting methodologies to develop the system and discussing the challenges in selecting optimal indicators in specific contexts (Chalmeta et al., 2012; Giovannoni & Maraghini, 2013; Sousa & Aspinwall, 2010). However, especially in the field of management accounting, numerous studies explore the dynamics and factors that shape and influence system development (Wouters & Wilderom, 2008). Some of these studies also investigate the impact of design choices on aspects such as motivation, organizational justice, and the effectiveness of strategy monitoring (Rowland & Hall, 2012).

Regarding the implementation phase, research efforts seem to be directed towards understanding the dynamics that contribute to the successful or unsuccessful introduction of PMS (Beusch et al., 2022; Kasurinen, 2002; Madsen & Stenheim, 2014). Some studies also offer prescriptive strategies to mitigate potential difficulties and facilitate smoother transitions (Neely & Bourne, 2000).

Finally, research focusing on the use of PMS seems to be mainly aimed at discovering the influence of PMS on overall organizational performance and behavior (Franco Santos & Otley, 2018; Franco-Santos et al., 2012). This includes also examining usage patterns, the impact on employee motivation, and the effects on perceptions of organizational justice.

In the fourth chapter, the focus shifts to the field of change management research (Hayes, 2022), examining the evolution of studies in this area and various models of planned organizational change. The chapter begins with a historical overview of the subject, tracing its origins back to Lewin's (1947) model and highlighting how subsequent theories have evolved to address emerging challenges in organizational change management. The chapter then categorizes the change management models into three main groups based on their focus and types of application. The first category addressed is that of organizational change models (Buchanan et al., 2005; Dawson, 2019; Kotter, 1996; Stouten et al., 2018), which focus on managing change at the organizational level. These models provide strategies and support for guiding companies through significant transitions, emphasizing elements such as leadership, communication of change, prevention of resistance, and management of cultural change. The second category consists of individual change management models (Hiatt, 2006; Parker & Lewis, 1981). These models focus on addressing the challenges experienced by members of the organization during significant organizational changes, such as role and task modifications. Their aim is to facilitate smoother transitions for individuals, ensuring their adaptation and well-being during periods of change.

Finally, this section examines the diagnostic change models (Burke & Litwin, 1992). These models are designed to assist organizations in identifying underlying issues or opportunities that require the introduction of an organizational change. Their aim is also to clarify how potential changes in some organizational elements could affect business performance. This category can be useful for organizations in identifying the need for change, the type of change required, and its potential impacts on organizational performance.

After reviewing the most popular change management models, the focus shifts to the Stouten et al. (2018) model, which is then used to examine the PMS implementation case study. This framework was chosen because it is based solely on empirical research, rather than the anecdotal experiences of gurus, consultants, or change experts. In addition, as a contemporary framework, it recognizes the evolving dynamics of society and business practices and takes into account theoretical advances in the field of change management. The chapter describes the different steps that constitute the Stouten et al. (2018) model, including a comparative analysis that highlights its similarities and differences with previous models. Each step has been given a short name by the author to facilitate their recognition later in the book. This examination is followed by a presentation of the enabling and hindering factors in the organizational change processes that emerge at different steps of this model. Each of these factors is then presented in a table, along with the step(s) at which they appear to impact the change process.

Each step and its associated enabling and hindering factors are then examined in light of the existing literature on PMS. In particular, an analysis is conducted here to explore the points of contact and similarities between the literature on PMS implementation and management accounting change, as well as the framework proposed by Stouten et al. (2018). This analysis aims to identify issues, topics, and elements discussed in change management literature that have not yet been fully explored in the context of PMS implementation and management accounting change.

The chapter then concludes by recapping the least explored factors, namely:

- Level of change readiness
- Achievement of small or quick wins during the implementation process
- Perceived fairness of the change process

- Enablement of testing and experimentation activities also with the support of transitional structures and/or the use of a prototype of the tool
- Level of employees' identification with the organization

The next chapter is then entirely devoted to analyzing a case study of implementing PMS.

First, the methodology is presented, specifying the method adopted for data collection and its analysis. The case study was mostly developed on the basis of semi-structured interviews conducted after the implementation process had essentially been completed. The interviews were then coded through the use of Stouten et al. (2018) framework, with the information organized in an Excel spreadsheet. In particular, this coding was aimed at identifying the enabling and hindering factors of the PMS implementation. However, this model was found to be insufficient to fully represent the phenomenon of management accounting change, such as the implementation of a PMS. Therefore, the data coding and analysis also employed Bourne et al.'s (2000) model, which served as an effective tool for decomposing the implementation process and identifying the phases at which the enabling and hindering factors occurred.

Following this, the analysis of a case study is presented. The initial section of the chapter offers a broad overview of the company, highlighting its history, the sector and market in which it operates, and its unique characteristics. This section does not delve into the specifics of the actual implementation process, but sets the stage by describing the background and context in which the company operates. Subsequently, the chapter reconstructs the implementation process, tracing the evolution of events and decisions that led to the introduction of the system without discussing the results or outcomes of the implementation. This is followed by a section dedicated to presenting and explaining the types of management control systems adopted by the company. Before presenting the findings, particularly the case study process of PMS implementation, the chapter includes a section that anticipates the theoretical discussion by outlining all the enabling and hindering factors identified in the case. This section is useful for facilitating analysis and understanding of the results, as well as for supporting practical applications in organizations. It provides a checklist of factors, supported by change management theories and the Stouten et al. (2018) framework, that appear to play an important role in the process of implementing a PMS. These factors may need to be managed—favored or avoided—depending on the outcomes they produce that could be considered by practitioners. Moreover, it also provides some suggestions for supporting PMS implementation processes.

Regarding the findings, especially the examination of the change process, the framework of Bourne et al. (2000) was used to break down the stages characterizing the implementation of the PMS in the case study. Yet, the joint use of this framework with that of Stouten et al. (2018) led to the recognition of the need to apply an extended version of Bourne et al.'s (2000) framework to the implementation process. Specifically, a predesign phase was added, which is generally recognized in change management literature as preparatory and essential, in addition to the existing design, implementation, and use phases. In this way, the process representation was more complete, making it easier to analyze the results fully. Within each phase of this modified version of Bourne et al.'s (2000) framework, the study outlined the factors that appeared to influence the change process, along with the recollection of events characterizing each phase, as identified with the support of Stouten et al.'s (2018) framework.

This approach allowed for greater clarity on the timing of certain factors or events, particularly in terms of when they most significantly impacted the implementation process, as well as the impact of each factor. The final section of the chapter, preceding the conclusions, was dedicated to delineating the theoretical and empirical contribution of this research.

From a theoretical point of view, this paper proposed to extend Bourne et al.'s (2000) framework by adding the predesign phase to facilitate the understanding and analysis of human dynamics and to provide a more extensive view of the PMS implementation process. According to the case study findings and change management literature, the change process begins long before the design and implementation of the PMS. For such a planned change to occur, the findings suggest to us that a series of preparatory events must occur (Cameron & Green, 2019; Hayes, 2022; Stouten et al., 2018). First, it is necessary for individuals in the company to *develop the need for change*. Second, it is essential that the chosen change path, such as the implementation or upgrade of a specific PMS or management accounting system, is considered *appropriate* by those with the authority to initiate the project. In light of this, it seems useful to extend Bourne et al. (2000) framework in the proposed way to better capture the dynamics that influence the adoption of a PMS.

From the point of view of the empirical contribution, this work has drawn attention to elements considered relevant by the change management literature, but little is considered by PMS. An example is *change readiness*, a concept that has received numerous revisions and developments over the years and has been addressed in multiple publications (Armenakis et al., 1993; Holt et al., 2007; Rafferty et al., 2013). This element, which is multidimensional and consists of various subfactors, appears to be essential during the predesign, design, and implementation phases of the system. Additionally, *organizational justice* has been largely examined in relation to system design and use (e.g., Burney et al., 2009; Parker & Kohlmeyer, 2005; Rowland & Hall, 2012) but less so with reference to the implementation phase. The case study showed the importance of this element and how crucial it is to consider different types of organizational justice when implementing the system. In the specific case study, respectful treatment of employees (i.e., *interpersonal justice*), transparency regarding the reasons for and implications of change (i.e., *informational justice*), fairness in rewarding desired behaviors through rewards and incentives (i.e., *distributive justice*), and involvement and collaboration in the change process (i.e., *procedural justice*) all favored PMS implementation. Consequently, these elements appear to be important in explaining the dynamics and success of PMS implementations.

In addition, this work provided evidence for the importance of focusing on individual employees, their perspectives, roles, and actions to explain the phenomenon of organizational change, in contrast to institutionalist approaches. In other words, it emphasized the ability of individuals to act as active *agents of change*, at least when organizational change processes are planned.

Still, this study did not determine the relevance of all the underexplored factors identified through the framework analysis. For example, in the case under study, a *formalized diagnosis* was not thoroughly conducted to identify problems to be solved or opportunities to be seized, an element considered essential in planned organizational change. However, it was shown that the core element of developing an *awareness of the need for change* was still present and was based on *multiple sources of evidence*. This supports the idea that both formal and structured *diagnoses*, as well as informal and unstructured ones, are useful in *developing awareness of the need for change*. This is especially true in small companies, where management can more easily keep track of all the key elements (Castellano, 2012) and, therefore, develop an awareness of problems affecting the organization or opportunities to be seized. Another element that could not be tested is the effect of *organizational history*, a component of *change readiness* (Stouten et al., 2018). In fact, the company in question had no previous unsuccessful or successful attempts to implement a PMS, so this element's positive or negative effect could not be investigated. In any case, it is clear that Stouten et al.'s (2018) prescriptive model itself is not intended to be applied in its entirety in every situation, and therefore, certain factors may not emerge in every context.

From a practical perspective, although the Stouten et al. (2018) model wasn't directly applied to managing change in this specific case study, this work suggests its potential usefulness in supporting management accounting change initiatives. While the model doesn't address the technical aspects associated with system development and use, it does address the human factors that influence the management accounting change process. Since change management theories, in general, are inherently prescriptive and designed to assist managers in managing organizational change, their proven usefulness in the context of PMS provides strong justification for adopting these approaches to increase the likelihood of success in real-world settings. Focusing solely on technical and design aspects may not be sufficient to ensure the success of such initiatives. As change management theories affirm, even with appropriate changes in terms of "content," factors such as resistance to change can lead to the failure of these initiatives. Considering elements related to *communication*, perceptions of *organizational justice*, and the level of *change readiness* during implementation may prove beneficial in managing the process more efficiently and mitigating potential problems. We recall that the elements supported by the case study analysis are listed and commented in Sect. 5.3, while the inhibiting and enabling factors identified in the Stouten et al. (2018) framework are present in Sect. 4.3.2.

While this research was exploratory in nature, it is important to acknowledge its primary limitation: its empirical part examines only a single case study. As such, generalization of the findings is neither feasible nor intended. Another major limitation is the retrospective reconstruction of the case study based on ex post interviews conducted after the implementation process was largely complete. A longitudinal analysis would potentially provide a better understanding of the implementation dynamics through direct observation, thus reducing the risk of cognitive and memory biases in respondents when reconstructing past events (Yin, 2003). Additionally, this study did not allow for the analysis of all factors identified in the Stouten et al. (2018) framework, constituting a further limitation. However, given that empirical evidence was found for most of the factors present in each step of the framework, its relevance still seems to be confirmed, as the steps of the framework appear to be substantially supported. Finally, it cannot be excluded that the adoption of this specific framework may have prevented the identification of other factors essential for the occurrence of change.

Concerning future research, further studies could continue investigating the less explored critical factors identified through the analysis of Stouten et al. (2018) framework, as only some of them were observed here and, in any case, in relation to a single case study. Indeed, the aspect of *change readiness* needs further exploration, as does the *perceived level of organizational justice and fairness* of the implementation process and *organizational history* on the success or failure of these initiatives. Future case study analyses adopting a change management perspective have the potential to deepen our understanding of PMS implementation by examining the role of these factors. These studies might enhance both theoretical knowledge and practical application, guiding organizations in the effective implementation of PMS.

References

Alsharari, N. M., Dixon, R., & Youssef, M. A. E. A. (2015). Management accounting change: Critical review and a new contextual framework. *Journal of Accounting & Organizational Change, 11*(4), 476–502.

Armenakis, A. A., Harris, S. G., & Mossholder, K. W. (1993). Creating readiness for organizational change. *Human Relations, 46*, 681–703.

Beusch, P., Frisk, J. E., Rosén, M., & Dilla, W. (2022). Management control for sustainability: Towards integrated systems. *Management Accounting Research, 54*, 100777.

Bourne, M., Mills, J., Wilcox, M., Neely, A., & Platts, K. (2000). Designing, implementing and updating performance measurement systems. *International Journal of Operations & Production Management, 20*(7), 754–771.

Bourne, M., Neely, A., Mills, J., & Platts, K. (2003). Why some performance measurement initiatives fail: Lessons from the change management literature. *International Journal of Business Performance Management, 5*(2–3), 245–269.

Bourne, M., Melnyk, S., & Bititci, U. S. (2018). Performance measurement and management: Theory and practice. *International Journal of Operations & Production Management, 38*(11), 2010–2021.

Brignall, S., & Modell, S. (2000). An institutional perspective on performance measurement and management in the new public service. *Management Accounting Research, 11*, 281–306.

Buchanan, D., Fitzgerald, L., Ketley, D., Gollop, R., Jones, J. L., Lamont, S. S., & Whitby, E. (2005). No going back: A review of the literature on sustaining organizational change. *International Journal of Management Reviews, 7*(3), 189–205.

Burke, W., & Litwin, G. (1992). A causal model of organizational performance and change. *Journal of Management, 18*, 523–545.

Burney, L. L., Henley, C. A., & Widener, S. K. (2009). A path model examining the relations among strategic performance measurement system characteristics, organizational justice, and extra- and in-role performance. *Accounting, Organizations and Society, 34*(3–4), 305–321.

Cameron, E., & Green, M. (2019). *Making sense of change management: A complete guide to the models, tools, and techniques of organizational change* (6th ed.). Kogan.

Castellano, N. G. (2012). *La misurazione delle performance per le piccole imprese Strumenti di misurazione e processi di controllo* (pp. 1–127). G. Giappichelli Editore.

Chalmeta, R., Palomero, S., & Matilla, M. (2012). Methodology to develop a performance measurement system in small and medium-sized enterprises. *International Journal of Computer Integrated Manufacturing, 5*, 716–740.

Dawson, P. (2019). *Reshaping change: A processual perspective* (2nd ed.). Routledge.

Franco Santos, M., & Otley, D. (2018). Reviewing and theorizing the unintended consequences of performance management systems. *International Journal of Management Reviews, 20*(3), 696–730.

Franco-Santos, M., Kennerley, M., Micheli, P., Martinez, V., Mason, S., Marr, B., Gray, D., & Neely, A. (2007). Towards a definition of a business performance measurement system. *International Journal of Operations & Production Management, 27*, 784–801.

Franco-Santos, M., Lucianetti, L., & Bourne, M. (2012). Contemporary performance measurement systems: A review of their consequences and a framework for research. *Management Accounting Research, 23*(2), 79–119. https://doi.org/10.1016/j.mar.2012.04.001

Giovannoni, E., & Maraghini, M. P. (2013). The challenges of integrated performance measurement systems: Integrating mechanisms for integrated measures. *Accounting, Auditing & Accountability Journal, 26*(6), 978–1008.

Hayes, J. (2022). *The theory and practice of change management* (6th ed.). Palgrave Macmillan.

Hiatt, J. M. (2006). *ADKAR: A model for change in business, government and our community: How to implement successful change in our personal lives and professional careers.* Prosci Research.

Holt, D. T., Armenakis, A. A., Feild, H. S., & Harris, S. G. (2007). Readiness for organizational change: The systematic development of a scale. *The Journal of Applied Behavioral Science, 43*(2), 232–255.

Kaplan, R. S., & Norton, D. P. (1996). *The balanced scorecard: Translating strategy into action.* Harvard Business School Press.

Kasurinen, T. (2002). Exploring management accounting change: The case of a balanced scorecard implementation. *Management Accounting Research, 13*, 323–343.

Kotter, J. P. (1996). *Leading change*. Harvard Business Review Press.

Lewin, K. (1947). Group decision and social change. *Readings in Social Psychology, 3*(1), 197–211.

Lynch, R. L., & Cross, K. F. (1991). *Measure up — Yardsticks for continuous improvement.* Basil Blackwell.

Madsen, D. Ø., & Stenheim, T. (2014). Perceived problems associated with the implementation of the balanced scorecard: Evidence from Scandinavia. *Problems and Perspectives in Management, 12*(1), 121–131.

Neely, A., Adams, C., & Kennerley, M. (2002). *The performance prism: The scorecard for measuring and managing business success*. Financial Times Prentice Hall.

Neely, A., & Bourne, M. (2000). Why measurement initiatives fail. *Measuring Business Excellence, 4*, 3–6.

Nudurupati, S. S., Bititci, U. S., Kumar, V., & Chan, F. T. S. (2011). State of the art literature review on performance measurement. *Computers and Industrial Engineering, 60*(2), 279–290.

Parker, R. J., & Kohlmeyer, J. M., III. (2005). Organizational justice and turnover in public accounting firms: A research note. *Accounting, Organizations and Society, 30*, 357–369.

Parker, C., & Lewis, R. (1981). Beyond the Peter principle—Managing successful transitions. *Journal of European Industrial Training, 5*(6), 17–21.

Pezet, A. (2009). The history of the French Tableau de Bord (1885-1975): Evidence from the archives. *Accounting, Business & Financial History, 19*(2), 103–125.

Rafferty, A. E., Jimmieson, N. L., & Armenakis, A. A. (2013). Change readiness: A multilevel review. *Journal of Management, 39*(1), 110–135.

Rowland, C. A., & Hall, R. D. (2012). Organizational justice and performance: Is appraisal fair? *EuroMed Journal of Business, 7*(3), 280–293.

Sousa, S., & Aspinwall, E. (2010). Development of a performance measurement framework for SMEs. *Total Quality Management and Business Excellence, 21*(5), 475–501.

Stouten, J., Rousseau, D. M., & De Cremer, D. (2018). Successful organizational change: Integrating the management practice and scholarly literatures. *Academy of Management Annals, 12*(2), 752–788.

Sveiby, K. E. (1997). The intangible assets monitor. *Journal of Human Resource Costing & Accounting, 2*(1), 73–97.

Wouters, M., Wilderom, C. (2008). Developing performance-measurement systems as enabling formalization: A longitudinal field study of a logistics department. *Accounting Organizations and Society, 33*(4–5), 488–516. https://doi.org/10.1016/j.aos.2007.05.002

Yin, R. (2003). *Case study research: Design and methods* (3rd ed.). Sage.

Appendix: Example of Interview Guidelines

A: Background

1. What does the company do, and what is its history?
2. In which industry do you operate?
3. Who are your competitors? Is this an area characterized by high competitiveness?
4. On which areas does the competition focus most?
5. Who are your primary customers, and what characteristics do they have?
6. What is your role in the company?
7. What kind of relationships exist within the company? Are communications transparent? Are communications mainly formal or informal?
8. How many people are employed by the company? Has the company experienced expansion in recent years? Has the company hired new individuals, or is it still composed mostly of long-standing members?

B: PMS

1. What kind of management control system do you have?
2. Do you have a budget?
3. Do you have nonfinancial measures? Do you employ a multidimensional performance measurement system?
4. What kind of indicators do you use? What kind of indicators of a noneconomic nature do you employ?
5. Is the PMS linked to an incentive system? On what basis are rewards given?

L. Leto, *Integrating Change Management and Management Accounting Change*, SIDREA Series in Accounting and Business Administration,
https://doi.org/10.1007/978-3-031-84387-7

6. What purposes does the system serve? Is it used solely for monitoring performance, or are there official occasions/meetings in the company when data is discussed and decisions are made based on it?
7. Who uses this system? What degree of development has it reached? Which business areas does it cover?
8. How important is data in decision-making within the company? Generally, when unsatisfactory performance results are achieved, do you investigate the reasons and take corrective action?

C: Reason for Change

1. Why did you decide to introduce a management control system?
2. Why did you start introducing the first dashboards for measuring performance?
3. Who were the main advocates for the new system? Why were these individuals convinced of the need to introduce the system?
4. Was the need for the tool perceived by only a few individuals, or was it a widely shared awareness among the management?
5. Was the PMS introduced in response to specific identified problems that could be solved through its introduction?
6. What benefits were expected from the introduction of the PMS?

D: Change Process

1. Did you use the help of external consultants, or was the system developed internally?
2. Was there a need to provide training to familiarize management with the new system? Was there anyone in the company at the time the system was introduced who already had knowledge of management accounting & control?
3. What were the main challenges faced during the implementation of the system?
4. Were there any skeptics regarding the implementation project or the system itself?
5. Was the tool developed in a participatory manner? Who was involved in the process? Did anyone raise concerns about the introduction of the tool? If so, what kind?
6. Was the system implemented gradually? Did you have to conduct tests and experiment with new indicators to identify those most useful to you?
7. Did you perceive the system's usefulness as its use and deployment increased?
8. Are you considering the possibility of expanding the system further?